Table of Contents

Table of Contents, *continued*

Teacher's Guide and Resource Book – *2nd edition* –

Touchphonics®

The Manipulative Multisensory Phonics System

EDUCATORS PUBLISHING SERVICE
Cambridge and Toronto

Acquisitions/Development: Bonnie Lass
Editorial: Will Tripp
Design: Karen Lomigora

Printed in USA

ISBN 978-0-8388-8809-4

2 3 4 5 6 PPG 12 11 10 09 08

Table of Contents, *continued*

Introduction

Vision and Rationale

Touchphonics® is a manipulative, multisensory instructional system designed to help students build their phonics knowledge as they discover patterns in the structure of words. It teaches core reading skills such as phonemic awareness, sound-to-symbol correspondences, substitution, segmentation, and blending. While phonics is the system of sound and symbol relationships, word structure knowledge includes the organization of the elements of phonics into patterns. In addition to dealing with words sound-by-sound, *Touchphonics* works with onsets, rimes, and other structural patterns to help students understand how sounds and spellings vary depending on the letter combination patterns within a word. Understanding word structure increases automaticity and fluency, which in turn enhances comprehension.

History and Development

Touchphonics was first developed by Dr. Robin Steed, Ed.D. as her doctoral dissertation in 1984. A Special Education teacher, Steed developed the Touch-units™ and methodology in response to a student who lacked essential orthographic understandings. She designed the program to teach four basic phonemic principles: sound to symbol correspondences, segmentation, blending, and substitution. She found that the Touch-units facilitated students' acquisition of phonics skills, helping to make decoding concepts more accessible by involving four senses—visual, auditory, kinesthetic, and tactile.

Robin Steed understood that the physical, tactile nature of the Touch-units helped to put phonics in the grasp of struggling readers. In her dissertation, she explains:

> A letter printed on a card or on the chalkboard is a symbol of a sound. It is abstract and processed at a symbolic level. A letter in the hand gives tactile input, and bridges the gaps between a presymbolic object and a symbol for a sound. Physically moving the letters helps the children experience the sound-symbol association concept. As they put letters or clusters in a sequence, they touch and concretely experience the temporal sequence of the word. The children 'build' a word and then self-check by touching and sounding the letters or clusters, which they easily rearrange if they discover they are not matching sound and symbol. This is feedback they can count on when their visual and/or auditory processing is faulty.[1]

Touchphonics has since been tested and proven in reading laboratories at Brigham Young University and developed into the system as it now exists. It has also been used in spelling studies, comparing favorably with a more traditional method and a control group with no method.[2] Since its development, the many teachers who have used it have found it to significantly and rapidly improve students' reading.

1. Steed, M. R. *A System for Teaching Word Recognition Skills to Children with Severe Reading Disorders.* Dissertation presented to the Department of Elementary Education at Brigham Young University, 1984 (online at www.epsbooks.com), p. 28.

2. Johnson, S. E. *The effect of method, language proficiency, and orthographic background on spelling acquisition.* Masters thesis presented at Brigham Young University, 1992.

Differentiated Instruction for Readers with Learning Disabilities

Every academic subject relies on its students' ability to read fluently and with comprehension. For many students, however, learning to read presents a substantial hurdle. It is estimated that roughly 30% of all students are at risk for reading failure, and that the bottom 15% are severely at risk of never learning to read fluently. Many of these at-risk readers are struggling with language-based learning disabilities.

Learning disabilities refers to neurobiological disorders that affect how the brain works.[3] For example, a nonimpaired reader utilizes neural pathways that allow instant word recognition, but a reader with dyslexia may compensate with areas of the brain that deal with word analysis, requiring the reader to analyze and decode each individual word each time it appears.

Recent studies have shown that effective reading intervention programs can allow students with language-based learning disabilities not only to reach a higher reading level, but to develop the same neural reading systems as nonimpaired readers. Sally Shaywitz has conducted experiments showing that effective instructional practices can help readers with language-based learning disabilities to develop rapid, automatic reading systems and utilize the same regions of the brain as nonimpaired readers. Shaywitz describes her findings: "[MRI brain images from dyslexic readers before and after intervention] provide powerful evidence that early intervention with an effective reading program leads to the development of primary, automatic [neural] reading systems and allows a child to catch up to his classmates.... After more than a century of frustration, it has now been shown that the brain can be rewired and that struggling children can become skilled readers."[4]

Effective instructional practices should both contain the five pillars of literacy outlined by the National Reading Panel, and capture students' attention so that they can practice and absorb the concepts. Shaywitz reinforces the idea that "You want [the student's] active involvement. When you have it, he is paying attention, and learning is going on."[5] Many students respond well to instruction that utilizes varied avenues of sensory input, involving them through multiple neural channels, allowing for more active learning.

Touchphonics is fully multisensory, incorporating visual, auditory, kinesthetic, and tactile elements in its instruction. The letter-shaped tactile Touch-units are kinesthetically manipulated during the lessons. Those qualities, along with the visual aspects—the Touch-units' shape and color coding—and the kinesthetic experience of writing the words made with the Touch-units, effectively capture students' attention and provide additional memory cues for rapid learning. Auditory elements, such as listening to and saying letter names, words, and sentences, complete *Touchphonics'* full range of multisensory stimuli.

---

3. Lerner, Janet. *Learning Disabilities: Theories, Diagnosis, and Teaching Strategies.* Boston: Houghton Mifflin Company, 2003, pp. 2–3.

4. Shaywitz, Sally. *Overcoming Dyslexia: A New and Complete Science-Based Program for Reading Problems at Any Level.* New York: Alfred A. Knopf, 2003, p. 86.

5. Shaywitz, p. 185.

Research

The National Reading Panel

The *Touchphonics* program meets the research standards of the National Reading Panel (NRP) and follows the guidelines established in the report *Put Reading First: The Research Building Blocks for Teaching Children to Read.*[6] This publication identifies good reading instruction as that which includes phonemic awareness, phonics, fluency, vocabulary, and comprehension, all of which are included in *Touchphonics* instruction. With these five elements, *Touchphonics* is designed to be a balanced literacy program, leading students towards automaticity in reading and increased reading comprehension.

Phonemic Awareness Phonemic awareness is the recognition that spoken words are made up of individual sounds (phonemes). Students with good phonemic awareness can identify and work with phonemes. The research done by the NRP found that phonemic awareness activities, such as orally manipulating parts of words, build the most useful foundation for reading.

In *Touchphonics*, each lesson starts with phonemic awareness. The first introduction to a new phonogram is aural, with students listening for a target phonogram and learning to hear the phonogram in the context of a word before they learn how it relates to letters. When they have learned the relationship of the sound to the letters, students can engage in building words activities, which contain phonemic awareness reinforcement through oral segmentation and blending of the phonograms in words. For students who need additional phonemic awareness instruction, there are extra Phonemic Awareness Activities on p. 165.

Phonics Phonics is the relationship between the sounds of spoken language and the letters of written language. Good phonics teaching consists of direct and systematic instruction that teaches letter-sound relationships in a clearly defined sequence. Methods that facilitate learning and give substantial opportunities to practice applying newly obtained concepts through reading and writing are other aspects of good phonics instruction.

In the *Touchphonics* Teacher's Guide and Resource Book, the lesson plans instruct students in the relationships between letters and sounds and word structure knowledge. Students build words with Touch-units and write the words they have just built. In this way, students transfer their concrete, multisensory understanding they gained from the Touch-units to the more abstract representation of letters in print. With the decodable Readers, they apply their phonics and word structure abilities to arrive at comprehension.

Fluency Fluency is the ability to read accurately and smoothly. A fluent reader is able to read at a good pace, grouping words to read with expression and comprehension. Students with poor fluency read slowly, relying too heavily on decoding each word instead of quickly identifying words and grouping them together to make sense. Students with a

6. National Reading Panel. *Teaching children to read: An evidence based assessment of the scientific research literature on reading and its implication for reading instruction—Reports of the Subgroups.* Washington, D.C.: National Institute of Child Health and Development. 2000.

lack of fluency concentrate on individual words instead of chunking words into phrases or sentences. These students have difficulty with comprehension.

In *Touchphonics*, fluency practice is incorporated into each lesson plan. As students read words they are asked to first sound out each letter, and then blend the sounds until they can read the word automatically. In the Workbook, students practice reading and writing words and sentences containing recently learned concepts, improving their automaticity and fluency through ample practice. The stories in the Readers provide excellent opportunities to practice fluent reading. Students are encouraged to go back over a story several times, improving their fluency with each round of reading.

Vocabulary Vocabulary refers to the words that a student knows. Students know different words to different extents in their listening/speaking, reading, and writing vocabularies. An adequate vocabulary is essential to comprehension, since the text makes sense only if the words are understood. Vocabulary is also important for fluency, since unknown words can slow down or trip up the flow of reading.

The words that students build with Touch-units are an excellent medium for teaching vocabulary. The word lists in the Teacher's Guide and Resource Book provide words to use as practice for each concept; these word lists contain a range of vocabulary, from common, well-known words to words that are much less likely to be in a student's listening/speaking vocabulary and thus are perfect candidates for vocabulary instruction. For example, the word lists associated with the silent *e* lesson contain words ranging from *bike* and *game* to less common words such as *mope* and *drake*. As Teachers choose words from the list and ask students to build or work with the words, they can incorporate definitions and examples of usage in the instruction. Many of the words have homonyms or multiple meanings, providing material for expanded vocabulary instruction.

Comprehension Comprehension is the ability to gain meaning from reading a text. Poor readers whose decoding skills are labored show poor comprehension. Once readers develop a certain degree of automaticity with word recognition, they can devote much more attention to the meaning of the word and to its significance in relation to the surrounding text. *Touchphonics* speeds students toward automaticity of decoding, and at the same time provides practice with comprehension. As students read the stories in the Readers, they practice making sense of the words in context. As they complete the Workbook pages, they are required to write or complete sentences about the stories, answer questions, and draw pictures to illustrate their comprehension of the story.

Unique Features

Touchphonics teaches more than just phonics—it also teaches word structure. By becoming familiar with common structural patterns in words, as well as becoming proficient in letter-by-letter decoding, students can build and read new words by transferring the concepts they have learned to unknown words. Students will learn four phonemic principles: (1) that words are made of separate parts, (2) that each part of a word has a specific sound, (3) that the sounds of the parts blend together to make a word, and (4) that parts of words can be substituted to make new words. The color-coding of the Touch-units helps convey the patterns of words without explicit rules. *Touchphonics* works to teach phonics and reading through the combination of the color-coded Touch-units, a multisensory lesson plan including manipulation of the Touch-units, listening, speaking, reading, pencil and paper work, and the application of newly developed phonics skills to the Readers. The program includes teacher choices for differentiation, so that teachers may flexibly adapt the *Touchphonics* system to their students' individual needs.

Components

Teacher's Guide and Resource Book

The Teacher's Guide and Resource Book describes the vision and rationale of *Touchphonics*, provides information about its research base and history, and presents teaching procedures, prereading lessons, and lessons. Word lists are included to support each lesson, and diagnostic tools are offered in the appendices.

Student Workbook

The Workbook provides independent practice in phonics, recording words, and responding to the Reader stories. Phonics exercises include matching pictures to words and vice versa, completing a sentence or word from a choice of words or letters, and picking the correct letter to represent a sound. Responding activities include drawing a picture to show story comprehension and independently writing words and sentences about the story.

Blackline Masters of Decodable Readers

The reproducible Blackline Masters contain 59 illustrated, decodable Readers, one for each *Touchphonics* lesson in the Teacher's Guide and Resource Book. The Readers contain recurring characters, humorous situations, and some nonfiction, inviting students to apply their new skills as they enjoy reading.

Whiteboards

The whiteboards are magnetic, dry-erase workspaces students will use for several of their word building activities. The top of the whiteboards contain a space for students to build words using the Touch-units or Magtiles. The bottom of the whiteboards contain a space for students to write words using a dry-erase marker. Students can store letters in the middle or around the edges of the whiteboard.

The Touch-units

The Touch-units are three-dimensional, textured-plastic, color-coded, shaped letters and letter combinations. The Touch-units are soft and have a bumpy side and a smooth side. If students place the Touch-unit upside down, they will realize that the bumps are not facing upwards and the Touch-unit does not lay flat, a clue that helps students self-correct letter reversals. The Touch-units are color-coded by how they are used in a word; for example, consonants are yellow and vowels are red. Each kit contains all of the letter-units needed to teach the structure of almost all of the single-syllable phonetic words and many of the multisyllable words in our language. The different types of Touch-units are detailed on pp. xi–xiii

To ensure that all the Touch-units are included in your kit, they are packaged attached to their injection-molded feed lines. Remove each Touch-unit by cutting the feed line at the point of attachment with scissors or by pulling it from the feed line with your fingertips tightly pressed at the point of attachment. Trim any remaining rough edges with a nail clipper or small scissors. Store the Touch-units in the compartmentalized storage box.

The Magtiles™

Magtiles are large-format color-coded magnetic tiles, which match the content of the Touch-units and can be used for demonstrations visible to the whole class. The lessons in this book are designed for use with Touch-units or Magtiles.

Color Coding

Single Consonants—yellow

There are 44 single consonant Touch-units.

Consonant Digraphs—yellow

There are five consonant digraph Touch-units. They are *ch, sh, wh, th* as in *thin*, and *th* as in *that.* Because consonant digraphs represent a single sound and function as a single-sound unit, they are yellow, the same color as single consonants.

Silent Letters—white with yellow sounded letters

There are 15 silent letter Touch-units. In these Touch-units, the yellow letters are sounded and the white letters are silent. Most of the silent letter Touch-units have the silent letter first, as in *kn* and *ck,* and others have the silent letter second, as in *mb* and *gu.*

Silent Letters—white

There are two final *e* Touch-units. Because this Touch-unit functions as a silent letter, it is white. Because its function is different, the final *e* should never be used in place of a red single vowel *e* Touch-unit. Additional white silent letters are *w, gh,* and *t.*

Consonant Blends—blue and green

There are 25 blue Initial Consonant Blends and 17 green Final Consonant Blends.

Borrowed Sounds—brown

There are five brown borrowed sound Touch-units: *gh, ph, ci, si,* and *ti.* Borrowed sounds have taken their spellings from other languages and been incorporated into English. For example, the /f/ sound when it is spelled *ph,* appears in words with Greek origins such as *physics.* The borrowed sounds of *gh* and *ph* both decode as the sound /f/. The borrowed sounds of *ci, si,* and *ti* all decode as the sound /sh/ and are used as part of the suffixes *tion* as in *caution, sion* as in *mission, cious* as in *conscious,* and *cial* as in *special.* These spellings can be found in words with Latin and French origins.

Schwa—brown

This Touch-unit is an upside-down, backwards *e.* It represents the vowel sound in an unaccented syllable. It decodes like the single *u* sound, /uh/. To teach the schwa sound, the Touch-unit can be placed on top of the vowel in the unaccented syllable to graphically show the student how the vowel sound is changed.

Punctuation Mark—brown

There are two punctuation marks. One is an accent mark for teaching stress in words of more than one syllable, and the other is an apostrophe for teaching contractions and possessives.

Single Vowels—red

There are two sets of red single vowels.

Special Case Vowels—red

The special case vowels are *u* and *y.* They are special because they each decode with two different sounds.

When *u* is decoded in a CV or CVe pattern, as an open syllable, or with a final *e,* it decodes with two different sounds. The two sounds are /o͞o/ as in *tune* and /ū/ as in *cue.*

When y is used as the final vowel in a syllable, it also is decoded with two different sounds. The two sounds are /ē/ as in *baby* and /ī/ as in *my.*

Note: When *y* is used as a suffix, be sure you use the purple suffix *y,* indicating its function as a suffix. As a suffix, it is always pronounced /ē/ as in *bumpy.* The *y* Touch-unit can be exchanged for an *i,* and then other suffixes may be added to make the word, as in *bumpier* or *bumpiest.*

Vowel Combinations—red

The red vowel combinations have been grouped into four different types:

Vowel combinations that have consistent sounds They are *ee* as in *keep; oa* as in *boat; ie* as in *chief;* and *ui* as in *fruit.* They consistently decode as the same sound in all the words in which they appear.

Vowel combinations that have two sounds There are two each of these Touch-units to represent their different sounds. They are *oo* as in *moon* and *book; ow* as in *snow* and *cow; ew* as in *new* and *few; ey* as in *they* and *key;* and *ei* as in *seize* and *eight.* Students learn to identify the words in this category through repeated exposure and repetition rather than rules.

Vowel combinations that have multiple sounds There are three *ea* Touch-units, and each decodes as a different sound. Most *ea* words decode as /ē/ as in *eat.* There are fewer words in which *ea* decodes as /ĕ/ as in *bread,* and only a very few that decode as /ā/ as in *steak.* There are five *ou* Touch-units, and each decodes as a different sound. Most *ou* words decode as /ou/ as in *ouch* or *loud* and could be referred to as the "pinch sound". Other decoded sounds of *ou* are /o͞o/ as in *you;* /ŏ/ as in *cough;* /ô/ as in *four* and /ŭ/ as in *trouble.* As above, students are taught that there are three *ea*'s and five *ou*'s, each with its own sound.

Vowel combinations that sound the same but look different This type includes the vowel combinations *ai* and *ay* (decoded as /ā/ as in *day* or *nail*); *au* and *aw* as in *haunt* or *saw*; and *oi* and *oy*, as in *boil* or *boy*. As with the vowel combinations that have more than one sound, students learn to choose the correct spelling of a certain sound through adequate exposure to words with each spelling. Remember that students will become familiar with correct vowel spellings through repeated exposure and repetition rather than through rules.

r Controlled Vowels—yellow and red

There are seven *r* controlled vowel Touch-units. All the *r* consonants in these Touch-units are yellow, indicating their function as a single consonant. The vowel letters *o, a, ai,* and *ea* of these Touch-units are red, indicating their function in each Touch-unit as a vowel. The *i, e,* and *u* letters of these Touch-units are white, or silent, because with an *r* they function as one sound: /er/.

The Affixes: Prefixes—orange; Suffixes—purple

There are 14 prefixes and 28 suffixes. These Touch-units are used when teaching students to structurally analyze words.

The prefixes and suffixes offered have been selected because of their frequency of use and their decoding consistency. There are sufficient prefix samples to give the student a clear understanding of how word meanings can be changed by substitution. For example, after building the word *port,* they can change it with prefixes to read *export, deport, report,* and *import,* among others.

The suffixes can be exchanged and substituted to show spelling and meaning changes as well as inflections of a base, or root, word. The single *s* is used to teach plurals. There are three *ed* Touch-units, to teach the three sounds of *ed*: /ĕd/ as in wanted; /t/ as in walked; and /d/ as in followed.

Base word spelling changes can be taught by exchanging *f* for *v* when adding a plural *es* (example: half/halves). Place the purple *v* over the yellow *f* and add the suffix *es*. Likewise, exchange *y* for *i* before adding *er* or *est* (example: happy/happier/happiest).

A syllable containing *le* can be used for any consonant-*le* syllable by adding the appropriate consonant to the *le* (example: apple, handle, uncle).

Teaching Procedures

Touchphonics is a sequential, systematic system for direct phonics instruction. You can use *Touchphonics* in conjunction with your school's reading program or as an independent system for phonics instruction. The lesson plans allow for complete scaffolding and support during the learning process, so students can rapidly progress and retain what they have learned.

General Lesson Guidelines

Make each lesson fun, and modify or discontinue the lesson if students tire. Do not allow students to fail, and be sure to give a great deal of praise and encouragement. If students are having difficulty performing an activity, first wait a few seconds to give them some thinking time, then give specific feedback or cue them with a statement that gives a clue.

If they're building a word, you can help them with prompts such as, "The word you're building starts with a /th/ sound. Do you remember what two letters make the /th/ sound?" If they're decoding a word, you can cue them by pointing to a critical attribute they've missed that will help them identify the word. If students are still unsure, help them complete the activity and then allow them to repeat the activity alone. Repeat these steps until students are consistently successful in performing the activities without help.

It is not necessary to use every word listed with a certain step of the lesson. Select only as many of the words as you feel are necessary to keep the session moving at an interesting and challenging pace. If you need more words, you can refer to the word lists. Keep in mind that the pace at which you move must be based upon students' progress, so be attentive to students' comfort levels with each task. When using words from the word lists in a lesson, it is best to use only those that fit the word pattern being covered; distracter words can be more confusing than helpful. For those steps in which additional Touch-units are added to a word to make a new word, reduce the number of Touch-units displayed for students to choose from if the number of choices seems too overwhelming.

When using the Touch-units procedures, each procedure is designed so that it may be used either by you or your students. Initially, you can model the procedure for students. Subsequently, students need to practice the activity with your guidance. And finally, students should do the activity independently with no assistance or cues from you. Likewise, you can guide students if they need help with the Reader story; then, students should be encouraged to read and reread the story independently. Workbook activities are designed to be able to be completed independently once students have been successful doing the corresponding part of the lesson independently; however, you may want to support students' Workbook activities with extra help, if needed.

Extra activities are provided for optional support surrounding the lesson plans; you can choose to have students participate in prereading activities, or phonemic awareness activities, or play reinforcing word games. The Teacher's Guide and Resource Book also includes assessments, diagnostics, and information about running records and keeping word rings.

Daily Teaching Plan

Each *Touchphonics* lesson can be divided into four segments of about 15 to 20 minutes each. Since the most rapid gains in long-term memory, fluency, and comprehension are made when students practice a concept immediately after learning it, the lessons are divided into segments each of which includes application and practice of the concept being learned. Students also gain beneficial practice if they are encouraged to reread the stories to themselves, each other, and their parents.

Segment 1: Phonemic Awareness, Link Sound(s) to Letter(s)

Segment 2: Build Words (Model), Build Words, Read Words in Isolation, Independent Practice, Dictation

Segment 3: Build Words from the Story/Selection, Learn/Review Sight Words, complete optional activities or games from the Teacher's Guide and Resource Book

Segment 4: Read the Story/Selection, Respond to the Story/Selection

There are 59 *Touchphonics* Lessons, so at a rate of one lesson a week, students can complete the program in approximately two school years. By covering two Touchponics lessons each week, the program can be completed in one school year.

PACING	
Options for Covering 1 Lesson Per Week (complete the program in approximately 2 school years)	***Options for Covering 2 Lessons Per Week*** (complete the program in approximately 1 school year)
4 days a week: 15–20 minutes per day; 1 segment per day	**4 days a week:** 40–45 minutes per day; 2 segments per day
2 days a week: 40–45 minutes per day; 2 segments per day	**2 days a week:** 80–90 minutes per day; 4 segments (1 lesson) per day

Touchphonics Lessons

There are 59 *Touchphonics* lessons, following an initial Consonant Warm-up. Each lesson builds on the prior lesson so that skills learned in the previous lessons are used in the one that follows. In some cases it may be necessary to repeat a lesson if students still find it difficult to identify and/or spell words that are from the word patterns of that lesson. You can find additional words for each lesson in the Word Lists at the end of a section of lessons (see Table of Contents). The words are grouped on the lists by pattern and correspond to the phonemes taught in a lesson. These lists will give you the flexibility to modify the words in a lesson to support the books being used in your classroom, and to choose more words for the lesson as needed.

Lesson Steps

The following steps appear in each of the 59 *Touchphonics* Lessons:

Step 1—**Phonemic Awareness:** Students become familiar with the target phoneme or phonemic pattern through teacher-led auditory activities and demonstrations.

Step 2—**Link Sound(s) to Letter(s):** In this phonics "mini-lesson," students become proficient at linking the sound or sounds to the letter or letters through teacher-led activities and demonstrations that involve tracing Touch-units and repeating sound in words formed on a whiteboard.

Step 3—**Build Words (Model):** The teacher models building words with the Touch-units. This step is omitted from review lessons.

Step 4—**Build Words:** After watching the teacher build a word, students build words with the Touch-units and write the words they build in their Workbook. This step can be expanded and varied using the Extended Techniques detailed on pp. 166–169.

Step 5—**Read Words in Isolation:** Partners take turns reading the words that they have written in the Workbook.

Step 6—**Independent Practice:** Students complete phonics activities in the Workbook.

Step 7—**Dictation:** Students write a dictated sentence that includes words with the target sounds and patterns in their Workbook.

Step 8—**Build Words from the Reader:** The teacher reviews the recently learned sounds and patterns with students, building words that they will encounter in the accompanying Reader.

Step 9—**Learn/Review Sight Words:** The teacher introduces students to the Sight Words, such as *the, of,* or *was,* that will be encountered in the accompanying Reader. This step may omitted from some lessons.

Step 10—**Read the Reader:** Students can independently read the Reader. This step can be varied with different ways of reading; for example, students can read the story aloud to a parent or teacher, read aloud in pairs or small groups, read in unison with the whole class, take turns reading aloud, or just read silently to themselves.

Step 11—**Respond to the Reader:** Students complete Reader response activities in the Workbook, often drawing a picture that relates to the Reader, and writing words or sentences.

Educators Publishing Service publishes a variety of a decodable readers that provide opportunities to practice newly acquired phonics skills in full-content reading. These titles are noted at the end of each lesson as "Additional Reading".

Extended Techniques for Building Words

The basic Build Words step in each lesson 1 to 59 consists of: 1. building the word; 2. touching and sounding each Touch-unit; 3. blending the sounds; 4. covering and spelling the word; and 5. covering and writing the word. Below are extended techniques and suggestions to vary, tailor, or lengthen the basic lesson.

Shake and Make

After you have built, touched and sounded, and blended the sounds of a word, you can "Shake and Make" the same word. Pick up all the units of the word that you have built and shake them up in your hands like dice. Then drop them in disarray on the desk or on the workspace (leaving the center clear). Ask a student to pick up the units and build the same word again, in the center of the workspace. After the student builds the word, prompt him to self-check by touching and sounding each unit, blending the sounds together. To make this more challenging, you can add two or three extra units and ask the student to leave out all the unneeded Touch-units.

Cover, Spell, Write

After building a word, cover the word and ask students to use "the camera in their heads" (visualization) to remember how the word looks and spell it out loud to you. The students should think of the Touch-units they have touched, sounded, and moved to build the word, and orally spell the word to you.

If a student is having some difficulty, you may choose to prompt with an oral sound or reveal part of the word while keeping the rest covered. If the student is unable to spell the word correctly, more modeling and student practice may be needed.

Touchphonics on the Board

Write the target words on the whiteboard or chalkboard. Words can be written in different colored chalk to draw the association to the color-coded patterning of the Touch-units, and later written in white chalk to graduate from the color cue. Have students take turns reading a word aloud. If they make a mistake, correct them right away and draw their attention to the part of the word that they missed or mistook. For example, if you write *swift* and the student says *sift*, point to the *w* and say "Here's a *w*, so this word says *swift*."

Appendices

Prereading Activities

You can do these activities with students who need to learn the names and sounds of letters, the conventions of print, the basics of reading comprehension, and the format of a story. If students already know the names of the letters, the sounds of most consonants, and they are familiar with the conventions of print, you may want to skip these activities and start with Lesson 1. The Prereading Activities are found on pp. 162–165.

Phonemic Awareness Activities

These activities give students additional practice in hearing, thinking about, and working with the individual sounds of words. Suggestions are given for working with rhyme, sound matching, sound/syllable segmentation, finger/syllable counting, word sorts, using song, poetry, and stories for phonemic awareness, and using mirrors for phonemic awareness. The Phonemic Awareness Activities are found on pp. 165–167.

Additional Word Activities

Word Games (p. 167) are included to provide fun practice for students who need extra reinforcement, or to vary and round out the instructional session's routine. Techniques for creating and using Word Rings and Word Walls are included on pp. 168–169.

Assessments

The Consonant Inventory (p. 170) and the Diagnostic Inventory (p. 172) are designed to assess a student's knowledge of letter sounds and names, phoneme and grapheme units, and English word structure. If students show in the Consonant Inventory that they have not yet mastered the names and sounds of the consonants, the Letter Names and Consonant Sounds Prereading Activities (pp. 162–164) are recommended. If students show in the Diagnostic Inventory that they have trouble decoding or encoding certain phonemes or graphemes, you can focus on those phonemes and graphemes in the lessons. The sounds and units that are not readily recognized and used correctly should become targets for instruction, and you may also want to include students' strengths in the lessons for positive reinforcement and sense of success. The diagnostics are also useful for identifying which students would benefit from extra time and instruction, and if given as pre- and post-tests, for gauging progress. If you are not using *Touchphonics* as a complete program but as an instructional tool, the diagnostics can be used prescriptively to decide which lessons would benefit students. Information on how to take Running Records, which can give insight into the strategies a student uses while reading, is included on p. 181.

Consonant Warm-up

Tell students that the letters of the alphabet are either consonants or vowels. Tell them that they are now going to learn the sounds that consonants make.

Sing or recite *The Alphabet Song* and point to each letter on an alphabet chart as you come to it. Afterwards, tell students that most of the letters in the alphabet are consonants. Tell them that the only letters that are not consonants are the vowels, *a, e, i, o,* and *u,* which they will learn later. Repeat *The Alphabet Song* with students, this time pointing only to the consonants. Tell students that they probably already know the sounds of most of the consonants, and that they will practice listening for consonants and saying the sounds that the consonants make.

To provide students with additional practice naming and sounding consonants, refer to the Touch-unit Letter Activity on page 163. You also may wish to individually test students using the Consonant Letter-Sound Inventory on page 170. Knowing which consonants your students need to practice, you can focus on about 4 to 6 consonants from the exercises below per teaching session.

Note:

A letter sound that you can sustain is an "open sound" (such as /m/, /r/, /s/, /f/, /l/, /n/, /x/, /v/, /z/). A letter that has a sound that you cannot sustain is a "stop sound" (such as /t/, /c/, /j/, /p/, /d/, /k/, /g/, /h/, /y/, /w/, /qu/). If the letter you are teaching has an "open sound," repeat the sound, and hold onto the sound. If the letter you are teaching has a "stop sound," just say the letter sound three times, so that students can learn to hear the first letter sound separate from the rest of the word. As you pronounce the letter sound three times, be sure you stop with the sound cut off. Be careful NOT to pronounce an "uh" at the end like /tuh/ for *t,* /cuh/ for *c,* /juh/ for *j,* etc.

Review the Consonants

Phonemic Awareness Say the word *bat,* emphasizing /b/ at the beginning. Then say the following words, and have students listen for the beginning sound: *band, big, box, bus, bug.* Ask students to tell you what sound they heard at the beginning of all those words.

Tell students to listen for the ending sound of some words you will say. Slowly say *rub, cab, fib, job, tub,* emphasizing /b/. Ask students to tell you what sound they heard at the end of all those words.

Repeat the above process with each consonant that students need to practice, having students listen and repeat the target consonant at the beginning of some words and at the end of other words. Practice words for each consonant are listed below.

c: cat, can, car, cub, cut; sac, tic, doc

d: dad, dip, dog, den, dug; bed, had, mud, sad, fed

j: jab, jam, job, jug, jet, jar, jog, jig

k: key, kid, kin, kit, kiss; wok, oak, yak, beak, hook

p: pad, pal, pin, pie, pet; cap, hip, map, pop, rip

t: tan, tea, top, tub, tag; pat, nut, met, bit, hut

v: van, vat, vet, vine, vase; cave, have, love, sieve, live

z: zig-zag, zap, zip, zoo; jazz, quiz, fizz, fuzz, maze

f: fun, fat, fig, fox, fan; off, beef, loaf, roof, leaf

l: leg, lab, lid, lot, lip; doll, goal, pal, tell, real

m: mad, man, map, mix, mud; dim, mom, yum, hum, ram

n: nap, net, nod, nut, new; hen, fan, pin, run, on

s: sun, sad, see, set, sip; bus, gas, moss, yes, kiss

r: rag, run, red, rib, rot; car, door, fur, more, ear

x: ax, ox, box, fox, six, tax, mix, wax

g: gap, gum, got, guy, gas; bag, dog, leg, mug, pig

h: hug, hen, his, hot, has, hid, hum, ham, hop

q: quit, quay, quiz, quail, quick, quell, quote, quid, quip, quad

y: yes, yell, yum, yet, yuck, yam, yay, yawn

w: wet, win, was, wig, wok, won, wag, wax

Link Letter to Sound Bring out all of the single Touchunit consonants or Magtile consonants to write the consonants out of order. Point to one letter at a time and call on individual students to say the sound the letter makes. Make sure that students say the sound, not the name of the letter.

Link Sound to Letter Form the following word on a whiteboard: *bun.* Say the word, emphasizing /b/. Then underline the *b* in the word. Tell students that the letter *b* makes the /b/ sound. Isolate the sound for students, and then have them repeat it after you.

Form the following words on a whiteboard: *lab, bib, sob, bed.* Say each word for students, and have them take turns underlining the *b*, saying /b/, and then saying the word.

Repeat the procedure above with each of the consonants, having students underline the target consonant in words you write on the board, say the consonant's sound, then say the word. Practice words for each consonant are listed below.

c: can, cup, cat, cub, car
d: dig, dip, had, nod, dad
j: job, jam, jet, jar, jug
k: kit, kin, yak, kid
p: pin, lip, pad, hop, tap
t: tag, hot, sit, tug, ten
v: van, vat, vet
z: zip, zap, zig, zag
f: fun, fan, fox, fit, fed
l: lid, pal, lot, lap, let
m: mug, him, men, ram, mop
n: nap, can, tin, not, nut
s: sip, bus, sat, yes, sob
r: ran, rip, car, rob, fur
x: box, fox, ax, ox, six
g: got, hug, pig, gas, leg
h: hen, hip, hot, hum, had
q: quit, quiz, quad, quid, quip
y: yes, yip, yet, yum, yam
w: win, wag, wit, wig, wax

Lesson 1: Short *a*

Remind students that they have learned the sounds that consonants make. Tell them that they are now going to learn the sounds that vowels make. Name the vowels for students: *a, e, i, o, u.*

Explain that when you say a vowel sound, you don't block the air with your teeth, tongue, or lips as it comes out of your mouth as you do with a consonant sound. Say several consonant and vowel sounds. Ask students if they can see and hear the difference.

Tell students that today they will learn the sound for short *a.*

Phonemic Awareness Say the word *ant.* Emphasize the short *a* sound.

Then say the following words, and have students listen for the short *a* sound at the beginning of each one: *apple, add, ant, arrow.*

Tell students to listen for short *a* in the middle of some words you will say. Slowly say *cat, tap, sat, mad, sad.* Emphasize the short *a* sound.

Link Sound to Letter Distribute the *a* Touch-unit. Have students trace its shape with their finger as they make the short *a* sound together.

Form the following word on a whiteboard: *hat.* Say the word, emphasizing the short *a* sound. Then underline the *a* in the word.

Tell students that the *a* makes the short *a* sound. Isolate the sound for students, and then have them repeat it after you.

Form these words on the whiteboard: *pal, tab, nag, lad.* Say each word for students, and have them take turns underlining the *a,* saying the short *a* sound, and then saying the word.

Build Words (Model) Tell students that they can use what they know about short *a* to build words.

Say *at.* Tell students you are going to build *at.* Use Touch-units or Magtiles to model.

Pick up the letter *a,* and say its sound as you place it on the whiteboard. Repeat the procedure with the letter *t,* and place it about an inch to the right of the letter *a.* Touch *a,* and say its sound. Touch *t,* and say its sound.

Move *a* and *t* closer together, and say their sounds, blending them slightly. Move the letters next to each other and blend the sounds to say *at.* (You may choose to do this in several steps, moving the letters closer together to demonstrate how to blend.)

Then cover the word and spell it orally. Uncover the word and have students compare your spelling with the Touch-units. Cover the word again and write it on the whiteboard. Uncover the word and have students compare the written word with the Touch-units.

Build Words Distribute Touch-units for the word *am.* Say *am.* Have students build it on their whiteboard using the Touch-units. Give help as necessary. After making the word, have students touch and sound each Touch-unit, then blend the sounds as they run their finger underneath the Touch-units. Have students cover the word and spell it orally, then compare their spelling to the Touch-units. Next have them cover the word again and write it on their whiteboard and then on the Build Words page of their Workbook (p. 2). Have students compare their writing to the Touch-units. Repeat the procedure with *ax* and *an.* Then use this procedure to have students build the following words:

	yellow	red
can	c, n	a
cat	t	
mat	m	
map	p	
nap	n	
nab	b	

Use one of the activities on page xvi to further practice sequencing and discriminating the words that students find challenging.

Read Words in Isolation Have students pair up and read all of the words they have written on Workbook page 2 aloud to their partner.

Independent Practice (Workbook page 1) For the first set of items, ask students to blend the sounds in each word, say the word, and circle the picture that the word names. For the second set, ask them to find the word that names the picture at the beginning of each row. When students complete the page, have them check their work with you or a partner.

Dictation Dictate the following sentence, and have students write it on their whiteboard or at the bottom of Workbook page 1: *An ant can nap.*

Reading Words in Context

Tell students that they will use what they know about short *a* words to read a story.

Build Words from the Story Use the Touch-units to build the following words on the whiteboard. Tell students that the words you will make together will help them read the story.

Start with the word *am.*

Substitute Touch-units to build the following words: *an, ant, add, adding, can, cap, cat, sat.*

As a prereading activity, you may want to have students find the words in the text and read them aloud.

Learn Sight Words Tell students that they will learn some new words to help them read the story. Display these sight words: *I, the.* Read the words as you point to them.

As a prereading activity, you may want to have students find the words in the text as they write them.

Read the Story Give students a copy of *Adding Ant.* Have them read it independently or with a partner. If necessary, you can support students as they read the story by identifying sight words or helping them to blend sounds to read words.

Respond to the Story After students read *Adding Ant,* have them complete Workbook page 3. Have students share their work with the rest of the group.

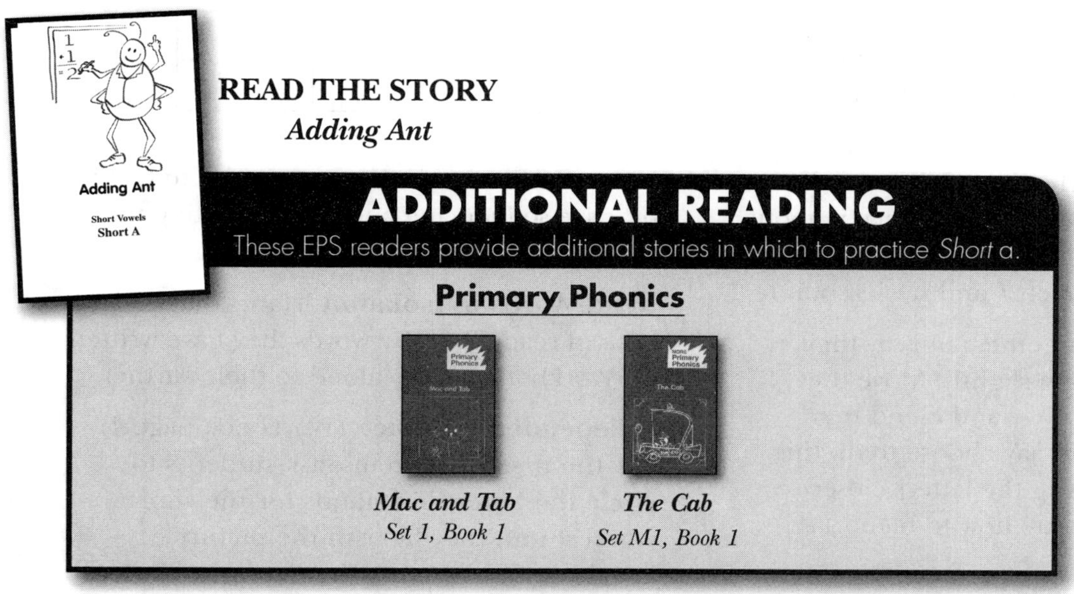

Lesson 2: Short *i*

Remind students that they have learned the sound for short *a.* Tell them that today they will learn the sound for short *i.*

Phonemic Awareness Say the word *igloo.* Emphasize the short *i* sound.

Then say the following words, and have students listen for the short *i* sound at the beginning of each one: *inch, ill, itch, in.*

Tell students to listen for short *i* in the middle of some words you will say. Slowly say *rib, hid, dim, tin, fit.* Emphasize the short *i* sound.

Link Sound to Letter Distribute the *i* Touch-unit. Have students trace its shape with their finger as they make the short *i* sound together.

Form the following word on a whiteboard: *win.* Say the word, emphasizing the short *i* sound. Then underline the *i* in the word.

Tell students that the *i* makes the short *i* sound. Isolate the sound for students, and then have them repeat it after you.

Form these words on the whiteboard: *bit, lid, him, pip.* Say each word for students, and have them take turns underlining the *i,* saying the short *i* sound, and then saying the word.

Build Words (Model) Tell students that they can use what they know about short *i* to build words.

Say *if.* Tell students you are going to build *if.* Use Touch-units or Magtiles to model.

Pick up the letter *i,* and say its sound as you place it on the whiteboard. Repeat the procedure with the letter *f,* and place it about an inch to the right of the letter *i.* Touch *i,* and say its sound. Touch *f,* and say its sound.

Move *i* and *f* closer together, and say their sounds, blending them slightly. Move the letters next to each other and blend the sounds to say *if.* (You may choose to do this in several steps, moving the letters closer together to demonstrate how to blend.)

Then cover the word and spell it orally. Uncover the word and have students compare your spelling with the Touch-units. Cover the word again and write it on the whiteboard. Uncover the word and have students compare the written word with the Touch-units.

Build Words Distribute Touch-units for the word *it.* Say *it.* Have students build it on their whiteboard using the Touch-units. Give help as necessary. After making the word, have students touch and sound each Touch-unit, then blend the sounds as they run their finger underneath the Touch-units. Have students cover the word and spell it orally, then compare their spelling to the Touch-units. Next have them cover the word again and write it on their whiteboard and then on the Build Words page of their Workbook (p. 5). Have students compare their writing to the Touch-units. Repeat the procedure with *in.* Then use this procedure to have students build the following words:

	yellow	red
did	d, d	i
kid	k	
kit	t	
lit	l	
pit	p	
pin	n	

Use one of the activities on page xvi to further practice sequencing and discriminating the words that students find challenging.

Read Words in Isolation Have students pair up and read all of the words they have written on Workbook page 5 aloud to their partner.

Independent Practice (Workbook page 4) For the first set of items, ask students to circle the letter that stands for the short vowel sound they hear in the picture.
For the second set, ask them to write the word

that completes each sentence. When students complete the page, have them check their work with you or a partner.

Dictation Dictate the following sentence, and have students write it on their whiteboard or at the bottom of Workbook page 4: *Jim did win it.*

Reading Words in Context

Tell students that they will use what they know about short *i* words to read a story.

Build Words from the Story Use the Touch-units to build the following words on the whiteboard. Tell students that the words you will make together will help them read the story.

Start with the word *in.*

Substitute Touch-units to build the following words: *bin, bid, big, bit, fit, fin, fig, jig, jigs, zig, wig, pig, pin, pit, hit, his, hip, hips, hid, lid, lip, lit.*

As a prereading activity, you may want to have students find the words in the text and read them aloud.

Learn Sight Words Tell students that they will learn some new words to help them read the story. Display these sight words: *are, you.* Read the words as you point to them.

As a prereading activity, you may want to have students find the words in the text as they write them.

Read the Story Give students a copy of *Izzy Can Jig.* Have them read it independently or with a partner. If necessary, you can support students as they read the story by identifying sight words or helping them to blend sounds to read words.

Respond to the Story After students read *Izzy Can Jig,* have them complete Workbook page 6. Have students share their work with the rest of the group.

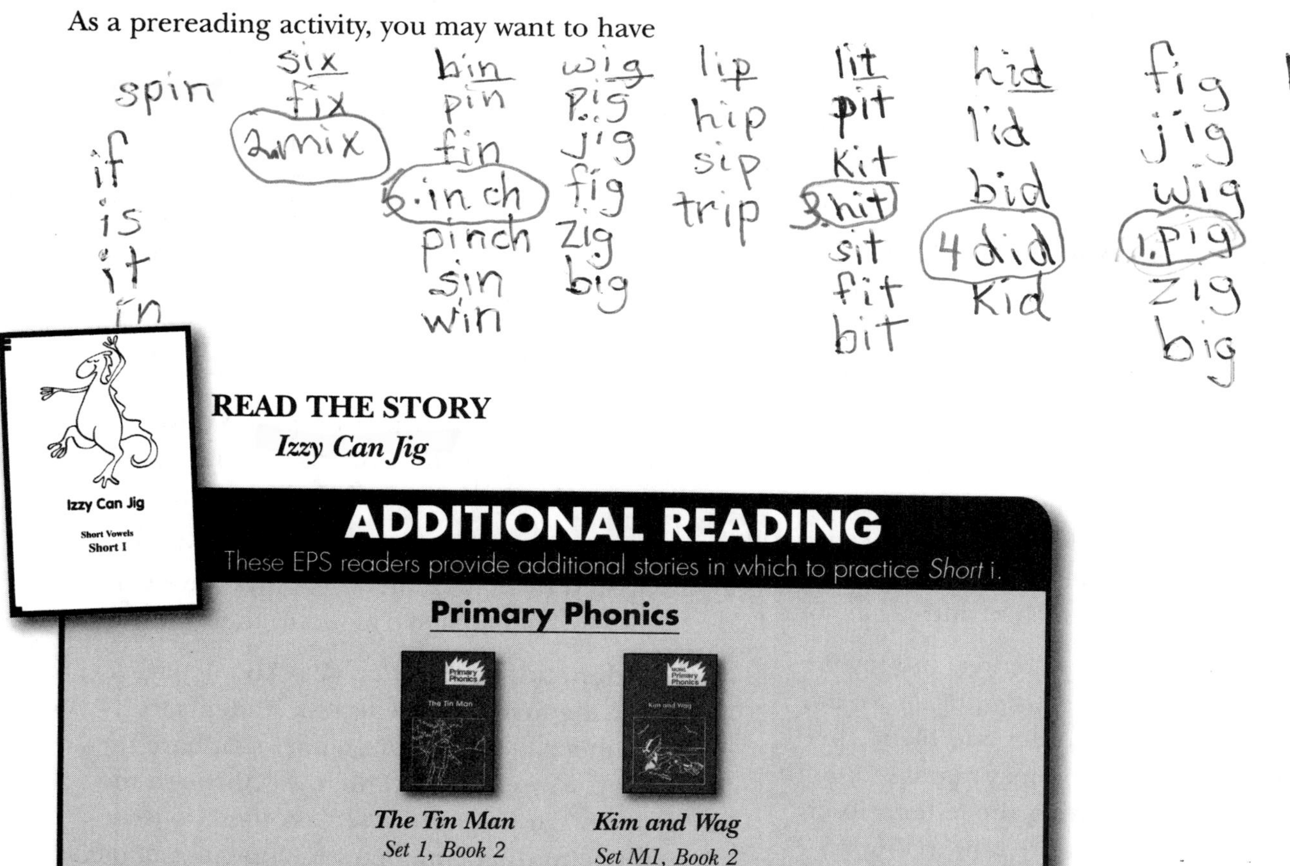

READ THE STORY
Izzy Can Jig

ADDITIONAL READING

These EPS readers provide additional stories in which to practice *Short i.*

Primary Phonics

The Tin Man
Set 1, Book 2

Kim and Wag
Set M1, Book 2

Lesson 3: Short *o*

Remind students that they have learned the sounds for short *a* and *i*. Tell them that today they will learn the sound for short *o*.

Phonemic Awareness Say the word *octopus*. Emphasize the short *o* sound.

Then say the following words, and have students listen for the short *o* sound at the beginning of each one: *on, odd, ox.*

Tell students to listen for short *o* in the middle of some words you will say. Slowly say *job, hot, nod, pop.* Emphasize the short *o* sound.

Link Sound to Letter Distribute the *o* Touch-unit. Have students trace its shape with their finger as they make the short *o* sound together.

Form the following word on a whiteboard: *not.* Say the word, emphasizing the short *o* sound. Then underline the *o* in the word.

Tell students that the *o* makes the short *o* sound. Isolate the sound for students, and then have them repeat it after you.

Form these words on the whiteboard: *dot, box, mom, fog.* Say each word for students, and have them take turns underlining the *o*, saying the short *o* sound, and then saying the word.

Build Words (Model) Tell students that they can use what they know about short *o* to build words.

Say *on.* Tell students you are going to build *on.* Use Touch-units or Magtiles to model.

Pick up the letter *o*, and say its sound as you place it on the whiteboard. Repeat the procedure with the letter *n*, and place it about an inch to the right of the letter *o*. Touch *o*, and say its sound. Touch *n*, and say its sound.

Move *o* and *n* closer together, and say their sounds, blending them slightly. Move the letters next to each other and blend the sounds to say *on.* (You may choose to do this in several steps, moving the letters closer together to demonstrate how to blend.)

Then cover the word and spell it orally. Uncover the word and have students compare your spelling with the Touch-units. Cover the word again and write it on the whiteboard. Uncover the word and have students compare the written word with the Touch-units.

Build Words Distribute Touch-units for the word *ox.* Say *ox.* Have students build it on their whiteboard using the Touch-units. Give help as necessary. After making the word, have students touch and sound each Touch-unit, then blend the sounds as they run their finger underneath the Touch-units. Have students cover the word and spell it orally, then compare their spelling to the Touch-units. Next have them cover the word again and write it on their whiteboard and then on the Build Words page of their Workbook (p. 8). Have students compare their writing to the Touch-units. Then use this procedure to have students build the following words:

	yellow	red
pot	p, t	o
pop	p	
mop	m	
mob	b	
cob	c	
cog	g	

Use one of the activities on page xvi to further practice sequencing and discriminating the words that students find challenging.

Read Words in Isolation Have students pair up and read all of the words they have written on Workbook page 8 aloud to their partner.

Independent Practice (Workbook page 7) For the first set of items, ask students to connect all the picture names that have the short *o* sound to find their way through the maze. For the second set, ask them to write the letter that completes each picture name.

When students complete the page, have them check their work with you or a partner.

Dictation Dictate the following sentence, and have students write it on their whiteboard or at the bottom of Workbook page 7: *Bob got on top.*

Reading Words in Context

Tell students that they will use what they know about short *o* words to read a story.

Build Words from the Story Use the Touch-units to build the following words on the whiteboard. Tell students that the words you will make together will help them read the story.

Start with the word *got.*

Substitute Touch-units to build the following words: *cot, hot, hog, hop, mop, mob, job, jobs, rob, rod, rot, lot, not, nod, pod, pop, pot, top.*

As a prereading activity, you may want to have students find the words in the text and read them aloud.

Learn Sight Words Tell students that they will learn some new words to help them read the story. Display these sight words: *a, all, of, said.* Read the words as you point to them.

As a prereading activity, you may want to have students find the words in the text as they write them.

Read the Story Give students a copy of *Top Job.* Have them read it independently or with a partner. If necessary, you can support students as they read the story by identifying sight words or helping them to blend sounds to read words.

Respond to the Story After students read *Top Job,* have them complete Workbook page 9. Have students share their work with the rest of the group.

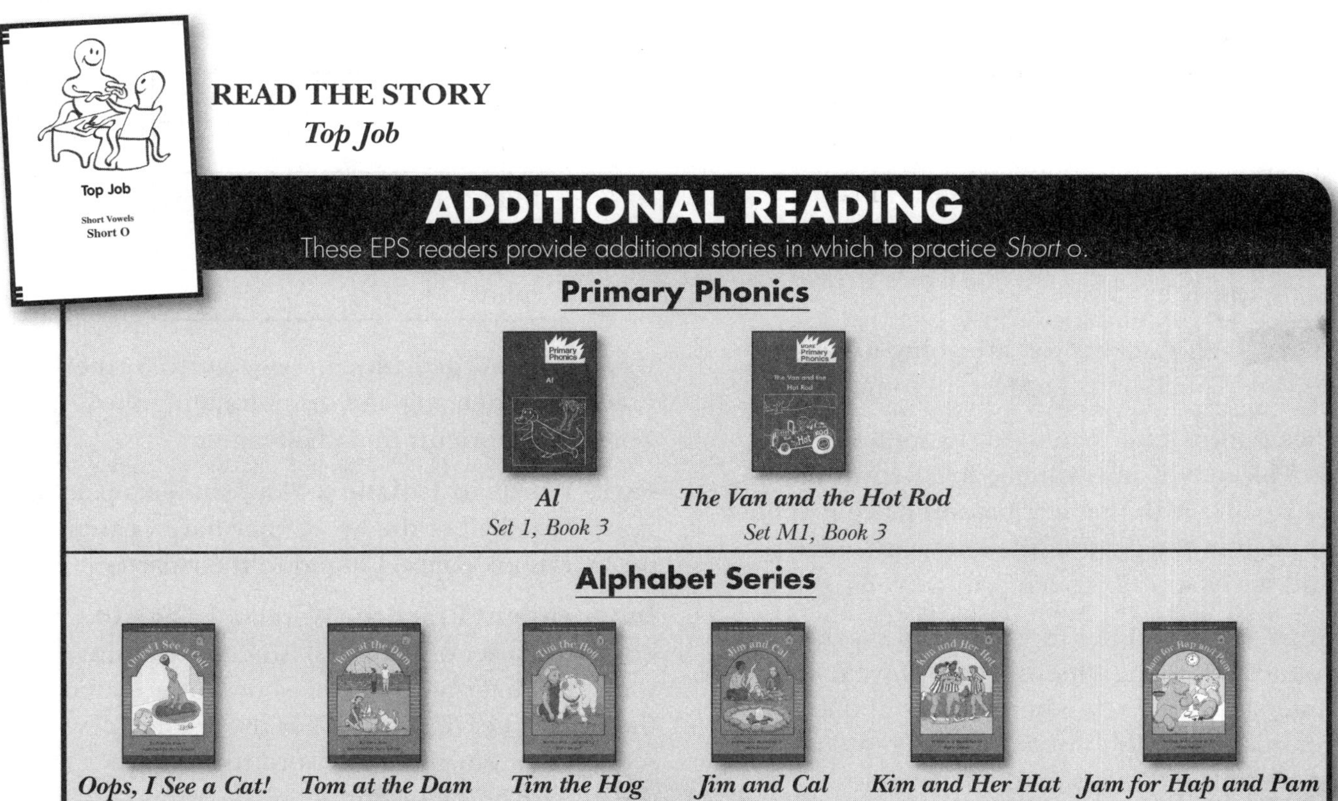

Lesson 4: Short *u*

Remind students that they have learned the sounds for short *a, i,* and *o.* Tell them that today they will learn the sound for short *u.*

Phonemic Awareness Say the word *uncle.* Emphasize the short *u* sound.

Then say the following words, and have students listen for the short *u* sound at the beginning of each one: *under, umbrella, upon, upside-down.*

Tell students to listen for short *u* in the middle of some words you will say. Slowly say *cut, luck, gum, hug.* Emphasize the short *u* sound.

Link Sound to Letter Distribute the *u* Touch-unit. Have students trace its shape with their finger as they make the short *u* sound together.

Form the following word on a whiteboard: *hum.* Say the word, emphasizing the short *u* sound. Then underline the *u* in the word.

Tell students that the *u* makes the short *u* sound. Isolate the sound for students, and then have them repeat it after you.

Form these words on the whiteboard: *run, sub, bud, dug.* Say each word for students, and have them take turns underlining the *u,* saying the short *u* sound, and then saying the word.

Build Words (Model) Tell students that they can use what they know about short *u* to build words.

Say *up.* Tell students you are going to build *up.* Use Touch-units or Magtiles to model.

Pick up the letter *u,* and say its sound as you place it on the whiteboard. Repeat the procedure with the letter *p,* and place it about an inch to the right of the letter *u.* Touch *u,* and say its sound. Touch *p,* and say its sound.

Move *u* and *p* closer together, and say their sounds, blending them slightly. Move the letters next to each other and blend the sounds to say *up.* (You may choose to do this in several steps, moving the letters closer together to demonstrate how to blend.)

Then cover the word and spell it orally. Uncover the word and have students compare your spelling with the Touch-units. Cover the word again and write it on the whiteboard. Uncover the word and have students compare the written word with the Touch-units.

Build Words Distribute Touch-units for the word *us.* Say *us.* Have students build it on their whiteboard using the Touch-units. Give help as necessary. After making the word, have students touch and sound each Touch-unit, then blend the sounds as they run their finger underneath the Touch-units. Have students cover the word and spell it orally, then compare their spelling to the Touch-units. Next have them cover the word again and write it on their whiteboard and then on the Build Words page of their Workbook (p. 11). Have students compare their writing to the Touch-units. Then use this procedure to have students build the following words:

	yellow	red
cub	c, b	u
tub	t	
tug	g	
dug	d	
dud	d	
mud	m	

Use one of the activities on page xvi to further practice sequencing and discriminating the words that students find challenging.

Read Words in Isolation Have students pair up and read all of the words they have written on Workbook page 11 aloud to their partner.

Independent Practice (Workbook page 10) For the first set of items, ask students to print the letter that stands for the short vowel sound they hear in each picture. For the second set, ask them to circle the word that names the picture at the beginning of each row.

When students complete the page, have them check their work with you or a partner.

Dictation Dictate the following sentence, and have students write it on their whiteboard or at the bottom of Workbook page 10: *Pup dug up the mug.*

Reading Words in Context

Tell students that they will use what they know about short *u* words to read a story.

Build Words from the Story Use the Touch-units to build the following words on the whiteboard. Tell students that the words you will make together will help them read the story.

Start with the word *bud.*

Substitute Touch-units to build the following words: *bug, bum, buzz, but, cut, cub, rub, rubs, run, rug, hug, hut, hum, sum, sub, sun.*

As a prereading activity, you may want to have students find the words in the text and read them aloud.

Learn Sight Words Tell students that they will learn a new word to help them read the story. Display this sight word: *was.* Read the word as you point to it.

As a prereading activity, you may want to have students find the word in the text as they write it.

Read the Story Give students a copy of *The Cub and the Bug.* Have them read it independently or with a partner. If necessary, you can support students as they read the story by identifying sight words or helping them to blend sounds to read words.

Respond to the Story After students read *The Cub and the Bug,* have them complete Workbook page 12. Have students share their work with the rest of the group.

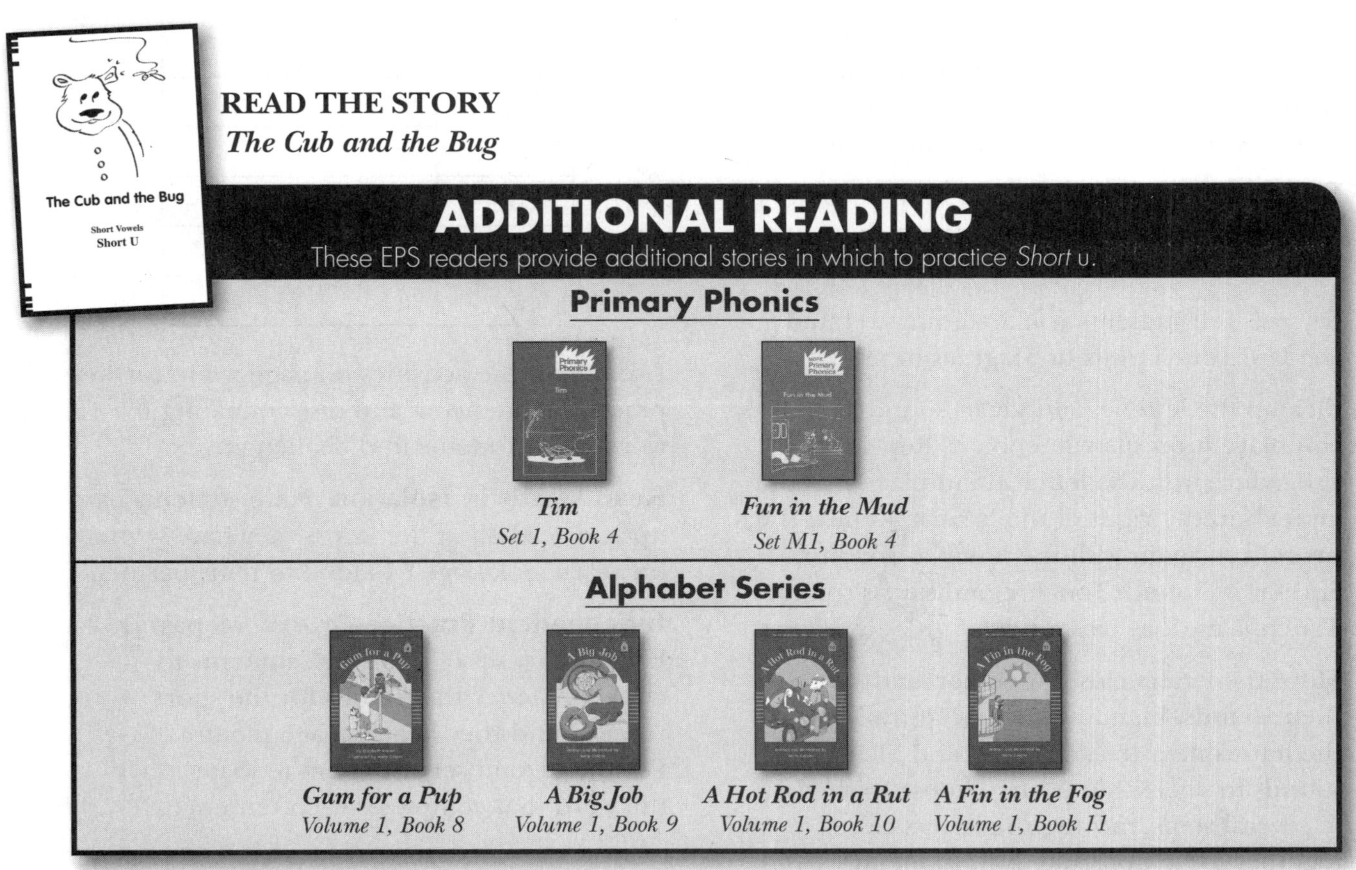

Lesson 5: Short e

Remind students that they have learned the sounds for short *a, i, o,* and *u.* Tell them that today they will learn the sound for short *e.*

Phonemic Awareness Say the word *egg.* Emphasize the short *e* sound.

Then say the following words, and have students listen for the short *e* sound at the beginning of each one: *end, edge, elephant, elbow.*

Tell students to listen for short *e* in the middle of some words you will say. Slowly say *get, wet, sell, fed.* Emphasize the short *e* sound.

Link Sound to Letter Distribute the *e* Touch-unit. Have students trace its shape with their finger as they make the short *e* sound together.

Form the following word on a whiteboard: *led.* Say the word, emphasizing the short *e* sound. Then underline the *e* in the word.

Tell students that the *e* makes the short *e* sound. Isolate the sound for students, and then have them repeat it after you.

Form these words on the whiteboard: *beg, yes, men, vet.* Say each word for students, and have them take turns underlining the *e,* saying the short *e* sound, and then saying the word.

Build Words (Model) Tell students that they can use what they know about short *e* to build words.

Say *red.* Tell students you are going to build *red.* Use Touch-units or Magtiles to model.

Pick up the letter *r,* and say its sound as you place it on the whiteboard. Repeat the procedure with the letter *e,* and place it about an inch to the right of the letter *r.* Repeat the procedure again with the letter *d.* Touch *r,* and say its sound. Touch *e,* and say its sound. Touch *d,* and say its sound.

Move the letters closer together, and say their sounds, blending them slightly. Move the letters next to each other and blend the sounds to say *red.* (You may choose to do this in several steps, moving the letters closer together to demonstrate how to blend.)

Then cover the word and spell it orally. Uncover the word and have students compare your spelling with the Touch-units. Cover the word again and write it on the whiteboard. Uncover the word and have students compare the written word with the Touch-units.

Build Words Distribute Touch-units for the word *set.* Say *set.* Have students build it on their whiteboard using the Touch-units. Give help as necessary. After making the word, have students touch and sound each Touch-unit, then blend the sounds as they run their finger underneath the Touch-units. Have students cover the word and spell it orally, then compare their spelling to the Touch-units. Next have them cover the word again and write it on their whiteboard and then on the Build Words page of their Workbook (p. 14). Have students compare their writing to the Touch-units. Then use this procedure to have students build the following words:

	yellow	red
pet	p, t	e
bet	t	
bed	d	
fed	f	
led	l	
leg	g	

Use one of the activities on page xvi to further practice sequencing and discriminating the words that students find challenging.

Read Words in Isolation Have students pair up and read all of the words they have written on Workbook page 14 aloud to their partner.

Independent Practice (Workbook page 13) For the first set of items, ask students to circle the letter that stands for the short vowel sound they hear in each picture. For the second set, ask them to write the word that completes each sentence.

When students complete the page, have them check their work with you or a partner.

Dictation Dictate the following sentence, and have students write it on their whitebaord or at the bottom of Workbook page 13: *Peg fed the red hen.*

Reading Words in Context

Tell students that they will use what they know about short *e* words to read a story.

Build Words from the Story Use the Touch-units to build the following words on the whiteboard. Tell students that the words you will make together will help them read the story.

Start with the word *bed.*

Substitute Touch-units to build the following words: *Ed, beg, bet, get, gets, set, let, yet, yes, leg, legs, led, red, wed, web, wet, pet, peg, pen, den.*

As a prereading activity, you may want to have students find the words in the text and read them aloud.

Learn Sight Words Tell students that they will learn a new word to help them read the story. Display this sight word: *to.* Read the word as you point to it.

As a prereading activity, you may want to have students find the word in the text as they write it.

Read the Story Give students a copy of *Wet Ed.* Have them read it independently or with a partner. If necessary, you can support students as they read the story by identifying sight words or helping them to blend sounds to read words.

Respond to the Story After students read *Wet Ed,* have them complete Workbook page 15. Have students share their work with the rest of the group.

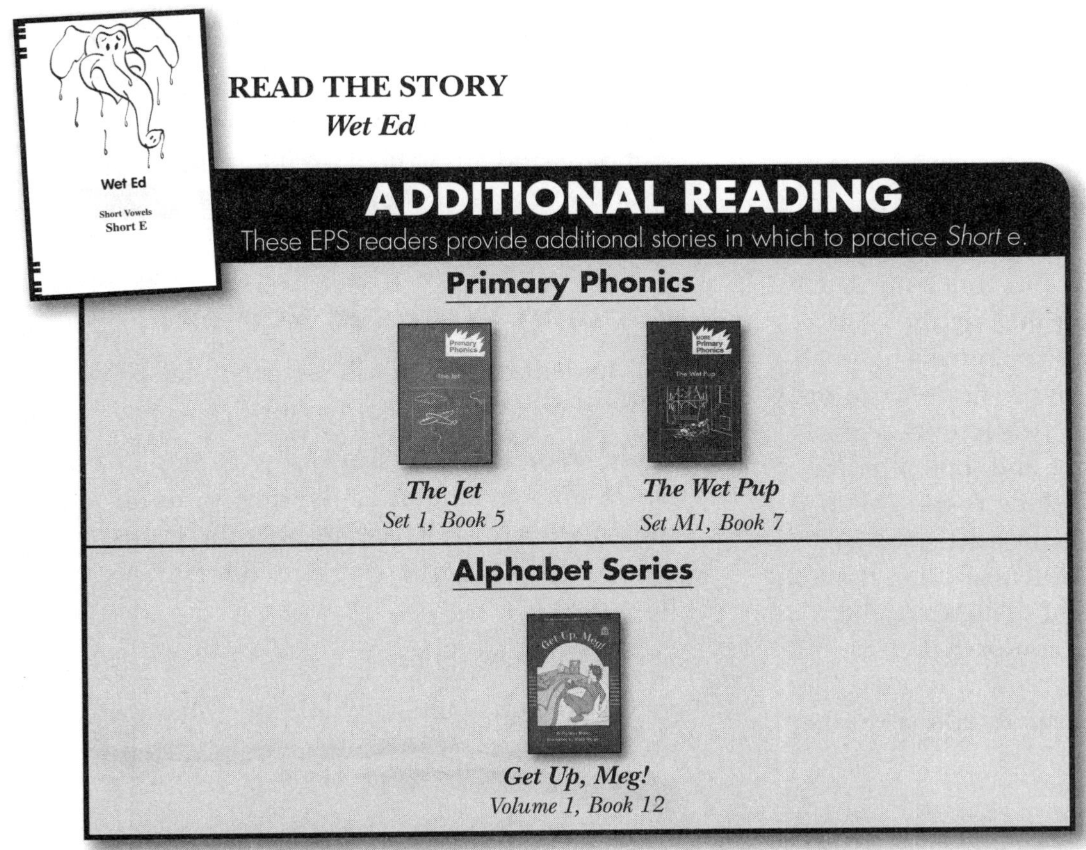

Lesson 6: Review Short Vowels, 1

Remind students that they have learned the sounds for all of the short vowels. Tell students that they are now going to review the sounds to help them remember them better.

Phonemic Awareness Tell students that they are going to play a game to help them remember the sounds for short vowels.

Say the following words: *pat, fit, gap.* Ask students to name the two words that have the same sound in the middle.

Repeat the procedure with the following sets of words: *top, pin, pop; sit, cut, luck; tip, win, cat; sip, let, hen.*

Link Sound to Letter Distribute the *i* Touch-unit. Have students trace its shape with their finger as they make the short *i* sound together.

Form the following word on a whiteboard: *pit.* Say the word, emphasizing the short *i* sound. Then underline the *i* in that word.

Tell students that the *i* makes the short *i* sound. Isolate the sound for students, and then have them repeat it after you.

Now distribute the *a, e, o,* and *u* Touch-units. Repeat the procedure above to form the following words: *lap, set, hop, pup.*

Build Words Distribute Touch-units for the word *sap.* Say *sap.* Have students build it on their whiteboard using the Touch-units. Give help as necessary. After making the word, have students touch and sound each Touch-unit, then blend the sounds as they run their finger underneath the Touch-units. Have students cover the word and spell it orally, then compare their spelling to the Touch-units. Next have them cover the word again and write it on their whiteboard and then on the Build Words page of their Workbook (p. 17). Have students compare their writing to the Touch-units. Then use this procedure to have students build the following words:

	yellow	red
sat	s, t	a
sit		i
bit	b	
but		u
bet		e
beg	g	
bog		o

Use one of the activities on page xvi to further practice sequencing and discriminating the words that students find challenging.

Read Words in Isolation Have students pair up and read all of the words they have written on Workbook page 17 aloud to their partner.

Independent Practice (Workbook page 16) For the first set of items, ask students to write the letter that completes each picture name. For the second set, ask them to circle the word that names the picture at the beginning of each row. When students complete the page, have them check their work with you or a partner.

Dictation Dictate the following sentence, and have students write it on their whiteboard or at the bottom of Workbook page 16: *Tom had a big, red cup.*

Reading Words in Context

Tell students that they will use what they know about short vowels to read a story.

Build Words from the Story Use the Touch-units to build the following words on the whiteboard. Tell students that the words you will make together will help them read the story.

Start with the word *ram.*

Substitute Touch-units to build the following words: *ran, run, rub, rug, dug, dig, big, dog, hog, hot, got, not, lot, lit, pit, pet, pep, pup, cup, cut, cat, can.*

As a prereading activity, you may want to have students find the words in the text and read them aloud.

Review Sight Words Tell students that they will review some words that will help them read the story. Display these sight words: *I, the, you, a.* Read the words as you point to them.

As a prereading activity, you may want to have students find the words in the text as they write them.

Read the Story Give students a copy of *Dan the Dog.* Have them read it independently or with a partner. If necessary, you can support students as they read the story by identifying sight words or helping them to blend sounds to read words.

Respond to the Story After students read *Dan the Dog,* have them complete Workbook page 18. Have students share their work with the rest of the group.

Lesson 7: Review Short Vowels, 2

Remind students that they have learned the sounds for all of the short vowels. Tell students that they are now going to review the sounds to help them remember them better.

Phonemic Awareness Tell students that they are going to play a rhyming game to help them remember the sounds for short vowels.

Say the word *cap.* Ask students to name words that rhyme with *cap.* Have them emphasize the short vowel sound in each one.

Repeat the procedure with the following words: *get, pin, not, luck.*

Link Sound to Letter Distribute the *o* Touch-unit. Have students trace its shape with their finger as they make the short *o* sound together.

Form the following word on a whiteboard: *tot.* Say the word, emphasizing the short *o* sound. Then underline the *o* in that word.

Tell students that the *o* makes the short *o* sound. Isolate the sound for students, and then have them repeat it after you.

Now distribute the *a, e, i,* and *u* Touch-units. Repeat the procedure above to form the following words: *sat, hen, pig, bud.*

Build Words Distribute Touch-units for the word *cup.* Say *cup.* Have students build it on their whiteboard using the Touch-units. Give help as necessary. After making the word, have students touch and sound each Touch-unit, then blend the sounds as they run their finger underneath the Touch-units. Have students cover the word and spell it orally, then compare their spelling to the Touch-units. Next have them cover the word again and write it on their whiteboard and then on the Build Words page of their Workbook (p. 20). Have students compare their writing to the Touch-units. Then use this procedure to have students build the following words:

	yellow	red
cut	c, t	u
cat		a
cap	p	
lap	l	
map	m	
mop		o
top	t	
tip		i
tin	n	
ten		e

Use one of the activities on page xvi to further practice sequencing and discriminating the words that students find challenging.

Read Words in Isolation Have students pair up and read all of the words they have written on Workbook page 20 aloud to their partner.

Independent Practice (Workbook page 19) For the first set of items, ask students to circle the letter that stands for the short vowel sound they hear in each picture name. For the second set, ask them to blend the sounds in each word, say the word, and circle the picture that the word names. When students complete the page, have them check their work with you or a partner.

Dictation Dictate the following sentence, and have students write it on their whiteboard or at the bottom of Workbook page 19: *Jen sat on a big rug.*

Reading Words in Context

Tell students that they will use what they know about short vowel sounds to read a story.

Build Words from the Story Use the Touch-units to build the following words on the whiteboard. Tell students that the words you will make together will help them read the story.

Start with the word *bat.*

Substitute Touch-units to build the following words: *bet, bit, big, bin, bun, but, nut, not, hot, lot, nap, map, mad, mud, bud, beg, peg, pig, pigs, pin, pen, ten.*

As a prereading activity, you may want to have students find the words in the text and read them aloud.

Learn Sight Words Tell students that they will learn some words that will help them read the story. Display these sight words: *do, have, they.* Read the words as you point to them.

As a prereading activity, you may want to have students find the words in the text as they write them.

Read the Story Give students a copy of *The Pig Pen.* Have them read it independently or with a partner. If necessary, you can support students as they read the story by identifying sight words or helping them to blend sounds to read words.

Respond to the Story After students read *The Pig Pen,* have them complete Workbook page 21. Have students share their work with the rest of the group.

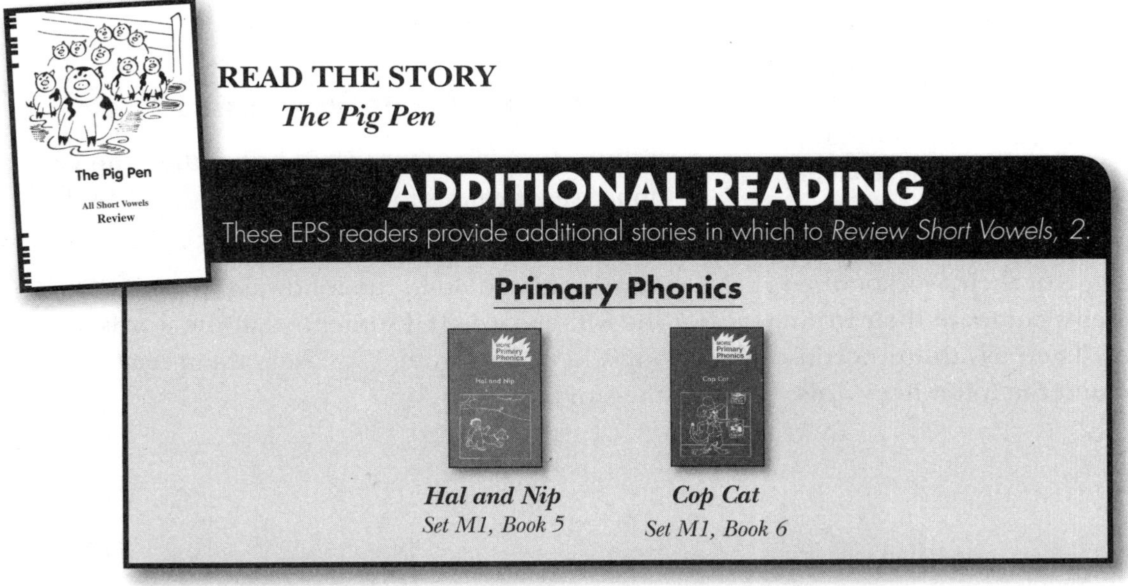

Lesson 8: Review Short Vowels, 3

Remind students that they have learned the sounds for all of the short vowels. Tell students that they are now going to review the sounds to help them remember them better.

Phonemic Awareness Tell students that they are going to play a game to help them remember the sounds for short vowels.

Say the word *set.* Ask students to name the sounds they hear in the word.

Repeat the procedure with the following words: *pat, tin, tot, sun.*

Link Sound to Letter Distribute the *e* Touch-unit. Have students trace its shape with their finger as they make the short *e* sound together.

Form the following word on a whiteboard: *leg.* Say the word, emphasizing the short *e* sound. Then underline the *e* in that word.

Tell students that the *e* makes the short *e* sound. Isolate the sound for students, and then have them repeat it after you.

Now distribute the *a, i, o,* and *u* Touch-units. Repeat the procedure above to form the following words: *mat, hit, lot, run.*

Build Words Distribute Touch-units for the word *cat.* Say *cat.* Have students build it on their whiteboard using the Touch-units. Give help as necessary. After making the word, have students touch and sound each Touch-unit, then blend the sounds as they run their finger underneath the Touch-units. Have students cover the word and spell it orally, then compare their spelling to the Touch-units. Next have them cover the word again and write it on their whiteboard and then on the Build Words page of their Workbook (p. 23). Have students compare their writing to the Touch-units. Then use this procedure to have students build the following words:

	yellow	red
sat	s, t	a
sit		i
pit	p	
pot		o
pet		e
pen	n	
pep	p	
pup		u

Use one of the activities on page xvi to further practice sequencing and discriminating the words that students find challenging.

Read Words in Isolation Have students pair up and read all of the words they have written on Workbook page 23 aloud to their partner.

Independent Practice (Workbook page 22) For the first set of items, ask students to print the letter that stands for the short vowel sound they hear in each picture name. For the second set, ask them to write the word that completes each sentence. When students complete the page, have them check their work with you or a partner.

Dictation Dictate the following sentence, and have students write it on their whiteboard or at the bottom of Workbook page 22: *Ted hid a fat bug in a box.*

Reading Words in Context

Tell students that they will use what they know about short vowels to read a story.

Build Words from the Story Use the Touch-units to build the following words on the whiteboard. Tell students that the words you will make together will help them read the story.

Start with the word *bed.*

Substitute Touch-units to build the following words: *bit, bud, bug, bugs, but, sit, set, six, Max, cat, can, nap, nods, not, got, get, leg, led, lid, lip, hip, hid.*

As a prereading activity, you may want to have students find the words in the text and read them aloud.

Learn Sight Words Tell students that they will learn a new word that will help them read the story. Display this sight word: *what.* Read the word as you point to it.

As a prereading activity, you may want to have students find the word in the text as they write it.

Read the Story Give students a copy of *Max and the Bed Bugs.* Have them read it independently or with a partner. If necessary, you can support students as they read the story by identifying sight words or helping them to blend sounds to read words.

Respond to the Story After students read *Max and the Bed Bugs,* have them complete Workbook page 24. Have students share their work with the rest of the group.

Lesson 9: Review Short Vowels, 4

Remind students that they have learned the sounds for all of the short vowels. Tell students that they are now going to review the sounds to help them remember them better.

Phonemic Awareness Tell students that they are going to play a game to help them remember the sounds for short vowels.

Say the sounds in the word *puck* one at a time. Ask students to guess which word you are saying.

Repeat the procedure with the following words: *pan, red, mill, hop.*

Link Sound to Letter Distribute the *a* Touch-unit. Have students trace its shape with their finger as they make the short *a* sound together.

Form the following word on a whiteboard: *ram.* Say the word, emphasizing the short *a* sound. Then underline the *a* in that word.

Tell students that the *a* makes the short *a* sound. Isolate the sound for students, and then have them repeat it after you.

Now distribute the *e, i, o,* and *u* Touch-units. Repeat the procedure above to form the following words: *pen, rip, rot, run.*

Build Words Distribute Touch-units for the word *dot.* Say *dot.* Have students build it on their whiteboard using the Touch-units. Give help as necessary. After making the word, have students touch and sound each Touch-unit, then blend the sounds as they run their finger underneath the Touch-units. Have students cover the word and spell it orally, then compare their spelling to the Touch-units. Next have them cover the word again and write it on their whiteboard and then on the Build Words page of their Workbook (p. 26). Have students compare their writing to the Touch-units. Then use this procedure to have students build the following words:

	yellow	red
dog	d, g	o
dig		i
dug		u
lug	l	
log		o
lag		a
rag	r	
rig		i

Use one of the activities on page xvi to further practice sequencing and discriminating the words that students find challenging.

Read Words in Isolation Have students pair up and read all of the words they have written on Workbook page 26 aloud to their partner.

Independent Practice (Workbook page 25) For the first set of items, ask students to write the letter that completes each picture name. For the second set, ask them to circle the word that names the picture at the beginning of each row. When students complete the page, have them check their work with you or a partner.

Dictation Dictate the following sentence, and have students write it on their whiteboard or at the bottom of Workbook page 25: *Len sat on a log in the sun.*

Reading Words in Context

Tell students that they will use what they know about short vowels to read a story.

Build Words from the Story Use the Touch-units to build the following words on the whiteboard. Tell students that the words you will make together will help them read the story.

Start with the word *cub.*

Substitute Touch-units to build the following words: *tub, tin, tap, taps, hop, hum, hums, fun, can, jam, pans, pat, pats, sat, has, his, is, it, hits.*

As a prereading activity, you may want to have students find the words in the text and read them aloud.

Learn Sight Words Tell students that they will learn a new word that will help them read the story. Display this sight word: *put.* Read the word as you point to it.

As a prereading activity, you may want to have students find the word in the text as they write it.

Read the Story Give students a copy of *Jam in the Den.* Have them read it independently or with a partner. If necessary, you can support students as they read the story by identifying sight words or helping them to blend sounds to read words.

Respond to the Story After students read *Jam in the Den,* have them complete Workbook page 27. Have students share their work with the rest of the group.

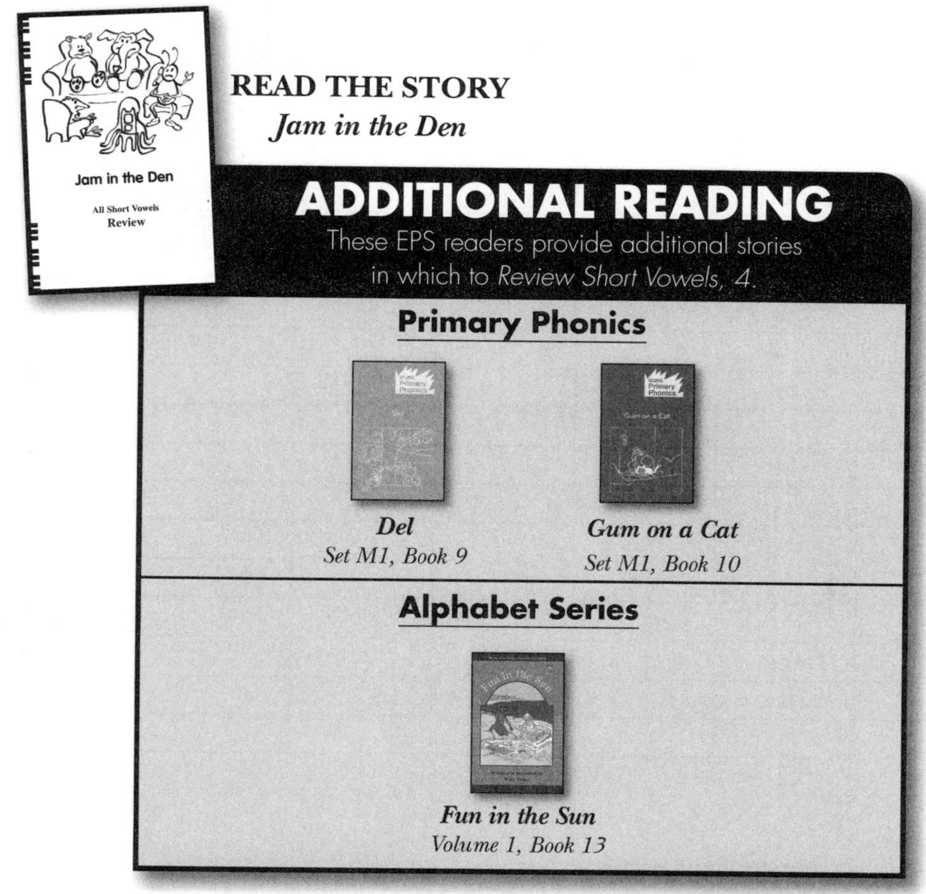

Word Lists

Consonant-Vowel-Consonant words—VC, CVC							
VC	**Substitute First Letter**						
	a		**o**	**u**	**i**		**e**
an	mat	pad	cob	pup	bib	tip	fed
on	cat	bad	mob	cup	fib	dip	led
in	bat	fad	sob		rib	hip	red
	fat	had	job	cub		lip	bed
it	pat	lad	rob	rub	rim	rip	beg
at	rat	mad		tub	dim	sip	keg
	sat	sad	rod		him		leg
ax	hat		nod	tug		sit	peg
ox		sap	cod	bug	hid	bit	pet
	ham	lap		dug	kid	hit	bet
as	dam	nap	cop	hug	lid	kit	get
us	Sam	cap	mop	jug	did	lit	jet
is	jam	map	pop	lug		pit	let
	ram	tap	top	mug	dig	fit	net
if			hop	rug	big		set
up	jab	tax			fig	fix	wet
ad	cab	wax	hot	run	jig	mix	met
am	nab	lax	got	fun	pig	six	
	tab	sax	lot	sun	wig		men
VCC		Max	not	bun			pen
odd	tag	fax	rot		win		den
add	bag		dot	gum	bin		ten
	gag		pot	yum	fin		hen
ebb	wag			bum	pin		
egg	rag		box	hum	tin		hem
	lag		fox				
inn	sag		lox	hut			
off				nut			
ill	ran		fog	cut			
ash	ban		dog	but			
ass	can		hog				
ax	fan		log	bud			
	man			mud			
	tan		mom				
	van		Tom				
	pan						

Consonant-Vowel-Consonant words—VC, CVC

Substitute Last Letter						
a		**o**	**u**	**i**		**e**
bad	map	cob	bud	bib	pin	bed
bag	mad	cod	bug	bin	pit	beg
ban	man	cog	bum	bit	pig	bet
bat	mat	cot	bun	big		
		cop	bus		rig	get
cat	pat		but	dig	rib	
cab	pad	hop		did	rid	hem
can	pal	hot	cut	dim	rim	hen
cap	pan		cub	dip	rip	
		lot	cup			men
lap	van	lox	cud	hip	lip	met
lax	vat			hid	lid	
lag		pod	dud	him	lit	let
lad	sat	pop	dug	his		led
	sad	pot		hit	wit	leg
fad	sag		hug		wig	
fan	sap	not	hub	fit	win	peg
fat		nod	hum	fib		pen
	tap		hut	fig	tin	pep
hat	tab	rod		fin	tip	pet
had	tag	rob	gut	fix		
ham	tan	rot	gum			set
has	tax			six		
		tot	nun	sip		wet
gas	wax	top	nub	sit		web
gag	wag		nut			wed
gal		mop		kit		
gap		mom	mud	kid		yes
gab		mop	mug	kin		yet
jab		sob	rug			
jam		sod	rut			
ram		sox	rub			
ran			run			
rap		job				
rat		jog	sun			
			sum			

Consonant-Vowel-Consonant words—VC, CVC							
Substitute Vowel							
b	**c**	**d**	**f**	**g**	**h**	**j**	**l**
bad	cab	dab	fed	gab	hid	jab	lob
bed	cob	dub	fad	gob	had	jib	lab
bid	cub	did				job	lad
bud		dud	fan	got	hog		lid
	cud		fun	gut	hug	jog	led
bug	cod	dug	fin	get		jag	
beg	cad	dog			hum	jig	leg
big		dig	fig		ham	jug	lug
bog	cop		fog		hem		log
bag	cup	dim			him		lag
	cap	dam	fox				
ban			fix		his		lap
bin	cat				has		lip
bun	cot		fit				
Ben	cut		fat		hit		lit
					hat		lot
but					hut		let
bat					hot		
bet							
bit					hop		
					hip		
					hup		
					hep		

Consonant-Vowel-Consonant words—VC, CVC						
Substitute Vowel (continued)						
m	**n**	**p**	**r**	**s**	**t**	**w**
mad	net	pad	rib	sip	tab	wag
mid	not	pod	rub	sap	tub	wig
mod	nut	pub	rob			
mud				sad	tug	wit
		pug	rod	sod	tag	wet
mug		peg	red			
Meg		pig	rid	sob	tan	
				sub	ten	
mop		pin	rig		tin	
map		pan	rag	sun		
		pen	rug		tip	
mat				sit	tap	
met		pep	run	sat	top	
		pip	ran	set		
men		pup				
man		pop	ram	six		
			rim	sox		
		pot				
		pet	rut			
		pit	rot			
		pat	rat			
			rap			
			rip			

Lesson 10: Consonant Digraph *th*

Remind students that they have learned the sounds that consonants make. Tell them that sometimes two consonants are found side by side in words.

Explain that pairs of consonants sometimes make only one special sound. Demonstrate the sounds for *th, ch,* and *sh* for students.

Tell students that today they will learn the sound that *th* makes, like in *thick.*

Phonemic Awareness Say the word *thick.* Emphasize the *th* sound.

Then say the following words, and have students listen for the *th* sound at the beginning of each one: *thank, think, thing.*

Tell students to listen for the *th* sound at the end of some words you will say. Slowly say *bath, path, with.* Emphasize the *th* sound.

Link Sound to Letters Distribute the *th* Touch-unit. Have students trace its shape with their finger as they make the *th* sound together.

Form the following word on a whiteboard: *this.* Say the word, emphasizing the *th* sound. Then underline the *th* in the word.

Tell students that the *th* makes the *th* sound they hear at the beginning of *this.* Isolate the sound for students, and then have them repeat it after you.

Form these words on the whiteboard: *that, Thad, Beth, with.* Say each word for students, and have them take turns underlining the *th,* saying the *th* sound, and then saying the word.

Build Words (Model) Tell students that they can use what they know about the sound for *th* to build words.

Say *thug.* Tell students you are going to build *thug.* Use Touch-units or Magtiles to model.

Pick up the letters *th,* and say their sound as you place them on the whiteboard. Repeat the procedure with the letter *u,* and place it about an inch to the right of the letters *th.* Repeat the procedure again with the letter *g.* Touch *th,* and say their sound. Touch *u,* and say its sound. Touch *g,* and say its sound.

Move the letters closer together, and say their sounds, blending them slightly. Move the letters next to each other and blend the sounds to say *thug.* (You may choose to do this in several steps, moving the letters closer together to demonstrate how to blend.)

Then cover the word and spell it orally. Uncover the word and have students compare your spelling with the Touch-units. Cover the word again and write it on the whiteboard. Uncover the word and have students compare the written word with the Touch-units.

Build Words Distribute Touch-units for the word *them.* Say *them.* Have students build it on their whiteboard using the Touch-units. Give help as necessary. After making the word, have students touch and sound each Touch-unit, then blend the sounds as they run their finger underneath the Touch-units. Have students cover the word and spell it orally, then compare their spelling to the Touch-units. Next have them cover the word again and write it on their whiteboard and then on the Build Words page of their Workbook (p. 29). Have students compare their writing to the Touch-units. Then use this procedure to have students build the following words:

	yellow	red
this	th, s	i
thus		u
that	t	a
path	p	
math	m	
bath	b	

Use one of the activities on page xvi to further practice sequencing and discriminating the words that students find challenging.

Read Words in Isolation Have students pair up and read all of the words they have written on Workbook page 29 aloud to their partner.

Independent Practice (Workbook page 28) For the first set of items, ask students to connect all the pictures whose names have the *th* sound to find their way through the maze. For the second set, ask them to write the word that completes each sentence. When students complete the page, have them check their work with you or a partner.

Dictation Dictate the following sentence, and have students write it on their whiteboard or at the bottom of Workbook page 28: *Thad had a hot bath.*

Reading Words in Context

Tell students that they will use what they know about *th* words to read a story.

Build Words from the Story Use the Touch-units to build the following words on the whiteboard. Tell students that the words you will make together will help them read the story.

Start with the word *bath.*

Substitute Touch-units to build the following words: *math, path, with, Beth, then, than, Thad, them, this, thin, thud, thug, thus.*

As a prereading activity, you may want to have students find the words in the text and read them aloud.

Learn Sight Words Tell students that they will learn some new words to help them read the story. Display these sight words: *both, saw.* Read the words as you point to them.

As a prereading activity, you may want to have students find the words in the text as they write them.

Read the Story Give students a copy of *Thad and Beth.* Have them read it independently or with a partner. If necessary, you can support students as they read the story by identifying sight words or helping them to blend sounds to read words.

Respond to the Story After students read *Thad and Beth*, have them complete Workbook page 30. Have students share their work with the rest of the group.

Lesson 11: Consonant Digraph *ch*

Remind students that they have learned the sound for *th.* Tell them that today they will learn the sound for *ch.*

Phonemic Awareness Say the word *chill.* Emphasize the *ch* sound.

Then say the following words, and have students listen for the *ch* sound at the beginning of each one: *chat, chop, check.*

Tell students to listen for the *ch* sound at the end of some words you will say. Slowly say *rich, much, catch.* Emphasize the *ch* sound.

Link Sound to Letters Distribute the *ch* Touch-unit. Have students trace its shape with their finger as they make the *ch* sound together.

Form the following word on a whiteboard: *chip.* Say the word, emphasizing the *ch* sound. Then underline the *ch* in the word.

Tell students that the *ch* makes the *ch* sound they hear at the beginning of *chip.* Isolate the sound for students, and then have them repeat it after you.

Form these words on the whiteboard: *chat, chin, such, much.* Say each word for students, and have them take turns underlining the *ch,* saying the *ch* sound, and then saying the word.

Build Words (Model) Tell students that they can use what they know about the sound for *ch* to build words.

Say *chin.* Tell students you are going to build *chin.* Use Touch-units or Magtiles to model.

Pick up the letters *ch,* and say their sound as you place them on the whiteboard. Repeat the procedure with the letter *i,* and place it about an inch to the right of the letters *ch.* Repeat the procedure again with the letter *n.* Touch *ch,* and say their sound. Touch *i,* and say its sound. Touch *n,* and say its sound.

Move the letters closer together, and say their sounds, blending them slightly. Move the letters next to each other and blend the sounds to say *chin.* (You may choose to do this in several steps, moving the letters closer together to demonstrate how to blend.)

Then cover the word and spell it orally. Uncover the word and have students compare your spelling with the Touch-units. Cover the word again and write it on the whiteboard. Uncover the word and have students compare the written word with the Touch-units.

Build Words Distribute Touch-units for the word *chop.* Say *chop.* Have students build it on their whiteboard using the Touch-units. Give help as necessary. After making the word, have students touch and sound each Touch-unit, then blend the sounds as they run their finger underneath the Touch-units. Have students cover the word and spell it orally, then compare their spelling to the Touch-units. Next have them cover the word again and write it on their whiteboard and then on the Build Words page of their Workbook (p. 32). Have students compare their writing to the Touch-units. Then use this procedure to have students build the following words:

	yellow	red
chip	ch, p	i
chap		a
chat	t	
chug	g	u
much	m	
such	s	

Use one of the activities on page xvi to further practice sequencing and discriminating the words that students find challenging.

Read Words in Isolation Have students pair up and read all of the words they have written on Workbook page 32 aloud to their partner.

Independent Practice (Workbook page 31) For the first set of items, ask students to circle the letters that stand for the sound they hear in each picture name. For the second set, ask them to write the word that completes each sentence. When students complete the page, have them check their work with you or a partner.

Dictation Dictate the following sentence, and have students write it on their whiteboard or at the bottom of Workbook page 31: *Chad had a chip and a chop.*

Reading Words in Context

Tell students that they will use what they know about *ch* words to read a story.

Build Words from the Story Use the Touch-units to build the following words on the whiteboard. Tell students that the words you will make together will help them read the story.

Start with the word *chap.*

Substitute Touch-units to build the following words: *chat, chin, chip, chips, chop, chill, Chub, chug, chum, much, such, rich.*

As a prereading activity, you may want to have students find the words in the text and read them aloud.

Review Sight Words Tell students that they will review some words that will help them read the story. Display these sight words: *what, do, you, put.* Read the words as you point to them.

As a prereading activity, you may want to have students find the words in the text as they write them.

Read the Story Give students a copy of *Chub and the Chips.* Have them read it independently or with a partner. If necessary, you can support students as they read the story by identifying sight words or helping them to blend sounds to read words.

Respond to the Story After students read *Chub and the Chips,* have them complete Workbook page 33. Have students share their work with the rest of the group.

Lesson 12: Consonant Digraph *sh*

Remind students that they have learned the sounds for *th* and *ch*. Tell them that today they will learn the sound for *sh*.

Phonemic Awareness Say the word *shark*. Emphasize the *sh* sound.

Then say the following words, and have students listen for the *sh* sound at the beginning of each one: *shade, she, sheep*.

Tell students to listen for the *sh* sound at the end of some words you will say. Slowly say *ash, swish, crush*. Emphasize the *sh* sound.

Link Sound to Letters Distribute the *sh* Touch-unit. Have students trace its shape with their finger as they make the *sh* sound together.

Form the following word on a whiteboard: *shop*. Say the word, emphasizing the *sh* sound. Then underline the *sh* in the word.

Tell students that the *sh* makes the *sh* sound they hear at the beginning of *shop*. Isolate the sound for students, and then have them repeat it after you.

Form these words on the whiteboard: *shin, shot, mush, gash*. Say each word for students, and have them take turns underlining the *sh*, saying the *sh* sound, and then saying the word.

Build Words (Model) Tell students that they can use what they know about the sound for *sh* to build words.

Say *shop*. Tell students you are going to build *shop*. Use Touch-units or Magtiles to model.

Pick up the letters *sh*, and say their sound as you place them on the whiteboard. Repeat the procedure with the letter *o*, and place it about an inch to the right of the letters *sh*. Repeat the procedure again with the letter *p*. Touch *sh*, and say their sound. Touch *o*, and say its sound. Touch *p*, and say its sound.

Move the letters closer together, and say their sounds, blending them slightly. Move the letters next to each other and blend the sounds to say *shop*. (You may choose to do this in several steps, moving the letters closer together to demonstrate how to blend.)

Then cover the word and spell it orally. Uncover the word and have students compare your spelling with the Touch-units. Cover the word again and write it on the whiteboard. Uncover the word and have students compare the written word with the Touch-units.

Build Words Distribute Touch-units for the word *shot*. Say *shot*. Have students build it on their whiteboard using the Touch-units. Give help as necessary. After making the word, have students touch and sound each Touch-unit, then blend the sounds as they run their finger underneath the Touch-units. Have students cover the word and spell it orally, then compare their spelling to the Touch-units. Next have them cover the word again and write it on their whiteboard and then on the Build Words page of their Workbook (p. 35). Have students compare their writing to the Touch-units. Then use this procedure to have students build the following words:

	yellow	red
shut	sh, t	u
shun	n	
shin		i
ship	p	
wish	w	
mash	m	a
rash	r	

Use one of the activities on page xvi to further practice sequencing and discriminating the words that students find challenging.

Read Words in Isolation Have students pair up and read all of the words they have written on Workbook page 35 aloud to their partner.

Independent Practice (Workbook page 34) For the first set of items, ask students to connect all the pictures whose names have the *sh* sound to find their way through the maze.

For the second set, ask them to circle the word that names the picture at the beginning of each row. When students complete the page, have them check their work with you or a partner.

Dictation Dictate the following sentence, and have students write it on their whiteboard or at the bottom of Workbook page 34: *I wish I had a ship.*

Reading Words in Context

Tell students that they will use what they know about *sh* words to read a story.

Build Words from the Story Use the Touch-units to build the following words on the whiteboard. Tell students that the words you will make together will help them read the story.

Start with the word *ash.*

Substitute Touch-units to build the following words: *bash, cash, mash, sham, rash, lash, rush, gush, hush, dish, fish, wish, mesh, shed, shell, shells, shin, shun, shut, shot, shod, shop, ship.*

As a prereading activity, you may want to have students find the words in the text and read them aloud.

Learn Sight Words Tell students that they will learn some words that will help them read the story. Display these sight words: *many, your.* Read the words as you point to them.

As a prereading activity, you may want to have students find the words in the text as they write them.

Read the Story Give students a copy of *The Shop.* Have them read it independently or with a partner. If necessary, you can support students as they read the story by identifying sight words or helping them to blend sounds to read words.

Respond to the Story After students read *The Shop,* have them complete Workbook page 36. Have students share their work with the rest of the group.

Lesson 13: Consonant Digraph *wh*

Remind students that they have learned the sounds for *ch, th,* and *sh.* Tell them that today they will learn the sound for *wh.*

Phonemic Awareness Say the word *whale.* Emphasize the *wh* sound.

Then say the following words, and have students listen for the *wh* sound at the beginning of each one: *what, wheel, whiz, whisper.*

Link Sound to Letters Distribute the *wh* Touch-unit. Have students trace its shape with their finger as they make the *wh* sound together.

Form the following word on a whiteboard: *when.* Say the word, emphasizing the *wh* sound. Then underline the *wh* in the word.

Tell students that the *wh* makes the *wh* sound they hear at the beginning of *when.* Isolate the sound for students, and then have them repeat it after you. Point out that *wh* makes the same sound as the letter *w.*

Form these words on the whiteboard: *which, whim, whiz.* Say each word for students, and have them take turns underlining the *wh,* saying the *wh* sound, and then saying the word.

Build Words (Model) Tell students that they can use what they know about the sound for *wh* to build words.

Say *when.* Tell students you are going to build *when.* Use Touch-units or Magtiles to model.

Pick up the letters *wh,* and say their sound as you place them on the whiteboard. Repeat the procedure with the letter *e,* and place it about an inch to the right of the letters *wh.* Repeat the procedure again with the letter *n.* Touch *wh,* and say their sound. Touch *e,* and say its sound. Touch *n,* and say its sound.

Move the letters closer together, and say their sounds, blending them slightly. Move the letters next to each other and blend the sounds to say *when.* (You may choose to do this in several steps, moving the letters closer together to demonstrate how to blend.)

Then cover the word and spell it orally. Uncover the word and have students compare your spelling with the Touch-units. Cover the word again and write it on the whiteboard. Uncover the word and have students compare the written word with the Touch-units.

Build Words Distribute Touch-units for the word *whiz.* Say *whiz.* Have students build it on their whiteboard using the Touch-units. Give help as necessary. After making the word, have students touch and sound each Touch-unit, then blend the sounds as they run their finger underneath the Touch-units. Have students cover the word and spell it orally, then compare their spelling to the Touch-units. Next have them cover the word again and write it on their whiteboard and then on the Build Words page of their Workbook (p. 38). Have students compare their writing to the Touch-units. Then use this procedure to have students build the following words:

	yellow	red
which	wh, ch	i
when	n	e
whip	p	i
whim	m	

Use one of the activities on page xvi to further practice sequencing and discriminating the words that students find challenging.

Read Words in Isolation Have students pair up and read all of the words they have written on Workbook page 38 aloud to their partner.

Independent Practice (Workbook page 37) For the first set of items, ask students to write the letters that stand for the sound at the beginning of each picture name. For the second set, ask them write the word that completes each sentence. When students complete the page, have them check their work with you or a partner.

Dictation Dictate the following sentence, and have students write it on their whiteboard or at the bottom of Workbook page 37: *When did Jan get the whip?*

Reading Words in Context

Tell students that they will use what they know about *wh* words to read a story.

Build Words from the Story Use the Touch-units to build the following words on the whiteboard. Tell students that the words you will make together will help them read the story.

Start with the word *when.*

Substitute Touch-units to build the following words: *whim, whip, whips, whiz, which, whiff.*

As a prereading activity, you may want to have students find the words in the text and read them aloud.

Learn Sight Words Tell students that they will learn a new word that will help them read the story. Display this sight word: *want.* Read the word as you point to it.

As a prereading activity, you may want to have students find the word in the text as they write it.

Read the Story Give students a copy of *Will the Whale.* Have them read it independently or with a partner. If necessary, you can support students as they read the story by identifying sight words or helping them to blend sounds to read words.

Respond to the Story After students read *Will the Whale,* have them complete Workbook page 39. Have students share their work with the rest of the group.

Lesson 14: Review Consonant Digraphs

Remind students that they have learned the sounds for *ch, th, sh,* and *wh.* Tell them that they are now going to review the sounds to help them remember them better.

Phonemic Awareness Tell students that they are going to play a game to help them remember the sounds for *ch, sh, th,* and *wh.*

Say the following words: *chin, chain, ship.* Ask students to name the two words that have the same sound at the beginning.

Repeat the procedure with the following sets of words: *that, chap, thin; shot, whale, shin; when, shell, whip.*

Link Sound to Letters Distribute the *ch* Touch-unit. Have students trace its shape with their finger as they make the *ch* sound together.

Form the following word on a whiteboard: *chat.* Say the word, emphasizing the *ch* sound. Then underline the *ch* in that word.

Tell students that the *ch* makes the *ch* sound they hear at the beginning of *chat.* Isolate the sound for students, and then have them repeat it after you.

Now distribute the *th, sh,* and *wh* Touch-units. Repeat the procedure above to form the following words: *think, shop, whiz.*

Build Words Distribute Touch-units for the word *chap.* Say *chap.* Have students build it on their whiteboard using the Touch-units. Give help as necessary. After making the word, have students touch and sound each Touch-unit, then blend the sounds as they run their finger underneath the Touch-units. Have students cover the word and spell it orally, then compare their spelling to the Touch-units. Next have them cover the word again and write it on their whiteboard and then on the Build Words page of their Workbook (p. 41). Have students compare their writing to the Touch-units. Then use this procedure to have students build the following words:

	yellow	red
chip	ch, p	i
whip	wh	
which	ch	
when	n	e
wish	sh	i
with	th	
then	n	e
thin		i
ship	sh, p	

Use one of the activities on page xvi to further practice sequencing and discriminating the words that students find challenging.

Read Words in Isolation Have students pair up and read all of the words they have written on Workbook page 41 aloud to their partner.

Independent Practice (Workbook page 40) For the first set of items, ask students to circle the letters that stand for the sound they hear in each word. For the second set, ask them to circle the word that names the picture at the beginning of each row. When students complete the page, have them check their work with you or a partner.

Dictation Dictate the following sentence, and have students write it on their whiteboard at the bottom of Workbook page 40: *Which pet shop is this fish in?*

Reading Words in Context

Tell students that they will use what they know about the sounds for *wh, th, ch,* and *sh* to read a story.

Build Words from the Story Use the Touch-units to build the following words on the whiteboard. Tell students that the words you will make together will help them read the story.

Start with the word *chap.*

Substitute Touch-units to build the following words: *chip, chin, rich, which, chips, chop, chum, chums, Chub, chug, much, such, cash, lash, shall, shells, wish, dish, shin, ship, shop, shot, shut, rush, math, than, that, Thad, this Beth, with, fifth, tenth, when.*

As a prereading activity, you may want to have students find the words in the text and read them aloud.

Review Sight Words Tell students that they will review some words that will help them read the story. Display these sight words: *both, many, said, saw, was, what.* Read the words as you point to them.

As a prereading activity, you may want to have students find the words in the text as they write them.

Read the Story Give students a copy of *Will's Birthday.* Have them read it independently or with a partner. If necessary, you can support students as they read the story by identifying sight words or helping them to blend sounds to read words.

Respond to the Story After students read *Will's Birthday,* have them complete Workbook page 42. Have students share their work with the rest of the group.

Word Lists

Consonant-Vowel-Consonant words—VC, CVC

Four-Plus Letter Words

_ss	_sh	_th	_ff	_ll		_ch	_tt	_zz
bass	ash	bath	miff	shall	sill	rich	mitt	jazz
lass	bash	lath	tiff		till			
pass	cash	math		bell	mill	much	mutt	fizz
mass	gash	path	buff	cell	hill	such	putt	
	lash		cuff	fell	quill			buzz
moss	mash	pith	huff	jell		gulch		fuzz
toss	dash	with	puff	sell	hull	mulch		
loss	rash			tell	cull			
		depth	gaff	yell	gull			
less	rush	tenth	chaff	well	lull			
mess	hush	fifth		shell	mull			
chess	lush	filth	off	quell	dull			
	mush							
fuss	gush	sixth		will	doll			
muss		width		ill				
	dish			bill				
hiss	fish			dill				
kiss	wish			fill				
miss	swish			gill				
				pill				
	posh			rill				
	mesh							

Consonant-Vowel-Consonant words—VC, CVC			
Four-Plus Letter Words (continued)			
ch_	**th_**	**sh_**	**wh_**
• chat	• that	• ship	• when
chap	• than	shin	whet
• chop	thin	shun	whim
	• this	• shut	whip
• chug			whiz
chum	thus	• shot	
	thug	• shop	• which
	• thud	shod	whiff
	• them	sham	
	• then	• shall	
		shell	
		• shed	

Review the words with a •

Lesson 15: Initial Consonant Blends: *L* Blends

Remind students that they have learned the sounds for some consonants that are found side by side in words.

Explain that there are other consonants that are sometimes found next to each other in words. Tell students that you say the sounds of these consonants so close together that they seem to blend into only one sound. Demonstrate the sounds for *st, bl,* and *fr* for students.

Tell students that today they will learn the sounds for blends that have *l* in them.

Phonemic Awareness Say the word *floor.* Emphasize the consonant sounds at the beginning of the word.

Then say the following words, and have students listen for the consonant sounds at the beginning of each one: *flight, fly, flock.*

Tell students to listen for the consonant sounds at the beginning of some words you will say. Slowly say *sled, blip, clip, plan, glue.* Emphasize the consonant sounds at the beginning of each word.

Link Sounds to Letters Distribute the *fl* Touch-unit. Have students trace its shape with their finger as they make the *fl* sounds together.

Form the following word on a whiteboard: *flap.* Say the word, emphasizing the *fl* sounds. Then underline the *fl* in the word.

Tell students that the *fl* makes the *fl* sounds they hear at the beginning of *flap.* Isolate the sounds for students, and then have them repeat the sounds after you.

Now distribute the remaining *l* blend Touch-units (*sl, bl, gl, cl, pl*). Repeat the procedure above to form the following words: *slid, bled, glop, clap, plum.*

Build Words (Model) Tell students that they can use what they know about blends to build words.

Say *clam.* Tell students you are going to build *clam.* Use Touch-units or Magtiles to model. Pick up the letters *cl,* and say their sounds as you place them on the whiteboard. Repeat the procedure with the letter *a,* and place it about an inch to the right of the letters *cl.* Repeat the procedure again with the letter *m.* Touch *cl,* and say their sounds. Touch *a,* and say its sound. Touch *m,* and say its sound.

Move the letters closer together, and say their sounds, blending them slightly. Move the letters next to each other and blend the sounds to say *clam.* (You may choose to do this in several steps, moving the letters closer together to demonstrate how to blend.)

Then cover the word and spell it orally. Uncover the word and have students compare your spelling with the Touch-units. Cover the word again and write it on the whiteboard. Uncover the word and have students compare the written word with the Touch-units.

Build Words Distribute Touch-units for the word *flag.* Say *flag.* Have students build it on their whiteboard using the Touch-units. Give help as necessary. After making the word, have students touch and sound each Touch-unit, then blend the sounds as they run their finger underneath the Touch-units. Have students cover the word and spell it orally, then compare their spelling to the Touch-units. Next have them cover the word again and write it on their whiteboard and then on the Build Words page of their Workbook (p. 44). Have students compare their writing to the Touch-units. Then use this procedure to have students build the following words:

	yellow	red	blue
flog	g	o	fl
clog			cl
blob	b		bl
slob			sl
slab		a	
glad	d		gl
plod		o	pl

Use one of the activities on page xvi to further practice sequencing and discriminating the words that students find challenging.

Read Words in Isolation Have students pair up and read all of the words they have written on Workbook page 44 aloud to their partner.

Independent Practice (Workbook page 43) For the first set of items, ask students to write the letters that complete each picture name. For the second set, ask them to write the word that completes each sentence. When students complete the page, have them check their work with you or a partner.

Dictation Dictate the following sentence, and have students write it on their whiteboard or at the bottom of Workbook page 43: *Glen did a flip on a sled.*

Reading Words in Context

Tell students that they will use what they know about blends to read a story.

Build Words from the Story Use the Touch-units to build the following words on the whiteboard. Tell students that the words you will make together will help them read the story.

Start with the word *clap.*

Substitute Touch-units to build the following words: *class, clip, Cliff, club, clot, slot, slim, slip, slap, slum, sled, bled, fled, flip, flit, flop, flat, flag, glad, glass, plan, plus, plush, blush, flash, clam, slam, slug, plug, glum.*

As a prereading activity, you may want to have students find the words in the text and read them aloud.

Learn Sight Words Tell students that they will learn some new words to help them read the story. Display these sight words: *come, fall, one, two.* Read the words as you point to them.

As a prereading activity, you may want to have students find the words in the text as they write them.

Read the Story Give students a copy of *The Hip Hop Club.* Have them read it independently or with a partner. If necessary, you can support students as they read the story by identifying sight words or helping them to blend sounds to read words.

Respond to the Story After students read *The Hip Hop Club,* have them complete Workbook page 45. Have students share their work with the rest of the group.

Lesson 16: Initial Consonant Blends: *S* Blends

Remind students that they have learned the sounds for blends with the consonant *l* in them. Tell students that today they will learn the sounds for blends that have *s* in them.

Phonemic Awareness Say the word *store.* Emphasize the consonant sounds at the beginning of the word.

Then say the following words, and have students listen for the consonant sounds at the beginning of each one: *stuck, stand, stamp.*

Tell students to listen for the consonant sounds at the beginning of some words you will say. Slowly say *ski, swamp, small, snail, sponge.* Emphasizing the consonant sounds at the beginning of each word.

Link Sounds to Letters Distribute the *sn* Touch-unit. Have students trace its shape with their finger as they make the *sn* sounds together.

Form the following word on a whiteboard: *snap.* Say the word, emphasizing the *sn* sounds. Then underline the *sn* in the word.

Tell students that the *sn* makes the *sn* sounds they hear at the beginning of *snap.* Isolate the sounds for students, and then have them repeat the sounds after you.

Now distribute the remaining *s* blend Touch-units (*sp, st, sk, sw, sm, sc, sl*). Repeat the procedure above to form the following words: *spin, stun, skim, swim, smell, scat, sled.*

Build Words (Model) Tell students that they can use what they know about blends to build words.

Say *skin.* Tell students you are going to build *skin.* Use Touch-units or Magtiles to model.

Pick up the letters *sk,* and say their sounds as you place them on the whiteboard. Repeat the procedure with the letter *i,* and place it about an inch to the right of the letters *sk.* Repeat the procedure again with the letter *n.* Touch *sk,* and say their sounds. Touch *i,* and say its sound. Touch *n,* and say its sound.

Move the letters closer together, and say their sounds, blending them slightly. Move the letters next to each other and blend the sounds to say *skin.* (You may choose to do this in several steps, moving the letters closer together to demonstrate how to blend.)

Then cover the word and spell it orally. Uncover the word and have students compare your spelling with the Touch-units. Cover the word again and write it on the whiteboard. Uncover the word and have students compare the written word with the Touch-units.

Build Words Distribute Touch-units for the word *swim.* Say *swim.* Have students build it on their whiteboard using the Touch-units. Give help as necessary. After making the word, have students touch and sound each Touch-unit, then blend the sounds as they run their finger underneath the Touch-units. Have students cover the word and spell it orally, then compare their spelling to the Touch-units. Next have them cover the word again and write it on their whiteboard and then on the Build Words page of their Workbook (p. 47). Have students compare their writing to the Touch-units. Then use this procedure to have students build the following words:

	yellow	red	blue
spin	n	i	sp
skin			sk
scan		a	sc
Stan			st
spell	l, l	e	sp
smell	d		sm

Use one of the activities on page xvi to further practice sequencing and discriminating the words that students find challenging.

Read Words in Isolation Have students pair up and read all of the words they have written on Workbook page 47 aloud to their partner.

Independent Practice (Workbook page 46) For the first set of items, ask students to circle the letters that stand for the sound they hear at the beginning of each picture name. For the second set, ask them to circle the word that names the picture at the beginning of each row. When students complete the page, have them check their work with you or a partner.

Dictation Dictate the following sentence, and have students write it on their whiteboard or at the bottom of Workbook page 46: *The dog sniffs the spot that smells.*

Reading Words in Context

Tell students that they will use what they know about blends to read a story.

Build Words from the Story Use the Touch-units to build the following words on the whiteboard. Tell students that the words you will make together will help them read the story.

Start with the word *scab.*

Substitute Touch-units to build the following words: *scat, Scott, skin, skip, skill, small, smell, smash, snap, sniff, sniffs, snug, spot, spots, spell, spill, split, splat, splash, step, steps, still, stop, swell, swig, swim.*

As a prereading activity, you may want to have students find the words in the text and read them aloud.

Learn Sight Words Tell students that they will learn a new word to help them read the story. Display this sight word: *once.* Read the word as you point to it.

As a prereading activity, you may want to have students find the word in the text as they write it.

Read the Story Give students a copy of *Scott the Squirrel.* Have them read it independently or with a partner. If necessary, you can support students as they read the story by identifying sight words or helping them to blend sounds to read words.

Respond to the Story After students read *Scott the Squirrel,* have them complete Workbook page 48. Have students share their work with the rest of the group.

Lesson 17: Initial Consonant Blends: *R* Blends

Remind students that they have learned the sounds for blends with the consonants *l* and *s* in them. Tell students that today they will learn the sounds for blends that have *r* in them.

Phonemic Awareness Say the word *trade.* Emphasize the consonants sounds at the beginning of the word.

Then say the following words, and have students listen for the consonant sounds at the beginning of each one: *traffic, treasure, treat.*

Tell students to listen for the consonant sounds at the beginning of some words you will say. Slowly say *brand, drink, grow, friend, crank, pretty.* Emphasize the consonant sounds at the beginning of each word.

Link Sounds to Letters Distribute the *fr* Touch-unit. Have students trace its shape with their finger as they make the *fr* sounds together.

Form the following word on a whiteboard: *fret.* Say the word, emphasizing the *fr* sounds. Then underline the *fr* in the word.

Tell students that the *fr* makes the *fr* sounds they hear at the beginning of *fret.* Isolate the sounds for students, and then have them repeat the sounds after you.

Now distribute the remaining *r* blend Touch-units (*tr, br, dr, gr, cr, pr*). Repeat the procedure above to form the following words: *trash, brat, drip, grim, crush, prep.*

Build Words (Model) Tell students that they can use what they know about blends to build words.

Say *crash.* Tell students you are going to build *crash.* Use Touch-units or Magtiles to model.

Pick up the letters *cr,* and say their sounds as you place them on the whiteboard. Repeat the procedure with the letter *a,* and place it about an inch to the right of the letters *cr.* Repeat the procedure again with the letters *sh.* Touch *cr,* and say their sounds. Touch *a,* and say its sound. Touch *sh,* and say their sounds.

Move the letters closer together, and say their sounds, blending them slightly. Move the letters next to each other and blend the sounds to say *crash.* (You may choose to do this in several steps, moving the letters closer together to demonstrate how to blend.)

Then cover the word and spell it orally. Uncover the word and have students compare your spelling with the Touch-units. Cover the word again and write it on the whiteboard. Uncover the word and have students compare the written word with the Touch-units.

Build Words Distribute Touch-units for the word *crab.* Say *crab.* Have students build it on their whiteboard using the Touch-units. Give help as necessary. After making the word, have students touch and sound each Touch-unit, then blend the sounds as they run their finger underneath the Touch-units. Have students cover the word and spell it orally, then compare their spelling to the Touch-units. Next have them cover the word again and write it on their whiteboard and then on the Build Words page of their Workbook (p. 50). Have students compare their writing to the Touch-units. Then use this procedure to have students build the following words:

	yellow	red	blue
grab	b	a	gr
drab			dr
crag	g		cr
frog		o	fr
prod	d		pr
trot	t		tr
broth	th		br

Use one of the activities on page xvi to further practice sequencing and discriminating the words that students find challenging.

Read Words in Isolation Have students pair up and read all of the words they have written on Workbook page 50 aloud to their partner.

Independent Practice (Workbook page 49) For the first set of items, ask students to write the letters that complete each picture name. For the second set, ask them to write the word that completes each sentence. When students complete the page, have them check their work with you or a partner.

Dictation Dictate the following sentence, and have students write it on their whiteboard or at the bottom of Workbook page 49: *Bret will grab a frog.*

Reading Words in Context

Tell students that they will use what they know about blends to read a story.

Build Words from the Story Use the Touch-units to build the following words on the whiteboard. Tell students that the words you will make together will help them read the story.

Start with the word *Brad.*

Substitute Touch-units to build the following words: *brass, brash, crash, crab, crush, cross, fresh, fret, frog, drag, drat, drip, drill, grill, grin, grins, grab, grub, grass, strap, strut, struts, stress, press, prim, trim, sprig, twig, twin, trip, trap.*

As a prereading activity, you may want to have students find the words in the text and read them aloud.

Learn Sight Words Tell students that they will learn some new words to help them read the story. Display these sight words: *any, from.* Read the words as you point to them.

As a prereading activity, you may want to have students find the words in the text as they write them.

Read the Story Give students a copy of *Brad the Crab.* Have them read it independently or with a partner. If necessary, you can support students as they read the story by identifying sight words or helping them to blend sounds to read words.

Respond to the Story After students read *Brad the Crab,* have them complete Workbook page 51. Have students share their work with the rest of the group.

Lesson 18: Review Initial Consonant Blends

Remind students that they have learned the sounds for blends with the consonants *l, s,* and *r* in them. Tell them that they are now going to review the sounds to help them remember them better.

Phonemic Awareness Tell students that you are going to play a game to help them remember the sounds for blends.

Say the word *still.* Ask students to name the sounds they hear in the word.

Repeat the procedure with the following words: *spin, snap, skill, swish, smack, scat, slip, black, glad, flip, clap, plod, truck, brash, drop, grid, Fred, crash, prim.*

Link Sounds to Letters Distribute the *cl* Touch-unit. Have students trace its shape with their finger as they make the *cl* sounds together.

Form the following word on a whiteboard: *clog.* Say the word, emphasizing the *cl* sounds. Then underline the *cl* in the word.

Tell students that the *cl* makes the *cl* sounds they hear at the beginning of *clog.* Isolate the sounds for students, and then have them repeat the sounds after you.

Repeat the procedure with other *l* blends. Then repeat the procedure with *s* blends and *r* blends.

Build Words Distribute Touch-units for the word *grin.* Say *grin.* Have students build it on their whiteboard using the Touch-units. Give help as necessary. After making the word, have students touch and sound each Touch-unit, then blend the sounds as they run their finger underneath the Touch-units. Have students cover the word and spell it orally, then compare their spelling to the Touch-units. Next have them cover the word again and write it on their whiteboard and then on the Build Words page of their Workbook (p. 53). Have students compare their writing to the Touch-units. Then use this procedure to have students build the following words:

	yellow	red	blue
cram	m	a	cr
slam			sl
plan	n		pl
span			sp
bran			br
brash	sh		
crush		u	cr
slush			sl

Use one of the activities on page xvi to further practice sequencing and discriminating the words that students find challenging.

Read Words in Isolation Have students pair up and read all of the words they have written on Workbook page 53 aloud to their partner.

Independent Practice (Workbook page 52) For the first set of items, ask students to blend the sounds in each word, say the word, and circle the picture that the word names. For the second set, ask them to circle the word that names the picture at the beginning of each row. When students complete the page, have them check their work with you or a partner.

Dictation Dictate the following sentence, and have students write it on their whiteboard or at the bottom of Workbook page 52: *Fred is glad to swim.*

Reading Words in Context

Tell students that they will use what they know about blends to read a story.

Build Words from the Story Use the Touch-units to build the following words on the whiteboard. Tell students that the words you will make together will help them read the story.

Start with the word *brag.*

Substitute Touch-units to build the following words: *brash, brass, brat, flat, Flash, crash, clap. slap, slug, slugs, slid, Fred, sped, glad, glum, snug, snub, snap, stop, still, stick, grin, gruff, skin, swig, small, swell, cloth.*

As a prereading activity, you may want to have students find the words in the text and read them aloud.

Learn Sight Words Tell students that they will learn some new words to help them read the story. Display these sight words: *into, live, wall, were, would.* Read the words as you point to them.

As a prereading activity, you may want to have students find the words in the text as they write them.

Read the Story Give students a copy of *Flash and Fred.* Have them read it independently or with a partner. If necessary, you can support students as they read the story by identifying sight words or helping them to blend sounds to read words.

Respond to the Story After students read *Flash and Fred,* have them complete Workbook page 54. Have students share their work with the rest of the group.

Word Lists

Initial Consonant Blends					
L Blends					
bl	**cl**	**fl**	**gl**	**pl**	**sl**
blab	clad	flab	glad	plan	slab
bled	clam	flag	glass		slag
bless	clan	flap		plod	slam
	clap	flash	glen	plop	slap
blip	clash	flat		plot	slash
bliss	class		glib		slat
		fled		plug	
blob	cliff	flesh	gloss	plum	sled
blot	clip			plunge	
		flip	glum	plus	slid
bluff	clod	flit	glut	plush	slim
					slip
blush	clot	flog			slit
	cloth	flop			
					slob
	club	flub			slot
		fluff			sloth
		flush			
					slug
					slum
					slush

Initial Consonant Blends							
***S* Blends**							
st	**sw**	**sn**	**sp**	**sk**	**sc**	**sm**	**spl**
stab	swag	snag	span	skid	scab	smash	splash
staff	swam	snap	spat	skiff	scam	smell	splat
stag				skill	scan	Smith	split
stance	swell	sniff	sped	skim	scat	smog	
stash		snip	spell	skin		smug	
	swig		spill	skip	Scott		
stem	swill	snob		skit			
step	swim		spot		scram		
	Swiss	snub		skull	scrap		
stiff		snuff	sprig		scroll		
still	swum	snug			scrub		
			spud				
stop		snot	spun		scuff		
					scum		
stub							
stud							
stuff							
stun							

Initial Consonant Blends					
***R* Blends**					
br	**dr**	**tr**	**cr**	**fr**	**gr**
brad	drab	tram	crab	France	grab
brag	drag	trap	crag		gram
bran	drat	trash	cram	Fred	
brat		trance	crash	fresh	grass
brash	dress			fret	
brass		tress	crib		grid
	drill		cringe	frill	grill
bred	drip	trill		Fringe	grim
		trim	crop		grin
brig	drop	trip	cross	frog	grip
brim				from	grit
	drub	trod	crud	froth	
bronze	drug	trot	crush		grub
broth	drum				gruff
		truss			
brush					

Initial Consonant Blends			
***R* Blends (continued)**			
pr	**thr**	**str**	**spr**
prance	thrash	strap	sprig
	thresh	stress	
prep	thrill		
press	throb	strip	
	thrush		
prim		strum	
prince		strut	
prod			
prop			

price
prize

Lesson 19: Final Consonant Blends: *sp, st, sk*

Remind students that they have learned the sounds for consonants that blend into one sound at the beginning of words.

Explain that there are other consonant blends that are found at the end of words. Tell students that like the consonant blends you find at the beginning of words, you say the sounds of these consonant blends so close together that they seem to blend into one sound. Demonstrate the sounds for *sp, st,* and *sk* for students.

Tell students that today they will learn the sounds for the blends *sp, st,* and *sk.*

Phonemic Awareness Say the word *blast.* Emphasize the consonant sounds at the end.

Then say the following words, and have students listen for the consonant sounds at the end of each one: *mast, list, chest.*

Tell students to listen for the consonant sounds at the end of some words you will say. Slowly say *grasp, crisp, mask, desk, vest.* Emphasize the consonant sounds at the end.

Link Sounds to Letters Distribute the *st* Touch-unit. Have students trace its shape with their finger as they make the *st* sounds together.

Form the following word on a whiteboard: *lost.* Say the word, emphasizing the *st* sounds. Then underline the *st* in the word.

Tell students that the *st* makes the *st* sounds they hear at the end of *lost.* Isolate the sounds for students, and then have them repeat the sounds after you.

Now distribute the *sp* and *sk* Touch-units. Repeat the procedure above to form the following words: *gasp, disk.*

Build Words (Model) Tell students that they can use what they know about blends to build words.

Say *fast.* Tell students you are going to build *fast.* Use Touch-units or Magtiles to model.

Pick up the letter *f,* and say its sound as you place it on the whiteboard. Repeat the procedure with the letter *a,* and place it about an inch to the right of the letter *f.* Repeat the procedure again with the letters *st.* Touch *f,* and say its sound. Touch *a,* and say its sound. Touch *st,* and say their sounds.

Move the letters closer together, and say their sounds, blending them slightly. Move the letters next to each other and blend the sounds to say *fast.* (You may choose to do this in several steps, moving the letters closer together to demonstrate how to blend.)

Then cover the word and spell it orally. Uncover the word and have students compare your spelling with the Touch-units. Cover the word again and write it on the whiteboard. Uncover the word and have students compare the written word with the Touch-units.

Repeat this procedure with *clasp* and *flask.*

Build Words Distribute Touch-units for the word *mask.* Say *mask.* Have students build it on their whiteboard using the Touch-units. Give help as necessary. After making the word, have students touch and sound each Touch-unit, then blend the sounds as they run their finger underneath the Touch-units. Have students cover the word and spell it orally, then compare their spelling to the Touch-units. Next have them cover the word again and write it on their whiteboard and then on the Build Words page of their Workbook (p. 56). Have students compare their writing to the Touch-units. Then use this procedure to have students build the following words:

	yellow	red	blue	green
task	t	a		sk
test		e		st
west	w			
wisp		i		sp
crisp			cr	
risk	r			sk
desk	d	e		

Use one of the activities on page xvi to further practice sequencing and discriminating the words that students find challenging.

Read Words in Isolation Have students pair up and read all of the words they have written on Workbook page 56 aloud to their partner.

Independent Practice (Workbook page 55) For the first set of items, ask students to write the letters that complete each picture name. For the second set, ask them to write the word that completes each sentence. When students complete the page, have them check their work with you or a partner.

Dictation Dictate the following sentence, and have students write it on their whiteboard or at the bottom of Workbook page 55: *Pat lost the mask in the mist.*

Reading Words in Context

Tell students that they will use what they know about blends to read a story.

Build Words from the Story Use the Touch-units to build the following words on the whiteboard. Tell students that the words you will make together will help them read the story.

Start with the word *ask.*

Substitute Touch-units to build the following words: *task, tusk, husk, husks, dusk, disk, risk, mask, gasp, grasp, crisp, wisp, west, best, rest, pest, past, fast, fist, last, frost, lost, mist.*

As a prereading activity, you may want to have students find the words in the text and read them aloud.

Learn Sight Words Tell students that they will learn some new words to help them read the story. Display these sight words: *here, pull, who, doing.* Read the words as you point to them.

As a prereading activity, you may want to have students find the words in the text as they write them.

Read the Story Give students a copy of *The Raccoon.* Have them read it independently or with a partner. If necessary, you can support students as they read the story by identifying sight words or helping them to blend sounds to read words.

Respond to the Story After students read *The Raccoon,* have them complete Workbook page 57. Have students share their work with the rest of the group.

Lesson 20: Final Consonant Blends: *nd, ng, nk*

Remind students that they have learned the sounds for the final blends *sp, st,* and *sk.* Tell students that today they will learn the sounds for the final blends *nd, ng,* and *nk.*

Phonemic Awareness Say the word *spend.* Emphasize the consonant sounds at the end.

Then say the following words, and have students listen for the consonant sounds at the end of each one: *bend, pond, land.*

Tell students to listen for the consonant sounds at the end of some words you will say. Slowly say *bond, end, gang, song, ring, wink.* Emphasize the consonant sounds at the end of each word.

Link Sounds to Letters Distribute the *nd* Touch-unit. Have students trace its shape with their finger as they make the *nd* sounds together.

Form the following word on a whiteboard: *spend.* Say the word, emphasizing the *nd* sounds. Then underline the *nd* in the word.

Tell students that the *nd* makes the *nd* sounds they hear at the end of *spend.* Isolate the sounds for students, and then have them repeat the sounds after you.

Now distribute the *ng* and *nk* Touch-units. Repeat the procedure above to form the following words: *wing, bank.*

Build Words (Model) Tell students that they can use what they know about blends to build words.

Say *thing.* Tell students you are going to build *thing.* Use Touch-units or Magtiles to model.

Pick up the letters *th,* and say their sound as you place them on the whiteboard. Repeat the procedure with the letter *i,* and place it about an inch to the right of the letters *th.* Repeat the procedure again with the letters *ng.* Touch *th,* and say their sound. Touch *i,* and say its sound. Touch *ng,* and say their sounds.

Move the letters closer together, and say their sounds, blending them slightly. Move the letters next to each other and blend the sounds to say *thing.* (You may choose to do this in several steps, moving the letters closer together to demonstrate how to blend.)

Then cover the word and spell it orally. Uncover the word and have students compare your spelling with the Touch-units. Cover the word again and write it on the whiteboard. Uncover the word and have students compare the written word with the Touch-units.

Repeat this procedure with *land* and *pink.*

Build Words Distribute Touch-units for the word *pond.* Say *pond.* Have students build it on their whiteboard using the Touch-units. Give help as necessary. After making the word, have students touch and sound each Touch-unit, then blend the sounds as they run their finger underneath the Touch-units. Have students cover the word and spell it orally, then compare their spelling to the Touch-units. Next have them cover the word again and write it on their whiteboard and then on the Build Words page of their Workbook (p. 59). Have students compare their writing to the Touch-units. Then use this procedure to have students build the following words:

	yellow	red	green
bend	b	e	nd
band		a	
bang			ng
sang	s		
song		o	
sink		i	nk
think	th		

Use one of the activities on page xvi to further practice sequencing and discriminating the words that students find challenging.

Read Words in Isolation Have students pair up and read all of the words they have written on Workbook page 59 aloud to their partner.

Independent Practice (Workbook page 58) For the first set of items, ask students to circle the letters that stand for the sound they hear at the end of each picture name. For the second set, ask them to write the word that completes each sentence. When students complete the page, have them check their work with you or a partner.

Dictation Dictate the following sentence, and have students write it on their whiteboard or at the bottom of Workbook page 58: *A skunk sat on the bank of the pond.*

A frog sat on a log in the pond.

Reading Words in Context

I sang a song to my mom.

Tell students that they will use what they know about blends to read a selection.

Build Words from the Selection Use the Touch-units to build the following words on the whiteboard. Tell students that the words you will make together will help them read the selection.

Start with the word *end.*

Substitute Touch-units to build the following words: *bend, spend, pond, land, grand, bond, bang, gang, sang, song, long, along, ring, bring, sing, thing, string, spring, sprung, think, plink, plunk, skunk, skunks, drank, bank, pink, wink, wing, wings.*

As a prereading activity, you may want to have students find the words in the text and read them aloud.

Learn Sight Words Tell students that they will learn some new words to help them read the selection. Display these sight words: *every, tall, together, very.* Read the words as you point to them.

As a prereading activity, you may want to have students find the words in the text as they write them.

Read the Selection Give students a copy of *Spring.* Have them read it independently or with a partner. If necessary, you can support students as they read the selection by identifying sight words or helping them to blend sounds to read words.

Respond to the Selection After students read *Spring,* have them complete Workbook page 60. Have students share their work with the rest of the group.

Lesson 21: Final Consonant Blends: *nt, mp, lt*

Remind students that they have learned the sounds for the final consonant blends *sp, st, sk, nd, ng,* and *nk.* Tell students that today they will learn the sounds for final consonant blends *nt, mp,* and *lt.*

Phonemic Awareness Say the word *lamp.* Emphasize the consonant sounds at the end.

Then say the following words, and have students listen for the consonant sounds at the end of each one: *camp, jump, bump.*

Tell students to listen for the consonant sounds at the end of some words you will say. Slowly say *belt, malt, romp, chimp, stunt, tent.* Emphasize the consonant sounds at the end of each word.

Link Sounds to Letters Distribute the *lt* Touch-unit. Have students trace its shape with their finger as they make the *lt* sounds together.

Form the following word on a whiteboard: *belt.* Say the word, emphasizing the *lt* sounds. Then underline the *lt* in the word.

Tell students that the *lt* makes the *lt* sounds they hear at the end of *belt.* Isolate the sounds for students, and then have them repeat the sounds after you.

Now distribute the *mp* and *nt* Touch-units. Repeat the procedure above to form the following words: *romp, punt.*

Build Words (Model) Tell students that they can use what they know about blends to build words.

Say *chimp.* Tell students you are going to build *chimp.* Use Touch-units or Magtiles to model.

Pick up the letters *ch,* and say their sound as you place them on the whiteboard. Repeat the procedure with the letter *i,* and place it about an inch to the right of the letters *ch.* Repeat the procedure again with the letters *mp.* Touch *ch,* and say their sound. Touch *i,* and say its sound. Touch *mp,* and say their sounds. Move the letters closer together, and say their sounds, blending them slightly. Move the letters next to each other and blend the sounds to say *chimp.* (You may choose to do this in several steps, moving the letters closer together to demonstrate how to blend.)

Then cover the word and spell it orally. Uncover the word and have students compare your spelling with the Touch-units. Cover the word again and write it on the whiteboard. Uncover the word and have students compare the written word with the Touch-units.

Repeat this procedure with *rent* and *tilt.*

Build Words Distribute Touch-units for the word *felt.* Say *felt.* Have students build it on their whiteboard using the Touch-units. Give help as necessary. After making the word, have students touch and sound each Touch-unit, then blend the sounds as they run their finger underneath the Touch-units. Have students cover the word and spell it orally, then compare their spelling to the Touch-units. Next have them cover the word again and write it on their whiteboard and then on the Build Words page of their Workbook (p. 62). Have students compare their writing to the Touch-units. Then use this procedure to have students build the following words:

	yellow	red	blue	green
melt	m	e		lt
malt		a		
ramp	r			mp
stamp			st	
stunt		u		nt
tent	t	e		

Use one of the activities on page xvi to further practice sequencing and discriminating the words that students find challenging.

Read Words in Isolation Have students pair up and read all of the words they have written on Workbook page 62 aloud to their partner.

Independent Practice (Workbook page 61) For the first set of items, ask students to write the letters that complete each picture name. For the second set, ask them to circle the word that names the picture at the beginning of each row. When students complete the page, have them check their work with you or a partner.

Dictation Dictate the following sentence, and have students write it on their whiteboard or at the bottom of Workbook page 61: *The lamp was on a quilt in the tent.*

Reading Words in Context

Tell students that they will use what they know about blends to read a story.

Build Words from the Story Use the Touch-units to build the following words on the whiteboard. Tell students that the words you will make together will help them read the story.

Start with the word *felt.*

Substitute Touch-units to build the following words: *quilt, belt, melt, malt, camp, champ, chimp, chimps, jump, romp, lamp, bump, punt, stunt, stunts, pants, tent, tents, went, thank, grand, pond.*

As a prereading activity, you may want to have students find the words in the text and read them aloud.

Learn Sight Words Tell students that they will learn a new word to help them read the story. Display this sight word: *give.* Read the word as you point to it.

As a prereading activity, you may want to have students find the word in the text as they write it.

Read the Story Give students a copy of *Chad at Camp.* Have them read it independently or with a partner. If necessary, you can support students as they read the story by identifying sight words or helping them to blend sounds to read words.

Respond to the Story After students read *Chad at Camp,* have them complete Workbook page 63. Have students share their work with the rest of the group.

Lesson 22: Final Consonant Blend: *nch*

Remind students that they have learned the sounds for final blends *sp, st, sk, nd, ng, nk, nt, mp,* and *lt.* Tell students that today they will learn the sound for final blend *nch.*

Phonemic Awareness Say the word *ranch.* Emphasize the consonant sounds at the end.

Then say the following words, and have students listen for the consonant sounds at the end of each one: *munch, inch, trench.*

Tell students to listen for the sound at the end of some words you will say. Slowly say *French, clench, blanch, clinch.* Emphasize the consonant sounds at the end of each word.

Link Sounds to Letters Distribute the *nch* Touch-unit. Have students trace its shape with their finger as they make the *nch* sounds together.

Form the following word on a whiteboard: *brunch.* Say the word, emphasizing the *nch* sound. Then underline the *nch* in the word.

Tell students that the *nch* makes the *nch* sounds they hear at the end of *brunch.* Isolate the sounds for students, and then have them repeat the sounds after you.

Form these words on a whiteboard: *ranch, munch, quench, crunch.* Say each word for students, and have them take turns underlining the blend, saying its sound, and then saying the word.

Build Words (Model) Tell students that they can use what they know about blends to build words.

Say *lunch.* Tell students you are going to build *lunch.* Use Touch-units or Magtiles to model.

Pick up the letter *l,* and say its sound as you place it on the whiteboard. Repeat the procedure with the letter *u,* and place it about an inch to the right of the letter *l.* Repeat the procedure again with the letters *nch.* Touch *l,* and say its sound. Touch *u,* and say its sound. Touch *nch,* and say their sounds.

Move the letters closer together, and say their sounds, blending them slightly. Move the letters next to each other and blend the sounds to say *lunch.* (You may choose to do this in several steps, moving the letters closer together to demonstrate how to blend.)

Then cover the word and spell it orally. Uncover the word and have students compare your spelling with the Touch-units. Cover the word again and write it on the whiteboard. Uncover the word and have students compare the written word with the Touch-units.

Build Words Distribute Touch-units for the word *bunch.* Say *bunch.* Have students build it on their whiteboard using the Touch-units. Give help as necessary. After making the word, have students touch and sound each Touch-unit, then blend the sounds as they run their finger underneath the Touch-units. Have students cover the word and spell it orally, then compare their spelling to the Touch-units. Next have them cover the word again and write it on their whiteboard and then on the Build Words page of their Workbook (p. 65). Have students compare their writing to the Touch-units. Then use this procedure to have students build the following words:

	yellow	red	blue	green
hunch	h	u		nch
bunch	b			
bench		e		
clench			cl	
clinch		i		
flinch			fl	

Use one of the activities on page xvi to further practice sequencing and discriminating the words that students find challenging.

Read Words in Isolation Have students pair up and read all of the words they have written on Workbook page 65 aloud to their partner.

Independent Practice (Workbook page 64) For the first set of items, ask students to connect all the picture names that have the *nch* sounds to find their way through the maze. For the second set, ask them to write the word that completes each sentence. When students complete the page, have them check their work with you or a partner.

Dictation Dictate the following sentence, and have students write it on their whiteboard or at the bottom of Workbook page 64: *They sat on the bench to have lunch.*

Reading Words in Context

Tell students that they will use what they know about blends to read a story.

Build Words from the Story Use the Touch-units to build the following words on the whiteboard. Tell students that the words you will make together will help them read the story.

Start with the word *ranch.*

Substitute Touch-units to build the following words: *branch, brunch, crunch, lunch, munch, punch, bunch, bench, French, quench, trench, inch, pinch, finch, clinch, flinch.*

As a prereading activity, you may want to have students find the words in the text and read them aloud.

Learn Sight Words Tell students that they will learn some new words to help them read the story. Display these sight words: *there, where.* Read the words as you point to them.

As a prereading activity, you may want to have students find the words in the text as they write them.

Read the Story Give students a copy of *Inchworm.* Have them read it independently or with a partner. If necessary, you can support students as they read the story by identifying sight words or helping them to blend sounds to read words.

Respond to the Story After students read *Inchworm,* have them complete Workbook page 66. Have students share their work with the rest of the group.

Word Lists

Final Consonant Blends						
sp, st, sk, nd, ng						
sp	**st**		**sk**	**nd**	**ng**	
asp	cast	cost	ask	and	bang	bong
gasp	fast	lost	bask	band	fang	gong
hasp	last	frost	cask	hand	gang	long
	mast		mask	land	hang	song
rasp	past	bust	task	sand	pang	tong
clasp	vast	dust	flask	bland	rang	thong
grasp	blast	gust		gland	sang	throng
		just	desk	brand	tang	prong
lisp	midst	must		grand	clang	strong
wisp		rust	disk	strand	slang	
crisp	best		risk	stand	sprang	dung
	jest	crust	brisk		twang	hung
	lest	thrust	frisk	end		lung
	chest	trust	whisk	bend	ding	clung
	nest			fend	king	flung
	pest		dusk	lend	ping	slung
	rest		husk	mend	ring	rung
	test		tusk	rend	sing	spring
	vest			send	wing	strung
	west			tend	zing	sung
	zest			vend	thing	stung
	blest			wend	cling	swung
	crest			blend	fling	string
	quest			spend	sling	
				trend	bring	
	fist				spring	
	list			bond	string	
	mist			fond	sting	
	grist			pond		
	twist			blond	swing	
				frond		
				fund		

Final Consonant Blends

nk, nt, mp

nk		nt		mp	
bank	plink	ant	font	camp	bump
dank	slink	pant		damp	dump
hank	brink	rant	bunt	lamp	hump
lank	drink	scant	hunt	ramp	jump
rank		chant	punt	tamp	lump
sank	honk	plant	runt	vamp	pump
tank	monk	slant	shunt	champ	rump
yank		grant	blunt	clamp	chump
shank	bunk		grunt	cramp	thump
thank	dunk	bent	stunt	tramp	clump
blank	funk	cent		stamp	plump
clank	hunk	dent			slump
flank	junk	gent		limp	frump
plank	punk	lent		chimp	grump
spank		rent		skimp	trump
crank	sunk	sent		blimp	stump
drank	chunk	tent		crimp	
frank	skunk	vent		shrimp	
shrank	flunk	went		primp	
prank	plunk	scent			
	slunk	Kent		pomp	
ink	spunk	spent		romp	
kink	drunk	hint		chomp	
link	shrunk	lint		stomp	
mink	trunk	mint			
pink	stunk	tint			
rink		flint			
sink		glint			
wink		splint			
chink		print			
think		sprint			
blink		squint			
clink					

Final Consonant Blends				
lt, nch, ld, pt, lm				
lt	**nch**	**ld**	**pt**	**lm**
malt	blanch	held	apt	balm
	ranch	meld	rapt	calm
belt		weld		palm
felt	bench	gild	kept	
melt	clench		wept	qualm
pelt	drench		slept	
welt	French		crept	elm
smelt	trench		swept	helm
	stench			
gilt	quench		script	film
hilt				
jilt	inch		tempt	
kilt	cinch		prompt	
silt	flinch			
tilt	clinch			
wilt	pinch			
spilt	winch			
stilt				
quilt	conch			
	bunch			
	hunch			
	lunch			
	munch			
	punch			
	brunch			
	crunch			

Final Consonant Blends				
ft, lk, lp, lf, ct				
ft	**lk**	**lp**	**lf**	**ct**
aft	elk	scalp	elf	act
daft			shelf	fact
raft	bilk	help	self	pact
waft	milk	kelp		tact
shaft	silk	yelp	golf	tract
craft				
draft	bulk	gulp	gulf	sect
graft	hulk	pulp		
	sulk			strict
deft				
heft				duct
left				
theft				
cleft				
gift				
lift				
rift				
sift				
shift				
drift				
thrift				
swift				
loft				
soft				
tuft				

Lesson 23: Silent Letters: *ck, lk, kn*

Remind students that they have learned the sounds for consonant blends found at the beginning and end of words.

Explain that there are other consonants that are sometimes found next to each other in words. Tell students that you say only one of the sounds for these consonants. The other consonant is silent. Demonstrate the sounds for *ck, lk,* and *kn* for students.

Tell students that today they will learn the sounds for consonant pairs with silent letters in *ck, lk,* and *kn.*

Phonemic Awareness Say the word *duck.* Emphasize the consonant sound at the end. Then say the following words, and have students listen for the consonant sound at the end of each one: *neck, black, talk, chalk.*

Now say the word *knack.* Emphasize the consonant sound at the beginning. Then say the following words, and have students listen for the consonant sound at the beginning of each one: *knee, knife, knight, know.*

Link Sound to Letters Distribute the *ck* Touch-unit. Have students trace its shape with their finger as they make the *k* sound together.

Form the following word on a whiteboard: *pack.* Say the word, emphasizing the *k* sound. Then underline the *ck* in the word.

Tell students that the *ck* makes the sound for *k.* Tell them that the *c* in *ck* is silent. Isolate the sound for students, and then have them repeat it after you.

Now distribute the *lk* and *kn* Touch-units. Repeat the procedure above to form the following words: *stalk, knelt.* Emphasize that the *l* in *lk* is silent, and that the *k* in *kn* is silent.

Build Words (Model) Tell students that they can use what they know about consonant pairs with silent letters to build words.

Say *pick.* Tell students you are going to build *pick.* Use Touch-units or Magtiles to model.

Pick up the letter *p,* and say its sound as you place it on the whiteboard. Repeat the procedure with the letter *i,* and place it about an inch to the right of the letter *p.* Repeat the procedure again with the letters *ck.* Touch *p,* and say its sound. Touch *i,* and say its sound. Touch *ck,* and say their sound.

Move the letters closer together, and say their sounds, blending them slightly. Move the letters next to each other and blend the sounds to say *pick.* (You may choose to do this in several steps, moving the letters closer together to demonstrate how to blend.)

Then cover the word and spell it orally. Uncover the word and have students compare your spelling with the Touch-units. Cover the word again and write it on the whiteboard. Uncover the word and have students compare the written word with the Touch-units.

Repeat this procedure with *knob* and *chalk.*

Build Words Distribute Touch-units for the word *stick.* Say *stick.* Have students build it on their whiteboard using the Touch-units. Give help as necessary. After making the word, have students touch and sound each Touch-unit, then blend the sounds as they run their finger underneath the Touch-units. Have students cover the word and spell it orally, then compare their spelling to the Touch-units. Next have them cover the word again and write it on their whiteboard and then on the Build Words page of their Workbook (p. 68). Have students compare their writing to the Touch-units. Then use this procedure to have students build the following words:

	yellow	red	green	white/yellow
tuck	t	u		ck
tack		a		
Jack	J			
knack				kn
knock		o		
knelt		e	lt	
talk	t	a		lk
walk	w			

Use one of the activities on page xvi to further practice sequencing and discriminating the words that students find challenging.

Read Words in Isolation Have students pair up and read all of the words they have written on Workbook page 68 aloud to their partner.

Independent Practice (Workbook page 67) For the first set of items, ask students to circle the word that names the picture at the beginning of each row. For the second set, ask them to write the word that completes each sentence. When students complete the page, have them check their work with you or a partner.

Dictation Dictate the following sentence, and have students write it on their whiteboard or at the bottom of Workbook page 67: *Jack knelt on the walk.* The truck got stuck in the mud.

Reading Words in Context

Tell students that they will use what they know about consonant pairs with silent letters to read a story.

Build Words from the Story Use the Touch-units to build the following words on the whiteboard. Tell students that the words you will make together will help them read the story.

Start with the word *back.*

Substitute Touch-units to build the following words: *pack, Jack, quack, black, clack, clock, cluck, duck, stuck, truck, trick, quick, sick, pick, chicks, check, neck, peck, knack, knock, knob, knot, knit, knelt, talk, walk, stalk, chalk.*

As a prereading activity, you may want to have students find the words in the text and read them aloud.

Learn Sight Words Tell students that they will learn a new word to help them read the story. Display this sight word: *could.* Read the word as you point to it.

As a prereading activity, you may want to have students find the word in the text as they write it.

Read the Story Give students a copy of *Jack the Vet.* Have them read it independently or with a partner. If necessary, you can support students as they read the story by identifying sight words or helping them to blend sounds to read words.

Respond to the Story After students read *Jack the Vet,* have them complete Workbook page 69. Have students share their work with the rest of the group.

Lesson 24: Silent Letters: *tch, dge*

Remind students that they have learned about silent letters in *ck, lk,* and *kn.* Tell students that sometimes three consonants found next to each other in words make only one sound. Today they will learn about silent letters in *tch* and *dge.*

Phonemic Awareness Say the word *batch.* Emphasize the consonant sound at the end.

Then say the following words, and have students listen for the consonant sound at the end of each one: *ditch, notch, blotch, lodge, wedge, judge.*

Link Sound to Letters Distribute the *tch* Touch-unit. Have students trace its shape with their finger as they make the *ch* sound together.

Form the following word on a whiteboard: *match.* Say the word, emphasizing the *ch* sound. Then underline the *tch* in the word.

Tell students that the *tch* makes the sound for *ch.* Tell them that the *t* in *tch* is silent. Isolate the sound for students, and then have them repeat it after you.

Now distribute the *dge* Touch-unit. Repeat the procedure above to form the word *dodge.* Tell students that the *dge* makes the sound for *j.* Tell them that the *d* and *e* in *dge* are silent.

Form these words on the whiteboard: *catch, fetch, badge, fudge.* Say each word for students, and have them take turns underlining the *tch* or *dge,* saying the appropriate sound, and then saying the word.

Build Words (Model) Tell students that they can use what they know about consonant pairs with silent letters to build words.

Say *patch.* Tell students you are going to build *patch.* Use Touch-units or Magtiles to model.

Pick up the letter *p,* and say its sound as you place it on the whiteboard. Repeat the procedure with the letter *a,* and place it about an inch to the right of the letter *p.* Repeat the procedure again with the letters *tch.* Touch *p,* and say its sound. Touch *a,* and say its sound. Touch *tch,* and say their sound.

Move the letters closer together, and say their sounds, blending them slightly. Move the letters next to each other and blend the sounds to say *patch.* (You may choose to do this in several steps, moving the letters closer together to demonstrate how to blend.)

Then cover the word and spell it orally. Uncover the word and have students compare your spelling with the Touch-units. Cover the word again and write it on the whiteboard. Uncover the word and have students compare the written word with the Touch-units.

Repeat this procedure with the word *pledge.*

Build Words Distribute Touch-units for the word *edge.* Say *edge.* Have students build it on their whiteboard using the Touch-units. Give help as necessary. After making the word, have students touch and sound each Touch-unit, then blend the sounds as they run their finger underneath the Touch-units. Have students cover the word and spell it orally, then compare their spelling to the Touch-units. Next have them cover the word again and write it on their whiteboard and then on the Build Words page of their Workbook (p. 71). Have students compare their writing to the Touch-units. Then use this procedure to have students build the following words:

	yellow	red	blue	white/yellow
hedge	h	e		dge
ridge	r	i		
bridge			br	
batch	b	a		tch
hatch	h			
hitch		i		

Use one of the activities on page xvi to further practice sequencing and discriminating the words that students find challenging.

Read Words in Isolation Have students pair up and read all of the words they have written on Workbook page 71 aloud to their partner.

Independent Practice (Workbook page 70) For the first set of items, ask students to write the letters that complete each picture name. For the second set, ask them to circle the word that names the picture at the beginning of each row. When students complete the page, have them check their work with you or a partner.

Dictation Dictate the following sentence, and have students write it on their whiteboard or at the bottom of Workbook page 70: *Madge had a batch of fudge.* Did you match his badge with his patch?

Reading Words in Context

Tell students that they will use what they know about silent letters to read a story.

Build Words from the Story Use the Touch-units to build the following words on the whiteboard. Tell students that the words you will make together will help them read the story.

Start with the word *badge.*

Substitute Touch-units to build the following words: *Madge, budge, fudge, Judge, edge, ledge, pledge, hedge, ridge, bridge, batch, catch, hatch, latch, match, patch, pitch, itch, witch, hitch, ditch, etch, fetch, Butch, crutch, clutch.*

As a prereading activity, you may want to have students find the words in the text and read them aloud.

Learn Sight Words Tell students that they will learn some new words to help them read the story. Display these sight words: *even, love.* Read the words as you point to them.

As a prereading activity, you may want to have students find the words in the text as they write them.

Read the Story Give students a copy of *Madge at the Farm.* Have them read it independently or with a partner. If necessary, you can support students as they read the story by identifying sight words or helping them to blend sounds to read words.

Respond to the Story After students read *Madge at the Farm,* have them complete Workbook page 72. Have students share their work with the rest of the group.

Lesson 25: Silent Letters: *mb, gh, wr*

Remind students that they have learned the sounds for consonants with silent letters in *ck, lk, kn, tch,* and *dge.* Tell students that today they will learn about silent letters in *mb, gh,* and *wr.*

Phonemic Awareness Say the word *numb.* Emphasize the consonant sound at the end. Then say the following words, and have students listen for the consonant sound at the end of each one: *climb, lamb, thumb.*

Now say the word *wreck.* Emphasize the consonant sound at the beginning. Then say the following words, and have students listen for the consonant sound at the beginning of each one: *wrap, wrist, wring.*

Link Sound to Letters Distribute the *mb* Touch-unit. Have students trace its shape with their finger as they make the *mb* sound together.

Form the following word on a whiteboard: *crumb.* Say the word, emphasizing the *m* sound. Then underline the *mb* in the word.

Tell students that the *mb* makes the sound for *m.* Tell them that the *b* in *mb* is silent. Isolate the sound for students, and then have them repeat it after you.

Then distribute the *wr* Touch-unit. Repeat the procedure above to form the word *wrench.* Tell students that the *wr* makes the sound for *r.* Tell them that the *w* in *wr* is silent.

Now distribute the *gh* Touch-unit. Repeat the procedure again to form the word *taught.* Tell students that the consonants *gh* are silent.

Form these words on the whiteboard: *thumb, dumb, wrong, wrist, fight, might.* Say each word for students, and have them take turns underlining the *mb, gh,* or *wr,* saying the appropriate sound, and then saying the word.

Build Words (Model) Tell students that they can use what they know about consonants with silent letters to build words.

Say *numb.* Tell students you are going to build *numb.* Use Touch-units or Magtiles to model. Pick up the letter *n,* and say its sound as you place it on the whiteboard. Repeat the procedure with the letter *u,* and place it about an inch to the right of the letter *n.* Repeat the procedure again with the letters *mb.* Touch *n,* and say its sound. Touch *u,* and say its sound. Touch *mb,* and say their sound.

Move the letters closer together, and say their sounds, blending them slightly. Move the letters next to each other and blend the sounds to say *numb.* (You may choose to do this in several steps, moving the letters closer together to demonstrate how to blend.)

Then cover the word and spell it orally. Uncover the word and have students compare your spelling with the Touch-units. Cover the word again and write it on the whiteboard. Uncover the word and have students compare the written word with the Touch-units.

Repeat this procedure with *wreck* and *sight.*

Build Words Distribute Touch-units for the word *night.* Say *night.* Have students build it on their whiteboard using the Touch-units. Give help as necessary. After making the word, have students touch and sound each Touch-unit, then blend the sounds as they run their finger underneath the Touch-units. Have students cover the word and spell it orally, then compare their spelling to the Touch-units. Next have them cover the word again and write it on their whiteboard and then on the Build Words page of their Workbook (p. 74). Have students compare their writing to the Touch-units. Then use this procedure to have them build these words:

	yellow	red	white	white/yellow
tight	t	i	gh	
light	l			
limb				mb
lamb		a		
wrap	p			wr
wren	n	e		

Use one of the activities on page xvi to further practice sequencing and discriminating the words that students find challenging.

Read Words in Isolation Have students pair up and read all of the words they have written on Workbook page 74 aloud to their partner.

Independent Practice (Workbook page 73) Ask students to write the word that completes each sentence in the story. When students complete the page, have them check their work with you or a partner.

Dictation Dictate the following sentence, and have students write it on their whiteboard or at the bottom of Workbook page 73: *The lamb and wren sat in the bright light.*

Reading Words in Context

Tell students that they will use what they know about consonant pairs with silent letters to read a story.

Build Words from the Story Use the Touch-units to build the following words on the whiteboard. Tell students that the words you will make together will help them read the story.

Start with the word *high.*

Substitute Touch-units to build the following words: *sigh, sight, right, tight, night, light, fight, fright, bright, limb, lamb, dumb, numb, crumb, thumb, wrap, wreck, wrench, wren, wrist, wrists, wring, wrong.*

As a prereading activity, you may want to have students find the words in the text and read them aloud.

Learn Sight Words Tell students that they will learn some new words to help them read the story. Display these sight words: *full, some, something, thought.* Read the words as you point to them.

As a prereading activity, you may want to have students find the words in the text as they write them.

Read the Story Give students a copy of *The Little Lamb.* Have them read it independently or with a partner. If necessary, you can support students as they read the story by identifying sight words or helping them to blend sounds to read words.

Respond to the Story After students read *The Little Lamb,* have them complete Workbook page 75. Have students share their work with the rest of the group.

READ THE STORY
The Little Lamb

ADDITIONAL READING

This EPS reader provides an additional story in which to practice *Silent Letters:* mb, gh, wr.

SPIRE Decodables

The Tomb of King Tut
Set 6A, Book 8

Word Lists

Silent Letters							
wr, kn, gn, gu, lk, ck							
wr	**kn**	**gn**	**gu**	**lk**	**ck**		
	knack	gnat	guess	balk	back	Dick	dock
wrap		gnash	guest	talk	hack	hick	hock
wrath	knell			walk	Jack	kick	lock
	knelt		guild	chalk	jack	nick	mock
wren			guilt	stalk	Mack	sick	rock
wreck	knit				pack	tick	sock
wrench	knight				lack	wick	shock
wrest					tack	Rick	block
wretch	knob				rack	chick	clock
	knot				sack	thick	flock
wring	knock				black	click	knock
wrist					clack	flick	crock
					slack	slick	frock
wrong					smack	brick	stock
					knack	crick	
wrung					snack	prick	buck
					shack	trick	duck
					whack	stick	luck
					crack	quick	muck
					track		suck
					stack		tuck
					quack		
							puck
					deck		shuck
					neck		cluck
					peck		pluck
					check		truck
					fleck		struck
					speck		stuck
					wreck		Chuck

Silent Letters			
tch, dge, mb, gh			
tch	**dge**	**mb**	**gh**
batch	badge	✓ lamb	✓high
catch			nigh
hatch	edge	✓ limb	✓sigh
thatch	hedge		
latch	ledge	bomb	✓fight
match	pledge	✓ dumb	✓ light
snatch	sledge	✓numb	✓might
patch	dredge	✓thumb	✓night
scratch		plumb	✓ right
	ridge	✓ crumb	✓ sight
etch	bridge		✓tight
fetch			
sketch	dodge		knight
retch	lodge		blight
wretch			✓bright
	budge		✓ flight
itch	fudge		✓ fright
ditch	judge		plight
hitch	sludge		slight
glitch	smudge		
pitch	nudge		
stitch	drudge		
witch	grudge		
switch	trudge		
twitch			
botch			
blotch			
splotch			
notch			
Dutch			
hutch			
clutch			

Lesson 26: Long Vowels: Open e, o

Remind students that they have learned the sounds that short vowels make. Tell them that vowels sometimes make other sounds. Some of these sounds are called long vowel sounds.

Explain that when you say a long vowel sound, you say the vowel letter's name. Demonstrate the long vowel sounds *a, e, i, o, u.* Tell students that today they will learn the sounds for long vowels *e* and *o.*

Phonemic Awareness Say the word *be.* Emphasize the long *e* sound.

Then say the following words, and have students listen for the long *e* sound at the end of each one: *key, knee, tea.*

Say the word *go.* Emphasize the long *o* sound. Then say the following words, and have students listen for long *o* sound at the end of each one: *blow, flow, show.*

Tell students to listen for the long vowel sound at the end of some words you will say. Slowly say *me, tree, see, hoe, low, glow.* Emphasize the long vowel sound at the end of each one.

Link Sound to Letter Distribute the *e* Touch-unit. Have students trace its shape with their finger as they make the long *e* sound together.

Form the following word on a whiteboard: *me.* Say the word, emphasizing the long *e* sound. Then underline the *e* in the word.

Tell students that the *e* makes the long *e* sound. Isolate the sound for students, and then have them repeat it after you.

Now distribute the *o* Touch-unit. Repeat the procedure above to form the word *so.*

Build Words (Model) Tell students that they can use what they know about long vowels to build words.

Say *pro.* Tell students you are going to build *pro.* Use Touch-units or Magtiles to model.

Pick up the letters *pr,* and say their sounds as you place them on the whiteboard. Repeat the procedure with the letter *o,* and place it about an inch to the right of the letters *pr.* Touch *pr,* and say their sounds. Touch *o,* and say its sound.

Move the letters closer together, and say their sounds, blending them slightly. Move the letters next to each other and blend the sounds to say *pro.* (You may choose to do this in several steps, moving the letters closer together to demonstrate how to blend.)

Then cover the word and spell it orally. Uncover the word and have students compare your spelling with the Touch-units. Cover the word again and write it on the whiteboard. Uncover the word and have students compare the written word with the Touch-units.

Repeat this procedure with the word *she.*

Build Words Distribute Touch-units for the word *he.* Say *he.* Have students build it on their whiteboard using the Touch-units. Give help as necessary. After making the word, have students touch and sound each Touch-unit, then blend the sounds as they run their finger underneath the Touch-units. Have students cover the word and spell it orally, then compare their spelling to the Touch-units. Next have them cover the word again and write it on their whiteboard and then on the Build Words page of their Workbook (p. 77). Have students compare their writing to the Touch-units. Then use this procedure to have students build the following words:

	yellow	red
be	b	e
me	m	
we	w	
go	g	o
no	n	
so	s	

Use one of the activities on page xvi to further practice sequencing and discriminating the words that students find challenging.

Read Words in Isolation Have students pair up and read all of the words they have written on Workbook page 77 aloud to their partner.

Independent Practice (Workbook page 76) Ask students to write the word that completes each sentence. When students complete the page, have them check their work with you or a partner.

Dictation Dictate the following sentence, and have students write it on their whiteboard or at the bottom of Workbook page 76: *Mom let me go on the big ship.*

Reading Words in Context

Tell students that they will use what they know about long vowels to read a story.

Build Words from the Story Use the Touch-units to build the following words on the whiteboard. Tell students that the words you will make together will help them read the story.

Start with the word *be.*

Substitute Touch-units to build the following words: *me, we, he, she, go, no, so, so-so, pro, yo-yo, yo-yos, Jo-Jo.*

As a prereading activity, you may want to have students find the words in the text and read them aloud.

Learn Sight Words Tell students that they will learn a new word to help them read the story. Display this sight word: *again.* Read the word as you point to it.

As a prereading activity, you may want to have students find the word in the text as they write it.

Read the Story Give students a copy of *The Yo-Yo.* Have them read it independently or with a partner. If necessary, you can support students as they read the story by identifying sight words or helping them to blend sounds to read words.

Respond to the Story After students read *The Yo-Yo,* have them complete Workbook page 78. Have students share their work with the rest of the group.

READ THE STORY
The Yo-Yo

ADDITIONAL READING

For extra reinforcement of *Lesson 26: Long Vowels: e, o* you will find additional word activities on pages 167–169.

At this printing, additional EPS readers are not available for this lesson. Please visit *www.epsbooks.com* periodically for updates.

Lesson 27: Long Vowel: Open y

Remind students that they have learned the sounds for long vowels *e* and *o*. Tell them that sometimes the consonant *y* acts like a long vowel.

Explain that when the letter *y* is at the end of words, it makes the sound they hear in *by*. Demonstrate the vowel sound for *y*.

Tell students that today they will learn the vowel sound for *y*.

Phonemic Awareness Say the word *by*. Emphasize the vowel sound at the end.

Then say the following words, and have students listen for the vowel sound at the end of each one: *my, cry, shy.*

Tell students to listen for the vowel sound at the end of some words you will say. Slowly say *spy, fry, ply.* Emphasize the vowel sound at the end of each word.

Link Sound to Letter Distribute the *y* Touch-unit. Have students trace its shape with their finger as they make the vowel sound for *y* together.

Form the following word on a whiteboard: *sky*. Say the word, emphasizing the vowel sound. Then underline the *y* in the word.

Tell students that the *y* makes the vowel sound they hear in *sky*. Isolate the sound for students, and then have them repeat it after you.

Form these words on the whiteboard: *fry, spry, dry, ply.* Say each word for students, and have them take turns underlining the *y*, saying its sound, and then saying the word.

Build Words (Model) Tell students that they can use what they know about long vowels to build words.

Say *try*. Tell students you are going to build *try*. Use Touch-units or Magtiles to model.

Pick up the letters *tr*, and say their sounds as you place them on the whiteboard. Repeat the procedure with the letter *y*, and place it about an inch to the right of the letters *tr*.

Touch *tr*, and say their sounds. Touch *y*, and say its sound.

Move the letters closer together, and say their sounds, blending them slightly. Move the letters next to each other and blend the sounds to say *try*. (You may choose to do this in several steps, moving the letters closer together to demonstrate how to blend.)

Then cover the word and spell it orally. Uncover the word and have students compare your spelling with the Touch-units. Cover the word again and write it on the whiteboard. Uncover the word and have students compare the written word with the Touch-units.

Build Words Distribute Touch-units for the word *my*. Say *my*. Have students build it on their whiteboard using the Touch-units. Give help as necessary. After making the word, have students touch and sound each Touch-unit, then blend the sounds as they run their finger underneath the Touch-units. Have students cover the word and spell it orally, then compare their spelling to the Touch-units. Next have them cover the word again and write it on their whiteboard and then on the Build Words page of their Workbook (p. 80). Have students compare their writing to the Touch-units. Then use this procedure to have students build the following words:

	yellow	red	blue
by	b	y	
cry			cr
spy			sp
fly			fl
shy	sh		
why	wh		

Use one of the activities on page xvi to further practice sequencing and discriminating the words that students find challenging.

Read Words in Isolation Have students pair up and read all of the words they have written on Workbook page 80 aloud to their partner.

Independent Practice (Workbook page 79) Ask students to write the word that completes each sentence. When students complete the page, have them check their work with you or a partner.

Dictation Dictate the following sentence, and have students write it on their whiteboard or at the bottom of Workbook page 79: *The fat fly sat on the dry mat.*

Reading Words in Context

Tell students that they will use what they know about long vowels to read a story.

Build Words from the Story Use the Touch-units to build the following words on the whiteboard. Tell students that the words you will make together will help them read the story.

Start with the word *by.*

Substitute Touch-units to build the following words: *my, cry, try, dry, fry, spy, spry, sly, sky, ply, fly, shy, why.*

As a prereading activity, you may want to have students find the words in the text and read them aloud.

Review Sight Words Tell students that they will review some words that will help them read the story. Display these sight words: *thought, would, love.* Read the words as you point to them.

As a prereading activity, you may want to have students find the words in the text as they write them.

Read the Story Give students a copy of *The Frog and the Fly.* Have them read it independently or with a partner. If necessary, you can support students as they read the story by identifying sight words or helping them to blend sounds to read words.

Respond to the Story After students read *The Frog and the Fly,* have them complete Workbook page 81. Have students share their work with the rest of the group.

Lesson 28: Long Vowels: *a, o*

Remind students that they have learned the long vowel sounds *e, o,* and *y* at the end of words. Tell students that today they will learn the sounds for long vowels *a* and *o.*

Phonemic Awareness Say the word *ate.* Emphasize the long *a* sound.

Then say the following words, and have students listen for the long *a* sound in each one: *ape, ace, age.*

Say the word *oak.* Emphasize the long *o* sound. Then say the following words, and have students listen for the long *o* sound in each one: *ode, old, oat.*

Tell students to listen for the long *a* or long *o* sound in some words you will say. Slowly say *cane, cape, late, code, note, rope.* Emphasize the long *a* or long *o* sound in each word.

Link Sound to Letter Distribute the *a* Touch-unit. Have students trace its shape with their finger as they make the long *a* sound together.

Form the following word on a whiteboard: *game.* Say the word, emphasizing the long *a* sound. Then underline the *a* and *e* in the word.

Tell students that when the *a* is followed by a consonant and a silent *e,* the *a* makes the long *a* sound. Isolate the sound for students, and then have them repeat it after you.

Now distribute the *o* Touch-unit. Repeat the procedure above to form *cone.*

Form these words on the whiteboard: *same, tape, mate, robe, hope, slope.* Say each word for students, and have them take turns underlining the long vowel and silent *e,* saying the vowel sound, and then saying the word.

Build Words (Model) Tell students that they can use what they know about long vowels to build words.

Say *ape.* Tell students you are going to build *ape.* Use Touch-units or Magtiles to model.

Pick up the letter *a,* and say its sound as you place it on the whiteboard. Repeat the procedure with the letter *p,* and place it about an inch to the right of the letter *a.* Repeat the procedure with the letter *e.* Touch *a,* and say its sound. Touch *p,* and say its sound. Touch *e,* and remind students that it is silent.

Move the letters closer together, and say their sounds, blending them slightly. Move the letters next to each other and blend the sounds to say *ape.* (You may choose to do this in several steps, moving the letters closer together to demonstrate how to blend.)

Then cover the word and spell it orally. Uncover the word and have students compare your spelling with the Touch-units. Cover the word again and write it on the whiteboard. Uncover the word and have students compare the written word with the Touch-units.

Repeat this procedure with the word *code.*

Build Words Distribute Touch-units for the word *fade.* Say *fade.* Have students build it on their whiteboard using the Touch-units. Give help as necessary. After making the word, have students touch and sound each Touch-unit, then blend the sounds as they run their finger underneath the Touch-units. Have students cover the word and spell it orally, then compare their spelling to the Touch-units. Next have them cover the word again and write it on their whiteboard and then on the Build Words page of their Workbook (p. 83). Have students compare their writing to the Touch-units. Then use this procedure to have students build the following words:

	yellow	red	white
made	m, d	a	e
mane	n		
cape	c, p		
cope		o	
rope	r		
rode	d		

Use one of the activities on page xvi to further practice sequencing and discriminating the words that students find challenging.

Read Words in Isolation Have students pair up and read all of the words they have written on Workbook page 83 aloud to their partner.

Independent Practice (Workbook page 82) For the first set of items, ask students to write the letters that complete each picture name. For the second set, ask them to circle the word that names the picture at the beginning of each row. When students complete the page, have them check their work with you or a partner.

Dictation Dictate the following sentence, and have students write it on their whiteboard or at the bottom of Workbook page 82: *Jane rode on a plane to the game.*

Reading Words in Context

Tell students that they will use what they know about long vowels to read a story.

Build Words from the Story Use the Touch-units to build the following words on the whiteboard. Tell students that the words you will make together will help them read the story.

Start with the word *cane.*

Substitute Touch-units to build the following words: *can, cane, cap, cape, capes, hat, hate, late, mad, made, mat, mate, mates, plan, plane, rat, rate, take, tap, tape, cod, code, hop, hope, not, note, rob, robe, rod, rode.*

As a prereading activity, you may want to have students find the words in the text and read them aloud.

Learn Sight Words Tell students that they will learn a new word to help them read the story. Display this sight word: *should.* Read the word as you point to it.

As a prereading activity, you may want to have students find the word in the text as they write it.

Read the Story Give students a copy of *First Rate Rat.* Have them read it independently or with a partner. If necessary, you can support students as they read the story by identifying sight words or helping them to blend sounds to read words.

Respond to the Story After students read *First Rate Rat,* have them complete Workbook page 84. Have students share their work with the rest of the group.

Lesson 29: Long Vowels: *i*, *u*

Remind students that they have learned the long vowel sounds for *e, o, y,* and *a.* Tell students that today they will learn the sounds for long vowels *i* and *u.*

Phonemic Awareness Say the word *pine.* Emphasize the long *i* sound. Then say the following words, and have students listen for the long *i* sound in each one: *time, ride, dine.*

Say the word *dune.* Emphasize the long *u* sound. Then say the following words, and have students listen for the long *u* sound in each one: *huge, jute, cube.*

Tell students to listen for the long *i* or long *u* sound in some words you will say. Slowly say *bite, mine, hide, dude, dune, mute.* Emphasize the long *i* or long *u* sound in each word.

Link Sound to Letter Distribute the *i* Touch-unit. Have students trace its shape with their finger as they make the long *i* sound together.

Form the following word on a whiteboard: *slime.* Say the word, emphasizing the long *i.* Then underline the *i* and *e* in the word.

Tell students that when the *i* is followed by a consonant and a silent *e,* the *i* makes the long *i* sound. Isolate the sound for students, and then have them repeat it after you.

Now distribute the *u* Touch-unit. Repeat the procedure above to form *tube.*

Form these words on the whiteboard: *bite, dime, time, crude, flute, mute.* Say each word for students, and have them take turns underlining the long vowel and silent *e,* saying the vowel sound, and then saying the word.

Build Words (Model) Tell students that they can use what they know about long vowels to build words.

Say *slide.* Tell students you are going to build *slide.* Use Touch-units or Magtiles to model.

Pick up the letters *sl,* and say their sounds as you place them on the whiteboard. Repeat the procedure with the letter *i,* and place it about an inch to the right of the letters *sl.*

Repeat the procedure with the letter *d.* Repeat the procedure again with the letter *e.* Touch *sl,* and say their sounds. Touch *i,* and say its sound. Touch *d,* and say its sound. Touch *e* and remind students that it is silent.

Move the letters closer together, and say their sounds, blending them slightly. Move the letters next to each other and blend the sounds to say *slide.* (You may choose to do this in several steps, moving the letters closer together to demonstrate how to blend.)

Then cover the word and spell it orally. Uncover the word and have students compare your spelling with the Touch-units. Cover the word again and write it on the whiteboard. Uncover the word and have students compare the written word with the Touch-units.

Repeat this procedure with the word *cute.*

Build Words Distribute Touch-units for the word *like.* Say *like.* Have students build it on their whiteboard using the Touch-units. Give help as necessary. After making the word, have students touch and sound each Touch-unit, then blend the sounds as they run their finger underneath the Touch-units. Have students cover the word and spell it orally, then compare their spelling to the Touch-units. Next have them cover the word again and write it on their whiteboard and then on the Build Words page of their Workbook (p. 86). Have students compare their writing to the Touch-units. Then use this procedure to have students build the following words:

	yellow	red	blue	white
fife	f, f	i		e
life	l			
line	n			
twine			tw	
dune	d	u		
tube	t, b			
cube	c			

Use one of the activities on page xvi to further practice sequencing and discriminating the words that students find challenging.

Read Words in Isolation Have students pair up and read all of the words they have written on Workbook page 86 aloud to their partner.

Independent Practice (Workbook page 85) For the first set of items, ask students to circle the letter that stands for the long vowel sound they hear in each picture name. For the second set, ask them to write the word that completes each sentence. When students complete the page, have them check their work with you or a partner.

Dictation Dictate the following sentence, and have students write it on their whiteboard or at the bottom of Workbook page 85: *Chad likes to ride on the tube slide.*

Reading Words in Context

Tell students that they will use what they know about long vowels to read a story.

Build Words from the Story Use the Touch-units to build the following words on the whiteboard. Tell students that the words you will make together will help them read the story.

Start with the word *bit.*

Substitute Touch-units to build the following words: *bite, dim, dime, fin, fine, hid, hide, kit, kite, life, like, pipe, slid, slide, slim, slime, smile, strip, stripe, time, twin, twine, cut, cute, dune, tub, tube, white, cub, cube.*

As a prereading activity, you may want to have students find the words in the text and read them aloud.

Review Sight Words Tell students that they will review some words that will help them read the story. Display these sight words: *there, would.* Read the words as you point to them.

As a prereading activity, you may want to have students find the words in the text as they write them.

Read the Story Give students a copy of *A Fine Fish.* Have them read it independently or with a partner. If necessary, you can support students as they read the story by identifying sight words or helping them to blend sounds to read words.

Respond to the Story After students read *A Fine Fish,* have them complete Workbook page 87. Have students share their work with the rest of the group.

Lesson 30: Long Vowel Review: *a, i, o, u*

Remind students that they have learned the sounds for long vowels *a, i, o,* and *u*. Tell students that they are now going to review the sounds to help them remember them better.

Phonemic Awareness Tell students that they are going to play a game to help them remember the sounds for long vowels.

Say the following words: *fake, cute, came.* Ask students to name the two words that have the same sound in the middle.

Repeat the procedure with the following sets of words: *flute, pale, duke; line, mike, home; huge, stone, mole.*

Link Sound to Letter Distribute the *o* Touch-unit. Have students trace its shape with their finger as they make the long *o* sound together.

Form the following word on a whiteboard: *bone.* Say the word, emphasizing the long *o* sound. Then underline the *o* and *e* in the word.

Tell students that when the *o* is followed by a consonant and a silent *e*, the *o* makes the long *o* sound. Isolate the sound for students, and then have them repeat it after you.

Now distribute the *a, i,* and *u* Touch-units. Repeat the procedure above to form the following words: *late, bite, cube.*

Build Words Distribute Touch-units for the word *flame.* Say *flame.* Have students build it on their whiteboard using the Touch-units. Give help as necessary. After making the word, have students touch and sound each Touch-unit, then blend the sounds as they run their finger underneath the Touch-units. Have students cover the word and spell it orally, then compare their spelling to the Touch-units. Next have them cover the word again and write it on their whiteboard and then on the Build Words page of their Workbook (p. 89). Have students compare their writing to the Touch-units. Then use this procedure to have students build the following words:

	yellow	red	blue	white
tape	t, p	a		e
cape	c			
cane	n			
cone		o		
slope	p		sl	
slide	d	i		
ride				
dude		u		
dune	n			

Use one of the activities on page xvi to further practice sequencing and discriminating the words that students find challenging.

Read Words in Isolation Have students pair up and read all of the words they have written on Workbook page 89 aloud to their partner.

Independent Practice (Workbook page 88) For the first set of items, ask students to write the letter that complete each picture name. For the second set, ask them to circle the word that names the picture at the beginning of each row. When students complete the page, have them check their work with you or a partner.

Dictation Dictate the following sentence, and have students write it on their whiteboard or at the bottom of Workbook page 88: *Sam made a huge pile of stones.*

Reading Words in Context

Tell students that they will use what they know about long vowels to read a story.

Build Words from the Story Use the Touch-units to build the following words on the whiteboard. Tell students that the words you will make together will help them read the story.

Start with the word *mad.*

Substitute Touch-units to build the following words: *made, mode, rid, ride, rod, rode, hug, huge, make, mike, hole, mile, mole, mule, pale, pile, pole, smile, came, home, lone, alone, tone, stone, line, tune, fin, fine, lane.*

As a prereading activity, you may want to have students find the words in the text and read them aloud.

Read the Story Give students a copy of *The Mule and the Mole.* Have them read it independently or with a partner. If necessary, you can support students as they read the story by identifying sight words or helping them to blend sounds to read words.

Respond to the Story After students read *The Mule and the Mole*, have them complete Workbook page 90. Have students share their work with the rest of the group.

READ THE STORY
The Mule and the Mole

ADDITIONAL READING

These EPS readers provide additional stories in which to practice *Long Vowel Review:* a, i, o, u.

Primary Phonics

Mac Get Well
Set 2, Book 1

The Big Game
Set 2, Book 2

The Joke
Set 2, Book 3

The Cake
Set 2, Book 4

Alphabet Series

A Snake for Jane
Volume 2, Book 22

Lesson 31: Vowels + *ck* and *ke*

Remind students that they have learned the sounds for short and long vowels. Tell them that looking at the letters at the ends of words can help them know which sound the vowel makes. Tell students that they are going to learn the sounds that vowels make when they are followed by *ck* and *ke.*

Phonemic Awareness Say the word *back.* Emphasize the vowel sound and the consonant sound at the end.

Then say the word *bake.* Emphasize the vowel sound and the consonant sound at the end.

Then say the following words, and have students listen for the vowel sound and ending consonant sound of each one: *rake, rack, duck, duke, poke, pock.*

Link Sound to Letters Distribute the *ck* Touch-unit. Have students trace its shape with their finger as they make the *k* sound together.

Form the following word on a whiteboard: *tack.* Say the word, emphasizing the short *a* sound and the sound for *ck.* Then underline the *a* and *ck* in the word.

Tell students that the *ck* makes the *k* sound. Isolate the *k* sound for students, and have them repeat it after you. Tell students that when a vowel is followed by *ck,* the vowel sound is short.

Now distribute the *k* and silent *e* Touch-units. Repeat the procedure above to form the word *take.* Tell students that when a vowel is followed by *ke,* the vowel sound is long.

Build Words (Model) Tell students that they can use what they know about letter sounds to build words.

Say *snack.* Tell students you are going to build *snack.* Use Touch-units or Magtiles to model.

Pick up the letters *sn,* and say their sounds as you place them on the whiteboard. Repeat the procedure with the letter *a,* and place it about an inch to the right of the letters *sn.*

Repeat the procedure again with *ck.* Touch *sn,* and say their sounds. Touch *a,* and say its sound. Touch *ck,* and say their sound.

Move the letters closer together and say their sounds, blending them slightly. Move the letters next to each other and blend the sounds to say *snack.* (You may choose to do this in several steps, moving the letters closer together to demonstrate how to blend.)

Then cover the word and spell it orally. Uncover the word and have students compare your spelling with the Touch-units. Cover the word again and write it on the whiteboard. Uncover the word and have students compare the written word with the Touch-units.

Repeat this procedure with the word *snake.* Remind students that the *e* in *snake* is silent.

Build Words Distribute Touch-units for the word *flake.* Say *flake.* Have students build it on their whiteboard using the Touch-units. Give help as necessary. After making the word, have students touch and sound each Touch-unit, then blend the sounds as they run their finger underneath the Touch-units. Have students cover the word and spell it orally, then compare their spelling to the Touch-units. Next have them cover the word again and write it on their whiteboard and then on the Build Words page of their Workbook (p. 92). Have students compare their writing to the Touch-units. Then use this procedure to have students build the following words:

	yellow	red	white
back	b	a	ck
bake			ke
pick	p	i	ck
pike			ke
pock		o	ck
poke			ke
duck	d	u	ck
duke			ke

Use one of the activities on page xvi to further practice sequencing and discriminating the words that students find challenging.

Read Words in Isolation Have students pair up and read all of the words they have written on Workbook page 92 aloud to their partner.

Independent Practice (Workbook page 91) For the first set of items, ask students to blend the sounds in each word, say the word, and circle the picture that the word names. For the second set, ask them to write the word that completes each sentence. When students complete the page, have them check their work with you or a partner.

Dictation Dictate the following sentence, and have students write it on their whiteboard or at the bottom of Workbook page 91: *A black snake is on the deck.*

Reading Words in Context

Tell students that they will use what they know about vowels followed by *ck* and *ke* to read a story.

Build Words from the Story Use the Touch-units to build the following words on the whiteboard. Tell students that the words you will make together will help them read the story.

Start with the word *back.*

Substitute Touch-units to build the following words: *bake, black, Blake, cake, lack, lake, Mack, make, quack, quake, rack, rake, sack, sake, shack, shake, snack, snake, tack, take, pick, pike, lick, like, strike, strikes, clock, pock, poke, spoke, stock, stoke, stuck, luck, duck, duke, deck.*

As a prereading activity, you may want to have students find the words in the text and read them aloud.

Learn Sight Words Tell students that they will learn some new words to help them read the story. Display these sight words: *done, friend.* Read the words as you point to them.

As a prereading activity, you may want to have students find the words in the text as they write them.

Read the Story Give students a copy of *Snake Bakes a Snack.* Have them read it independently or with a partner. If necessary, you can support students as they read the story by identifying sight words or helping them to blend sounds to read words.

Respond to the Story After students read *Snake Bakes a Snack,* have them complete Workbook page 93. Have students share their work with the rest of the group.

Lesson 32: Open Syllable + Silent *e*

Remind students that they have learned the sounds for long vowels. Explain that when a vowel is followed by *e* at the end of a word, the vowel sound is long and the *e* is silent. Tell them that today they will learn the sounds for vowels followed by silent *e* at the end of words.

Phonemic Awareness Say the word *doe.* Emphasize the vowel sound at the end. Then say the following words, and have students listen for the vowel sound at the end of each one: *foe, clue, tie, rye.*

Link Sound to Letters Distribute the *i* and silent *e* Touch-units. Have students trace the shapes with their finger as they make the long *i* sound together.

Form the following word on a whiteboard: *pie.* Say the word, emphasizing the long *i* sound. Then underline the *i* and *e* in the word.

Tell students that the *i* makes the long *i* sound when it is followed by a silent *e.* Isolate the long *i* sound for students, and then have them repeat it after you.

Now distribute the *y* and silent *e* Touch-units. Repeat the procedure above to form the word *bye.* Emphasize that the *y* also makes the long *i* sound when it is followed by a silent *e.*

Tell students that when a vowel is followed by *e* at the end of a word, the vowel sound is long. Then form these words on the whiteboard: *tie, doe, hoe, glue, eye.* Say each word for students, and have them take turns underlining the vowel, saying its sound, and then saying the word.

Build Words (Model) Tell students that they can use what they know about letter sounds to build words.

Say *blue.* Tell students you are going to build *blue.* Use Touch-units or Magtiles to model.

Pick up the letters *bl,* and say their sounds as you place them on the whiteboard. Repeat the procedure with the letter *u,* and place it about an inch to the right of the letters *bl.* Repeat the procedure with the letter *e.* Touch *bl,* and say their sounds. Touch *u,* and say its sound. Touch *e* and remind students that it is silent.

Move the letters closer together and say their sounds, blending them slightly. Move the letters next to each other and blend the sounds to say *blue.* (You may choose to do this in several steps, moving the letters closer together to demonstrate how to blend.)

Then cover the word and spell it orally. Uncover the word and have students compare your spelling with the Touch-units. Cover the word again and write it on the whiteboard. Uncover the word and have students compare the written word with the Touch-units.

Build Words Distribute Touch-units for the word *lie.* Say *lie.* Have students build it on their whiteboard using the Touch-units. Give help as necessary. After making the word, have students touch and sound each Touch-unit, then blend the sounds as they run their finger underneath the Touch-units. Have students cover the word and spell it orally, then compare their spelling to the Touch-units. Next have them cover the word again and write it on their whiteboard and then on the Build Words page of their Workbook (p. 95). Have students compare their writing to the Touch-units. Then use this procedure to have students build the following words:

	yellow	red	white
toe	t	o	e
hoe	h		
hue		u	
due	d		
dye		y	
die		i	

Use one of the activities on page xvi to further practice sequencing and discriminating the words that students find challenging.

Read Words in Isolation Have students pair up and read all of the words they have written on Workbook page 95 aloud to their partner.

Independent Practice (Workbook page 94) Ask students to write the word that completes each sentence. When students complete the page, have them check their work with you or a partner.

Dictation Dictate the following sentence, and have students write it on their whiteboard or at the bottom of Workbook page 94: *Sue gave a blue tie to Joe.*

Reading Words in Context

Tell students that they will use what they know about vowels followed by silent *e* at the end of words to read a story.

Build Words from the Story Use the Touch-units to build the following words on the whiteboard. Tell students that the words you will make together will help them read the story.

Start with the word *lie.*

Substitute Touch-units to build the following words: *pie, tie, toe, hoe, foe, blue, clue, clues, glue, true, cue, flue, sue, bye, eye, rye, dye, die, doe, due.*

As a prereading activity, you may want to have students find the words in the text and read them aloud.

Learn Sight Words Tell students that they will learn some new words to help them read the story. Display these sight words: *gone, laugh.* Read the words as you point to them.

As a prereading activity, you may want to have students find the words in the text as they write them.

Read the Story Give students a copy of *True Blue Friends.* Have them read it independently or with a partner. If necessary, you can support students as they read the story by identifying sight words or helping them to blend sounds to read words.

Respond to the Story After students read *True Blue Friends,* have them complete Workbook page 96. Have students share their work with the rest of the group.

Lesson 33: Vowel + *ce* and *ge*

Remind students that they have learned the sounds for vowels when a word ends in silent *e*. Tell them that today they will learn the sounds for consonants *c* and *g* when they are followed by silent *e*.

Phonemic Awareness Say the word *place*. Emphasize the consonant sound at the end.

Then say the following words, and have students listen for the consonant sound at the end of each one: *dance, prince, gage, huge*.

Link Sound to Letters Distribute the *c* and silent *e* Touch-units. Have students trace the shapes with their finger as they make the soft *c* sound together.

Form the following word on a whiteboard: *grace*. Say the word, emphasizing the consonant sound at the end. Then underline the *c* and *e* in the word.

Tell students that the *c* makes the soft *c* sound when it is followed by a silent *e*. Isolate the soft *c* sound for students, and then have them repeat it after you.

Now distribute the *g* and silent *e* Touch-units. Repeat the procedure above to form the word *gage*. Tell students that the *g* makes the soft *g* sound when it is followed by silent *e*.

Build Words (Model) Tell students that they can use what they know about letter sounds to build words.

Say *brace*. Tell students you are going to build *brace*. Use Touch-units or Magtiles to model.

Pick up the letters *br*, and say their sounds as you place them on the whiteboard. Repeat the procedure with the letter *a*, and place it about an inch to the right of the letters *br*. Repeat the procedure with the letter *c* and place it about an inch to the right of the letter *a*. Repeat the procedure again with the letter *e*. Touch *br*, and say their sounds. Touch *a*, and say its sound. Touch *c*, and say its sound. Then touch *e*, and remind students it is silent.

Move the letters closer together and say their sounds, blending them slightly. Move the letters next to each other and blend the sounds to say *brace*. (You may choose to do this in several steps, moving the letters closer together to demonstrate how to blend.)

Then cover the word and spell it orally. Uncover the word and have students compare your spelling with the Touch-units. Cover the word again and write it on the whiteboard. Uncover the word and have students compare the written word with the Touch-units.

Repeat this procedure with the word *page*.

Build Words Distribute Touch-units for the word *nice*. Say *nice*. Have students build it on their whiteboard using the Touch-units. Give help as necessary. After making the word, have students touch and sound each Touch-unit, then blend the sounds as they run their finger underneath the Touch-units. Have students cover the word and spell it orally, then compare their spelling to the Touch-units. Next have them cover the word again and write it on their whiteboard and then on the Build Words page of their Workbook (p. 98). Have students compare their writing to the Touch-units. Then use this procedure to have students build the following words:

	yellow	red	blue	white
pace	p, c	a		e
race	r			
rice		i		
rage	g	a		
page	p			
stage			st	
huge	h	u		

Use one of the activities on page xvi to further practice sequencing and discriminating the words that students find challenging.

Read Words in Isolation Have students pair up and read all of the words they have written on Workbook page 98 aloud to their partner.

Independent Practice (Workbook page 97) Ask students to write the word that completes each sentence. When students complete the page, have them check their work with you or a partner.

Dictation Dictate the following sentence, and have students write it on their whiteboard or at the bottom of Workbook page 97: *Ed put the mice in a huge cage.*

Reading Words in Context

Tell students that they will use what they know about consonants *c* and *g* when they are followed by silent *e* to read a story.

Build Words from the Story Use the Touch-units to build the following words on the whiteboard. Tell students that the words you will make together will help them read the story.

Start with the word *ace.*

Substitute Touch-units to build the following words: *face, lace, brace, place, trace, fence, ice, dice, mice, nice, price, slice, twice, spice, space, age, wage, cage, stage, huge, hinge, rice, race, rage, page, pace.*

As a prereading activity, you may want to have students find the words in the text and read them aloud.

Learn Sight Words Tell students that they will learn a new word to help them read the story. Display this sight word: *their.* Read the word as you point to it.

As a prereading activity, you may want to have students find the word in the text as they write it.

Read the Story Give students a copy of *Space Age Mice.* Have them read it independently or with a partner. If necessary, you can support students as they read the story by identifying sight words or helping them to blend sounds to read words.

Respond to the Story After students read *Space Age Mice,* have them complete Workbook page 99. Have students share their work with the rest of the group.

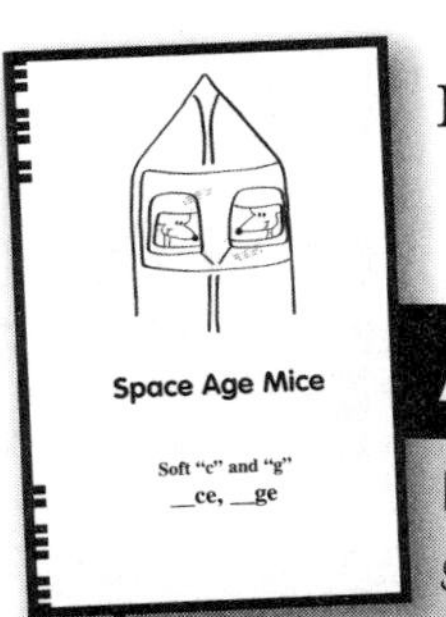

READ THE STORY
Space Age Mice

ADDITIONAL READING

For extra reinforcement of *Lesson 33: Vowel + ce and ge* you will find additional word activities on pages 167–169.

At this printing, additional EPS readers are not available for this lesson. Please visit *www.epsbooks.com* periodically for updates.

Word Lists

Open Syllable Words with *e, i, o, and y* CV	
e, i, o	**y**
be	by
he	my
me	
we	cry
	dry
hi	try
	wry
go	spry
no	fry
so	
	ply
	fly
	shy
	why
	guy

Final *e* Words—VCe, CVCe, CVe

a			o		u	i		e
ace	bale	ate	lobe	cope	cube	jibe	dine	eve
babe	dale	date	robe	dope	lube		fine	
face	gale	fate		hope	rube	ice	line	gene
lace	hale	gate	bode	lope	tube	dice	mine	
mace	male	hate	code	mope		lice	nine	mete
pace		Kate	lode	nope	dude	mice	pine	Pete
race	came	late	mode	pope	nude	nice	tine	
	dame	mate	node	rope	rude	rice	vine	
bade	fame	rate	rode			vice	wine	
fade	game			dose	huge			
jade	lame	cave	coke	hose		bide	pipe	
made	name	Dave	joke	nose	duke	hide	ripe	
wade	same	gave	poke	pose		ride	wipe	
	tame	pave	woke	rose	mule	side		
safe		rave	yoke		rule	tide	fire	
	bane	save		dote	Yule	wide	hire	
age	cane	wave	dole	note			tire	
cage	Jane		hole	rote	fume	fife	wire	
gage	lane	daze	mole	tote		life		
page	mane	faze	pole	vote	dune	rife	rise	
rage	pane	gaze	role		June	wife	vise	
sage	sane	haze	sole	cove	tune		wise	
wage	vane	maze		wove		bike		
	wane	raze	dome		lure	dike	bite	
bake			home	doze	pure	hike	cite	
cake	ape		Nome			like	kite	
fake	cape		Rome		use	Mike	mite	
Jake	gape		tome		fuse	pike	site	
lake	nape				muse			
make	tape		bone		ruse	bile	dive	
rake			cone			file	five	
sake	base		hone		cute	mile	hive	
take	case		lone		jute	Nile	live	
wake	vase		tone		lute	pile		
			zone		mute	tile	size	
						dime		
						lime		
						mime		
						time		

Final *e* Words—VCe, CVCe, CVe (continued)

a		o	u	i		e
place	skate	globe	truce	bribe	snipe	theme
space	plate	probe		tribe	gripe	
brace	slate		crude		tripe	scene
grace	crate	choke	prude	slice	swipe	
trace	grate	spoke		spice		these
shade	state	broke	fluke	price	spire	
blade		stoke		twice		Steve
glade	shave		flume		white	
spade	slave	whole	plume	chide	spite	
grade	knave	stole	spume	glide	write	
trade	brave			slide	quite	
	crave	gnome	prune	snide		
stage	grave			bride	chive	
	stave	phone	flute	pride	drive	
shake		shone	brute	guide		
flake	blaze	clone			prize	
snake	glaze	drone		knife		
brake	craze	prone				
drake	graze	stone		spike		
stake						
quake	strange	scope		shile		
		slope				
scale		grope		chime		
shale				clime		
whale		chore		slime		
stale		spore		crime		
				grime		
shame		chose		prime		
blame		those				
flame		close		shine		
frame		prose		whine		
				spine		
plane		wrote		brine		
crane		quote		swine		
shape				twine		
drape		clove				
grape		drove				
		grove				
chase		trove				
phase		stove				

Final *e* Words:	
Changing _ke to _ck	
_ke	**_ck**
bake	back
chode	chock
coke	cock
duke	duck
flake	flack
hike	hick
joke	jock
lake	lack
like	lick
make	Mack
pike	pick
poke	pock
quake	quack
rake	rack
sake	sack
shake	shack
snake	snack
stake	stack
stoke	stock
take	tack

Final *e* Words: Changing CVC & CCVC to CVCe							
a		o		u		i	
bad	bade	lob	lobe	cub	cube	jib	jibe
fad	fade	rob	robe	rub	rube	bid	bide
mad	made	cod	code	tub	tube	hid	hide
wad	wade	mod	mode	dud	dude	rid	ride
gag	gage	nod	node	hug	huge	dim	dime
rag	rage	rod	rode	dun	dune	Tim	time
sag	sage	wok	woke	cut	cute	din	dine
wag	wage	con	cone	jut	jute	fin	fine
gal	gale	ton	tone			pin	pine
pal	pale	cop	cope			tin	tine
cam	game	hop	hope			win	wine
dam	dame	lop	lope			pip	pipe
Sam	same	mop	mope			rip	ripe
tam	tame	pop	pope			bit	bite
ban	bane	dot	dote			kit	kite
can	cane	not	note			sit	site
Jan	Jane	rot	rote				
man	mane	tot	tote				
pan	pane						
van	vane						
cap	cape						
gap	gape						
nap	nape						
tap	tape						
fat	fate						
hat	gate						
mat	mate						
rat	rate						

Final *e* Words:			
Changing			
CVC & CCVC to CVCe			
(continued)			
a, o, u		**i**	
shad	shade	slid	slide
glad	glade	slim	slime
grad	grade	grim	grime
stag	stage	prim	prime
flak	flake	shin	shine
sham	shame	thin	thine
flam	flame	spin	spine
plan	plane	twin	twine
slat	slate	snip	snipe
		grip	gripe
glob	globe	trip	tripe
slop	slope	whit	white
		spit	spite
crud	crude	writ	write
plum	plume	quit	quite

Lesson 34: "R" Controlled Vowels: *or*

Remind students that they have learned the sounds that short and long vowels make. Tell them that vowels also make other sounds.

Explain that vowels make a special sound when they are followed by the letter *r*.

Tell students that today they will learn the sound that *o* makes when it is followed by *r*.

Phonemic Awareness Say the word *corn*. Emphasize the sound that *or* makes.

Then say the following words, and have students listen for the *or* sound in each one: *storm, horse, porch, door*.

Link Sound to Letters Distribute the *or* Touch-unit. Have students trace its shape with their finger as they make the *or* sound together.

Form the following word on a whiteboard: *fort*. Say the word, emphasizing the *or* sound. Then underline the *or* in the word.

Tell students that the *or* makes the sound they hear in the middle of *fort*. Isolate the sound for students, and then have them repeat it after you.

Form these words on the whiteboard: *porch, store, torn, form*. Say each word for students, and have them take turns underlining the *or*, saying the *or* sound, and then saying the word.

Build Words (Model) Tell students that they can use what they know about the *or* sound to build words.

Say *horn*. Tell students you are going to build *horn*. Use Touch-units or Magtiles to model.

Pick up the letter *h*, and say its sound as you place it on the whiteboard. Repeat the procedure with the letters *or*, and place them about an inch to the right of the letter *h*. Repeat the procedure again with the letter *n*. Touch *h*, and say its sound. Touch *or*, and say their sound. Touch *n*, and say its sound.

Move the letters closer together, and say their sounds, blending them slightly. Move the letters next to each other and blend the sounds to say *horn*. (You may choose to do this in several steps, moving the letters closer together to demonstrate how to blend.)

Then cover the word and spell it orally. Uncover the word and have students compare your spelling with the Touch-units. Cover the word again and write it on the whiteboard. Uncover the word and have students compare the written word with the Touch-units.

Build Words Distribute Touch-units for the word *worn*. Say *worn*. Have students build it on their whiteboard using the Touch-units. Give help as necessary. After making the word, have students touch and sound each Touch-unit, then blend the sounds as they run their finger underneath the Touch-units. Have students cover the word and spell it orally, then compare their spelling to the Touch-units. Next have them cover the word again and write it on their whiteboard and then on the Build Words page of their Workbook (p. 101). Have students compare their writing to the Touch-units. Then use this procedure to have students build the following words:

	yellow	red/yellow	blue
corn	c, n	or	
cork	k		
fork	f		
fort	t		
sport			sp
sort	s		

Use one of the activities on page xvi to further practice sequencing and discriminating the words that students find challenging.

Read Words in Isolation Have students pair up and read all of the words they have written on Workbook page 101 aloud to their partner.

Independent Practice (Workbook page 100) For the first set of items, ask students to connect all the picture names that have the *or* sound to find their way through the maze.

For the second set, ask them to circle the word that names the picture at the beginning of each row. When students complete the page, have them check their work with you or a partner.

Dictation Dictate the following sentence, and have students write it on their whiteboard or at the bottom of Workbook page 100: *I got corn for Mom at the store.*

Reading Words in Context

Tell students that they will use what they know about words with *or* to read a story.

Build Words from the Story Use the Touch-units to build the following words on the whiteboard. Tell students that the words you will make together will help them read the story.

Start with the word *for.*

Substitute Touch-units to build the following words: *fort, forth, north, short, sort, torn, worn, corn, born, store, storm, porch, word, horse.*

As a prereading activity, you may want to have students find the words in the text and read them aloud.

Read the Story Give students a copy of *The Storm from the North.* Have them read it independently or with a partner. If necessary, you can support students as they read the story by identifying sight words or helping them to blend sounds to read words.

Respond to the Story After students read *The Storm from the North,* have them complete Workbook page 102. Have students share their work with the rest of the group.

Lesson 35: "R" Controlled Vowels: *ar*

Remind students that they have learned the sound for *o* when it is followed by the letter *r*.

Tell students that today they will learn the sound that *a* makes when it is followed by *r*.

Phonemic Awareness Say the word *tar*. Emphasize the sound that *ar* makes.

Then say the following words, and have students listen for the *ar* sound in each one: *large, star, farm, spark, charm.*

Link Sound to Letters Distribute the *ar* Touch-unit. Have students trace its shape with their finger as they make the *ar* sound together.

Form the following word on a whiteboard: *bar*. Say the word, emphasizing the *ar* sound. Then underline the *ar* in the word.

Tell students that the *ar* makes the sound they hear at the end of *bar*. Isolate the sound for students, and have them repeat it after you.

Form these words on the whiteboard: *hard, dark, chart, carp, harm.* Say each word for students, and have them take turns underlining the *ar*, saying the *ar* sound and then saying the word.

Build Words (Model) Tell students that they can use what they know about the *ar* sound to build words.

Say *far*. Tell students you are going to build *far*. Use Touch-units or Magtiles to model.

Pick up the letter *f*, and say its sound as you place it in on the whiteboard. Repeat the procedure with the letters *ar*, and place them about an inch to the right of the letter *f*. Touch *f*, and say its sound. Touch *ar*, and say their sound.

Move the letters closer together, and say their sounds, blending them slightly. Move the letters next to each other and blend the sounds to say *far*. (You may choose to do this in several steps, moving the letters closer together to demonstrate how to blend.)

Then cover the word and spell it orally. Uncover the word and have students compare your spelling with the Touch-units. Cover the word again and write it on the whiteboard. Uncover the word and have students compare the written word with the Touch-units.

Build Words Distribute Touch-units for the word *hard*. Say *hard*. Have students build it on their whiteboard using the Touch-units. Give help as necessary. After making the word, have students touch and sound each Touch-unit, then blend the sounds as they run their finger underneath the Touch-units. Have students cover the word and spell it orally, then compare their spelling to the Touch-units. Next have them cover the word again and write it on their whiteboard and then on the Build Words page of their Workbook (p. 104). Have students compare their writing to the Touch-units. Then use this procedure to have students build the following words:

	yellow	red/yellow	blue
cart	c, t	ar	
part	p		
park	k		
start			st
star	t		
car	c		
carp	p		

Use one of the activities on page xvi to further practice sequencing and discriminating the words that students find challenging.

Read Words in Isolation Have students pair up and read all of the words they have written on Workbook page 104 aloud to their partner.

Independent Practice (Workbook page 103) For the first set of items, ask students to write the letters that complete each picture name. For the second set, ask them to write the word that completes each sentence. When students complete the page, have them check their work with you or a partner.

Dictation Dictate the following sentence, and have students write it on their whiteboard or at the bottom of Workbook page 103: *Art drove far in the car.*

Reading Words in Context

Tell students that they will use what they know about words with *ar* to read a story.

Build Words from the Story Use the Touch-units to build the following words on the whiteboard. Tell students that the words you will make together will help them read the story.

Start with the word *ark.*

ark
spark
dark
bark
hark
lark
mark
park
shark
clark

arp
carp
harp
tarp
sharp

ard
card
hard
lard
yard

Substitute Touch-units to build the following words: *dark, lark, mark, park, car, far, bar, star, arm, harm, cart, chart, smart, hard, card, large, scarf, warm.*

As a prereading activity, you may want to have students find the words in the text and read them aloud.

Read the Story Give students a copy of *A Ride to the Park.* Have them read it independently or with a partner. If necessary, you can support students as they read the story by identifying sight words or helping them to blend sounds to read words.

Respond to the Story After students read *A Ride to the Park,* have them complete Workbook page 105. Have students share their work with the rest of the group.

Lesson 36: "R" Controlled Vowels: *er, ir, ur*

Remind students that they have learned the sounds for *or* and *ar*.

Tell students that today they will learn the sound for *er, ir,* and *ur*.

Phonemic Awareness Say the word *girl*. Emphasize the sound that *ir* makes.

Then say the following words, and have students listen for the *ir* sound in each one: *fir, thirst, dirt*.

Tell students to listen for the sound in these words. Slowly say *her, purr, pert, curd, turn*. Emphasize the *er* or *ur* sound in each one.

Link Sound to Letters Distribute the *ur* Touch-unit. Have students trace its shape with their finger as they make the *ur* sound together.

Form the following word on a whiteboard: *hurt*. Say the word, emphasizing the *ur* sound. Then underline the *ur* in the word.

Tell students that the *ur* makes the sound they hear in the middle of *hurt*. Isolate the sound for students, and then have them repeat it after you.

Now distribute the *er* and *ir* Touch-units. Repeat the procedure above to form the words *fern* and *firm*. Point out that the *er, ir,* and *ur* letter combinations all make the same sound.

Build Words (Model) Tell students that they can use what they know about the *er, ir,* and *ur* sound to build words.

Say *curl*. Tell students you are going to build *curl*. Use Touch-units or Magtiles to model.

Pick up the letter *c*, and say its sound as you place it on the whiteboard. Repeat the procedure with the letters *ur*, and place them about an inch to the right of the letter *c*. Repeat the procedure with the letter *l*. Touch *c*, and say its sound. Touch *ur*, and say their sound. Touch *l*, and say its sound.

Move the letters closer together, and say their sounds, blending them slightly. Move the letters next to each other and blend the sounds to say *curl*. (You may choose to do this in several steps, moving the letters closer together to demonstrate how to blend.)

Then cover the word and spell it orally. Uncover the word and have students compare your spelling with the Touch-units. Cover the word again and write it on the whiteboard. Uncover the word and have students compare the written word with the Touch-units.

Repeat this procedure with *shirt* and *her*.

Build Words Distribute Touch-units for the word *dirt*. Say *dirt*. Have students build it on their whiteboard using the Touch-units. Give help as necessary. After making the word, have students touch and sound each Touch-unit, then blend the sounds as they run their finger underneath the Touch-units. Have students cover the word and spell it orally, then compare their spelling to the Touch-units. Next have them cover the word again and write it on their whiteboard and then on the Build Words page of their Workbook (p. 107). Have students compare their writing to the Touch-units. Then use this procedure to have students build the following words:

	yellow	white/yellow	blue
her	h	er	
herd	d		
bird	b	ir	
burp	p	ur	
Bern	n	er	
stern			st
stir		ir	
spur		ur	sp

Use one of the activities on page xvi to further practice sequencing and discriminating the words that students find challenging.

Independent Practice Have students pair up and read all of the words they have written on Workbook page 107 aloud to their partner.

Independent Practice (Workbook page 106) Ask students to write the word that completes each sentence. When students complete the page, have them check their work with you or a partner.

Dictation Dictate the following sentence, and have students write it on their whiteboard or at the bottom of Workbook page 106: *I gave her the hurt bird.*

Reading Words in Context

Tell students that they will use what they know about words with *er, ir,* and *ur* to read a story.

Build Words from the Story Use the Touch-units to build the following words on the whiteboard. Tell students that the words you will make together will help them read the story.

Start with the word *bird.*

Substitute Touch-units to build the following words: *birth, chirp, dirt, first, girl, shirt, skirt, third, thirst, curl, hurt, nurse, urge, fern, germ, her.*

As a prereading activity, you may want to have students find the words in the text and read them aloud.

Read the Story Give students a copy of *Fern and the Baby Bird.* Have them read it independently or with a partner. If necessary, you can support students as they read the story by identifying sight words or helping them to blend sounds to read words.

Respond to the Story After students read *Fern and the Baby Bird,* have them complete Workbook page 108. Have students share their work with the rest of the group.

Lesson 37: "R" Controlled Vowels: *wor, ear*

Remind students that they have learned the sounds for some vowels that are followed by the letter *r*.

Tell students that today they will learn the sounds for *wor* and *ear*.

Phonemic Awareness Say the word *work*. Emphasize the sound that *wor* makes. Then say the following words, and have students listen for the *wor* sound in each one: *worth, world, worm.*

Now say the word *bear*, emphasizing the sound that *ear* makes. Then say the following words, and have students listen for the *ear* sound in each one: *fear, learn, earn.*

Link Sound to Letters Distribute the *ear* Touch-unit. Have students trace its shape with their finger as they make the *ear* sound together.

Form the following word on a whiteboard: *wear*. Say the word, emphasizing the *ear* sound. Then underline the *ear* in the word.

Tell students that the *ear* makes the sound they hear at the end of *wear*. Isolate the sound for students, and then have them repeat it after you.

Now distribute the *w* and *or* Touch-units. Repeat the procedure above to form *work*.

Form these words on the whiteboard: *near, earn, worth, world.* Say each word for students, and have them take turns underlining the *wor* or *ear*, saying the sound, and saying the word.

Build Words (Model) Tell students that they can use what they know about the *wor* and *ear* sounds to build words.

Say *fear*. Tell students you are going to build *fear*. Use Touch-units or Magtiles to model.

Pick up the letter *f*, and say its sound as you place it on the whiteboard. Repeat the procedure with the letters *ear*, and place them about an inch to the right of the letter *f*. Touch *f*, and say its sound. Touch *ear*, and say its sound.

Move the letters closer together, and say their sounds, blending them slightly. Move the letters next to each other and blend the sounds to say *fear*. (You may choose to do this in several steps, moving the letters closer together to demonstrate how to blend.)

Then cover the word and spell it orally. Uncover the word and have students compare your spelling with the Touch-units. Cover the word again and write it on the whiteboard. Uncover the word and have students compare the written word with the Touch-units.

Repeat this procedure with the word *worm*.

Build Words Distribute Touch-units for the word *tear*. Say *tear*. Have students build it on their whiteboard using the Touch-units. Give help as necessary. After making the word, have students touch and sound each Touch-unit, then blend the sounds as they run their finger underneath the Touch-units. Have students cover the word and spell it orally, then compare their spelling to the Touch-units. Next have them cover the word again and write it on their whiteboard and then on the Build Words page of their Workbook (p. 110). Have students compare their writing to the Touch-units. Then use this procedure to have students build the following words:

	yellow	red/yellow	blue
year	y	ear	
clear			cl
hear	h		
heard	d		
word	w	or	
work	k		

Use one of the activities on page xvi to further practice sequencing and discriminating the words that students find challenging.

Read Words in Isolation Have students pair up and read all of the words they have written on Workbook page 110 aloud to their partner.

Independent Practice (Workbook page 109) For the first set of items, ask students to circle the letters that stand for the vowel sound they hear in each picture name. For the second set, ask them to write the word that completes each sentence. When students complete the page, have them check their work with you or a partner.

Dictation Dictate the following sentence, and have students write it on their whiteboard or at the bottom of Workbook page 109: *Ward and I wear work shirts all year.*

Reading Words in Context

Tell students that they will use what they know about words with *wor* and *ear* to read a selection.

Build Words from the Selection Use the Touch-units to build the following words on the whiteboard. Tell students that the words you will make together will help them read the selection.

Start with the word *ear.*

Substitute Touch-units to build the following words: *fear, clear, hear, year, near, sear, earn, earth, heard, learn, bear, wear, word, work, world, worm, worth.*

As a prereading activity, you may want to have students find the words in the text and read them aloud.

Read the Selection Give students a copy of *Earthworms.* Have them read it independently or with a partner. If necessary, you can support students as they read the selection by identifying sight words or helping them to blend sounds to read words.

Respond to the Selection After students read *Earthworms,* have them complete Workbook page 111. Have students share their work with the rest of the group.

Lesson 38: "R" Controlled Vowels: *air, are*

Remind students that they have learned the sounds for some vowels that are followed by the letter *r.*

Tell students that today they will learn the sounds for *air* and *are.*

Phonemic Awareness Say the word *hair.* Emphasize the sound that *air* makes. Then say the following words, and have students listen for the *air* sound in each one: *chair, fair, stair.*

Now say the word *rare.* Emphasize the sound that *are* makes. Then say the following words, and have students listen for the *are* sound in each one: *care, dare, stare.*

Link Sounds to Letters Distribute the *air* Touch-unit. Have students trace its shape with their finger as they make the sound for *air* together.

Form the following word on a whiteboard: *hair.* Say the word, emphasizing the *air* sound. Then underline the *air* in the word.

Tell students that the *air* makes the sound they hear at the end of *hair.* Isolate the sound for students, and then have them repeat it after you.

Now distribute the *ar* and *e* Touch-units. Repeat the procedure above to form the word *hare.* Tell students that *are* makes the same sound as *air.*

Then form these words on the whiteboard: *fair, stair, stare, fair.* Say each word for students, and have them take turns underlining the *air* or *are,* saying the appropriate sound, and then saying the word.

Build Words (Model) Tell students that they can use what they know about the sounds for *air* and *are* to build words.

Say *fair.* Tell students you are going to build *fair.* Use Touch-units or Magtiles to model.

Pick up the letter *f,* and say its sound as you place it on the whiteboard. Repeat the procedure with the letters *air,* and place them about an inch to the right of the letter *f.* Touch *f,* and say its sound. Touch *air,* and say their sound.

Move the letters closer together, and say their sounds, blending them slightly. Move the letters next to each other and blend the sounds to say *fair.* (You may choose to do this in several steps, moving the letters closer together to demonstrate how to blend.)

Then cover the word and spell it orally. Uncover the word and have students compare your spelling with the Touch-units. Cover the word again and write it on the whiteboard. Uncover the word and have students compare the written word with the Touch-units.

Repeat this procedure with the word *share.*

Build Words Distribute Touch-units for the word *spare.* Say *spare.* Have students build it on their whiteboard using the Touch-units. Give help as necessary. After making the word, have students touch and sound each Touch-unit, then blend the sounds as they run their finger underneath the Touch-units. Have students cover the word and spell it orally, then compare their spelling to the Touch-units. Next have them cover the word again and write it on their whiteboard and then on the Build Words page of their Workbook (p. 113). Have students compare their writing to the Touch-units. Then use this procedure to have students build the following words:

	yellow	red/yellow	blue	white
hair	h	air		
hare		ar		e
pare	p			
pair		air		
stair			st	
stare		ar		e

Use one of the activities on page xvi to further practice sequencing and discriminating the words that students find challenging.

Read Words in Isolation Have students pair up and read all of the words they have written on Workbook page 113 aloud to their partner.

Independent Practice (Workbook page 112) Ask students to write the word that completes each sentence. When students complete the page, have them check their work with you or a partner.

Dictation Dictate the following sentence, and have students write it on their whiteboard or at the bottom of Workbook page 112: *You have to care for your hair.*

Reading Words in Context

Tell students that they will use what they know about words with *air* and *are* to read a story.

Build Words from the Story Use the Touch-units to build the following words on the whiteboard. Tell students that the words you will make together will help them read the story.

Start with the word *air.*

Substitute Touch-units to build the following words: *bare, care, chair, dare, fair, fare, hair, mare, pair, share, spare, stair, stare.*

As a prereading activity, you may want to have students find the words in the text and read them aloud.

Read the Story Give students a copy of *Pierre and the Fair Lady.* Have them read it independently or with a partner. If necessary, you can support students as they read the story by identifying sight words or helping them to blend sounds to read words.

Respond to the Story After students read *Pierre and the Fair Lady,* have them complete Workbook page 114. Have students share their work with the rest of the group.

READ THE STORY
Pierre and the Fair Lady

ADDITIONAL READING

This EPS reader provides an additional story in which to practice *"R" Controlled Vowels:* air, are.

SPIRE Decodables

A Scare
Set 2A, Book 9

Word Lists

"R" Controlled Vowel Words: C(V+r)C, VV+r					
or		ar			ir
cord	bored	bar	barb	scarf	bird
lord	core	car			gird
	fore	far	bard	starch	
worm	more	jar	card		birch
	wore	mar	hard	shark	
porch			lard	Clark	birth
torch	horde	par	ward	spark	firth
	borne	tar	yard	stark	girth
forth	snore	war			
north	store		scar	gnarl	girl
	sword	cart	chart	snarl	
cork		dart	spar		firm
fork	scorch	mart	star	charm	fir
pork		part		swarm	sir
	stork	tart	chart		
dorm		wart	smart	sharp	dirt
norm	storm		start		
		bark	quart	larch	first
born	scorn	dark		March	
corn	shorn	hark		parch	chirp
horn	thorn	lark			
morning	sworn	mark		harsh	flirt
torn		park		marsh	
worn	boor				quirk
	poor	farm		warmth	shirk
for		harm			
nor	short	warm			shirt
	snort				skirt
fort	sport	barn			
Mort		darn			smirk
report		warn			
sort		yarn			stir
					whir
York		carp			swirl
		harp			third
forks	horse	tarp			thirst
					twirl
gloria					whirl

Words in story.

"R" Controlled Vowel Words: C(V+r)C, VV+r (continued)										
er	**ur**		**air***	**are***	**ear***	**ear***	**ear***	**eer***	**oar***	**wor***
herb	curb	burnt	air	bare	sear	bear	learn	beer	oar	word
Serb			fair	care	near	pear	heard	deer	board	work
verb	curd	curt	hair	dace	hear	wear	early	jeer	hoard	
		hurt	lair	face	gear	swear	earn	seer		world
herd	surf		pair	mare	fear		earth			worse
	turf	church		pare	dear		earthworm			worth
serf			stair		rear					worry
	lurk	fourth	flair	share	tear					worst
perch	murk		chair	spare	year					worm
	Turk	churn		stare	clear					
berth					spear					
	burl	blur			smear					
jerk	curl	slur			beard					
	furl				weary					
berm	hurl	spur								
germ										
term	burn	blurt								
	turn	spurt								
fern										
tern	burp	curse								
		nurse								
her	burr	purse								
per	purr									
	cur	lurch								
here	fur									
mere		burst								
verse										
serve										
clerk										
sperm										
stern										

* Do not teach the words in these categories until after these vowel combinations have been introduced in later lessons.

Lesson 39: Vowel Combinations: *oa*

Remind students that they have learned the sounds that vowels make. Tell them that some words have two vowels in a row. The vowels in these words work together to make one sound.

Tell students that today they will learn the sound that *oa* makes.

Phonemic Awareness Say the word *coat.* Emphasize the sound that *oa* makes.

Then say the following words, and have students listen for the *oa* sound in each one: *loan, soak, toast, coal, groan.*

Link Sound to Letters Distribute the *oa* Touch-unit. Have students trace its shape with their finger as they make the long *o* sound together.

Form the following word on a whiteboard: *road.* Say the word, emphasizing the long *o* sound. Then underline the *oa* in the word.

Tell students that the *oa* makes the long *o* sound they hear in the middle of *road.* Isolate the sound for students, and then have them repeat it after you.

Form these words on the whiteboard: *goat, toast, moan, float, cloak.* Say each word for students, and have them take turns underlining the *oa,* saying the long *o* sound, and then saying the word.

Build Words (Model) Tell students that they can use what they know about the *oa* sound to build words.

Say *foam.* Tell students you are going to build *foam.* Use Touch-units or Magtiles to model.

Pick up the letter *f,* and say its sound as you place it on the whiteboard. Repeat the procedure with the letters *oa,* and place them about an inch to the right of the letter *f.* Repeat the procedure again with the letter *m.* Touch *f,* and say its sound. Touch *oa,* and say their sound. Touch *m,* and say its sound.

Move the letters closer together, and say their sounds, blending them slightly. Move the letters next to each other and blend the sounds to say *foam.* (You may choose to do this in several steps, moving the letters closer together to demonstrate how to blend.)

Then cover the word and spell it orally. Uncover the word and have students compare your spelling with the Touch-units. Cover the word again and write it on the whiteboard. Uncover the word and have students compare the written word with the Touch-units.

Build Words Distribute Touch-units for the word *oak.* Say *oak.* Have students build it on their whiteboard using the Touch-units. Give help as necessary. After making the word, have students touch and sound each Touch-unit, then blend the sounds as they run their finger underneath the Touch-units. Have students cover the word and spell it orally, then compare their spelling to the Touch-units. Next have them cover the word again and write it on their whiteboard and then on the Build Words page of their Workbook (p. 116). Have students compare their writing to the Touch-units. Then use this procedure to have students build the following words:

	yellow	red	blue
toad	t, d	oa	
road	r		
load	l		
loan	n		
soak	s,k		
cloak			cl

Use one of the activities on page xvi to further practice sequencing and discriminating the words that students find challenging.

Read Words in Isolation Have students pair up and read all of the words they have written on Workbook page 116 aloud to their partner.

Independent Practice (Workbook page 115) For the first set of items, ask students to connect all the picture names that have the *oa* sound to find their way through the maze. For the second set, ask them to circle the word that names the picture at the beginning of each row. When students complete the page, have them check their work with you or a partner.

Dictation Dictate the following sentence, and have students write it on their whiteboard or at the bottom of Workbook page 115: *Joan will coax the goat to go.*

Reading Words in Context

Tell students that they will use what they know about words with *oa* to read a story.

Build Words from the Story Use the Touch-units to build the following words on the whiteboard. Tell students that the words you will make together will help them read the story.

Start with the word *road.*

Substitute Touch-units to build the following words: *load, toad, toast, oak, soak, cloak, croak, goat, float, coax, Joan, loan, groan, moan, foam, coal, soap, whoa.*

As a prereading activity, you may want to have students find the words in the text and read them aloud.

Read the Story Give students a copy of *Toad and the Goat.* Have them read it independently or with a partner. If necessary, you can support students as they read the story by identifying sight words or helping them to blend sounds to read words.

Respond to the Story After students read *Toad and the Goat,* have them complete Workbook page 117. Have students share their work with the rest of the group.

READ THE STORY
Toad and the Goat

ADDITIONAL READING

This EPS reader provides an additional story in which to practice *Vowel Combinations:* oa.

Primary Phonics

The Goat
Set 2, Book 6

Lesson 40: Vowel Combinations: *ie, ui*

Remind students that they have learned the sound that the vowels *oa* make.

Tell students that today they will learn the sounds that *ie* and *ui* make.

Phonemic Awareness Say the word *piece.* Emphasize the sound that *ie* makes. Then say the following words, and have students listen for the *ie* sound in each one: *chief, field, niece.*

Now say the word *juice.* Emphasize the sound that *ui* makes. Then say the following words, and have students listen for the *ui* sound in each one: *suit, fruit.*

Link Sound to Letters Distribute the *ie* Touch-unit. Have students trace its shape with their finger as they make the long *e* sound together.

Form the following word on a whiteboard: *thief.* Say the word, emphasizing the long *e* sound. Then underline the *ie* in the word.

Tell students that the *ie* makes the long *e* sound they hear in the middle of *thief.* Isolate the sound for students, and then have them repeat it after you.

Now distribute the *ui* Touch-unit. Repeat the procedure above to form the word *juice.*

Form these words on the whiteboard: *yield, piece, suit, fruit.* Say each word for students, and have them take turns underlining the *ie* or *ui,* saying the appropriate sound, and then saying the word.

Build Words (Model) Tell students that they can use what they know about the *ie* and *ui* sounds to build words.

Say *field.* Tell students you are going to build *field.* Use Touch-units or Magtiles to model.

Pick up the letter *f,* and say its sound as you place it on the whiteboard. Repeat the procedure with the letters *ie,* and place them about an inch to the right of the letter *f.* Repeat the procedure again with the letter *l.* Repeat it again with *d.* Touch *f,* and say its sound. Touch *ie,* and say their sound. Touch *l,* and say its sound. Touch *d,* and say its sound. Move the letters closer together, and say their sounds, blending them slightly. Move the letters next to each other and blend the sounds to say *field.* (You may choose to do this in several steps, moving the letters closer together to demonstrate how to blend.)

Then cover the word and spell it orally. Uncover the word and have students compare your spelling with the Touch-units. Cover the word again and write it on the whiteboard. Uncover the word and have students compare the written word with the Touch-units.

Repeat this procedure with the word *suit.*

Build Words Distribute Touch-units for the word *yield.* Say *yield.* Have students build it on their whiteboard using the Touch-units. Give help as necessary. After making the word, have students touch and sound each Touch-unit, then blend the sounds as they run their finger underneath the Touch-units. Have students cover the word and spell it orally, then compare their spelling to the Touch-units. Next have them cover the word again and write it on their whiteboard and then on the Build Words page of their Workbook (p. 119). Have students compare their writing to the Touch-units. Then use this procedure to have students build the following words:

	yellow	red	blue	white
grief	f	ie	gr	
brief			br	
chief	ch			
niece	n, c			e
juice	j	ui		
suit	s, t			
fruit			fr	

Use one of the activities on page xvi to further practice sequencing and discriminating the words that students find challenging.

Read Words in Isolation Have students pair up and read all of the words they have written on Workbook page 119 aloud to their partner.

Independent Practice (Workbook page 118) Ask students to write the word that completes each sentence. When students complete the page, have them check their work with you or a partner.

Dictation Dictate the following sentence, and have students write it on their whiteboard or at the bottom of Workbook page 118: *My niece had a piece of fruit.*

Reading Words in Context

Tell students that they will use what they know about words with *ie* and *ui* to read a story.

Build Words from the Story Use the Touch-units to build the following words on the whiteboard. Tell students that the words you will make together will help them read the story.

Start with the word *brief.*

Substitute Touch-units to build the following words: *chief, grief, thief, field, yield, tied, piece, niece, fruit, juice, suit.*

As a prereading activity, you may want to have students find the words in the text and read them aloud.

Read the Story Give students a copy of *The Fruit Thief.* Have them read it independently or with a partner. If necessary, you can support students as they read the story by identifying sight words or helping them to blend sounds to read words.

Respond to the Story After students read *The Fruit Thief,* have them complete Workbook page 120. Have students share their work with the rest of the group.

READ THE STORY
The Fruit Thief

ADDITIONAL READING

For extra reinforcement of *Lesson 40: Vowel combinations ie, ui* you will find additional word activities on pages 167–169.

At this printing, additional EPS readers are not available for this lesson. Please visit *www.epsbooks.com* periodically for updates.

Lesson 41: Vowel Combinations: ee

Remind students that they have learned some of the sounds that two vowels make.

Tell students that today they will learn the sound that *ee* makes.

Phonemic Awareness Say the word *free.* Emphasize the sound that *ee* makes.

Then say the following words, and have students listen for the *ee* sound in each one: *feel, keep, deep, three.*

Link Sound to Letters Distribute the *ee* Touch-unit. Have students trace its shape with their finger as they make the long *e* sound together.

Form the following word on a whiteboard: *see.* Say the word, emphasizing the long *e* sound. Then underline the *ee* in the word.

Tell students that the *ee* makes the long *e* sound they hear at the end of *see.* Isolate the sound for students, and then have them repeat it after you.

Form these words on the whiteboard: *tree, feet, sleep, green.* Say each word for students, and have them take turns underlining the *ee,* saying the *ee* sound, and then saying the word.

Build Words (Model) Tell students that they can use what they know about the *ee* sound to build words.

Say *meet.* Tell students you are going to build *meet.* Use Touch-units or Magtiles to model.

Pick up the letter *m,* and say its sound as you place it on the whiteboard. Repeat the procedure with the letters *ee,* and place them about an inch to the right of the letter *m.* Repeat the procedure again with the letter *t.* Touch *m,* and say its sound. Touch *ee,* and say their sound. Touch *t,* and say its sound.

Move the letters closer together, and say their sounds, blending them slightly. Move the letters next to each other and blend the sounds to say *meet.* (You may choose to do this in several steps, moving the letters closer together to demonstrate how to blend.)

Then cover the word and spell it orally. Uncover the word and have students compare your spelling with the Touch-units. Cover the word again and write it on the whiteboard. Uncover the word and have students compare the written word with the Touch-units.

Build Words Distribute Touch-units for the word *keep.* Say *keep.* Have students build it on their whiteboard using the Touch-units. Give help as necessary. After making the word, have students touch and sound each Touch-unit, then blend the sounds as they run their finger underneath the Touch-units. Have students cover the word and spell it orally, then compare their spelling to the Touch-units. Next have them cover the word again and write it on their whiteboard and then on the Build Words page of their Workbook (p. 122). Have students compare their writing to the Touch-units. Then use this procedure to have students build the following words:

	yellow	red	blue
reed	r, d	ee	
feed	f		
feel	l		
greed			gr
speed			sp
need	n		

Use one of the activities on page xvi to further practice sequencing and discriminating the words that students find challenging.

Read Words in Isolation Have students pair up and read all of the words they have written on Workbook page 122 aloud to their partner.

Independent Practice (Workbook page 121) For the first set of items, ask students to write the letters that complete each picture name. For the second set, ask them to write the word that completes each sentence. When students complete the page, have them check their work with you or a partner.

Dictation Dictate the following sentence, and have students write it on their whiteboard or at the bottom of Workbook page 121: *They need to see the queen.*

Reading Words in Context

Tell students that they will use what they know about words with *ee* to read a selection.

Build Words from the Selection Use the Touch-units to build the following words on the whiteboard. Tell students that the words you will make together will help them read the selection.

Start with the word *see.*

Substitute Touch-units to build the following words: *tree, three, free, keen, green, queen, seek, week, sleek, meek, meet, feet, feel, feed, reed, greed, keep, sleep, deep, speed.*

As a prereading activity, you may want to have students find the words in the text and read them aloud.

Read the Selection Give students a copy of *A Coral Reef.* Have them read it independently or with a partner. If necessary, you can support students as they read the selection by identifying sight words or helping them to blend sounds to read words.

Respond to the Selection After students read *A Coral Reef,* have them complete Workbook page 123. Have students share their work with the rest of the group.

Lesson 42: Vowel Combinations: *ai, ay*

Remind students that they have learned some of the sounds that two vowels make.

Tell students that today they will learn the sounds that *ai* and *ay* make.

Phonemic Awareness Say the word *main.* Emphasize the sound that *ai* makes.Then say the following words, and have students listen for the vowel sound in each one: *stay, rain, tail, day.*

Now say the word *sway.* Emphasize the sound that *ay* makes. Then say the following words, and have students listen for the *ay* sound in each one: *say, play, gray.*

Link Sound to Letters Distribute the *ai* Touch-unit. Have students trace its shape with their finger as they make the long *a* sound together.

Form the following word on a whiteboard: *pail.* Say the word, emphasizing the long *a* sound. Then underline the *ai* in the word.

Tell students that the *ai* makes the long *a* sound they hear in the middle of *pail.* Isolate the sound for students, and then have them repeat it after you.

Now distribute the *ay* Touch-unit. Repeat the procedure above to form the word *way.* Point out that *ay* and *ai* make the same sound.

Form these words on the whiteboard: *main, hay, hail, gray.* Say each word for students, and have them take turns underlining the *ai* or *ay,* saying the sound, and then saying the word.

Build Words (Model) Tell students that they can use what they know about the *ai* and *ay* sounds to build words.

Say *pain.* Tell students you are going to build *pain.* Use Touch-units or Magtiles to model.

Pick up the letter *p,* and say its sound as you place it on the whiteboard. Repeat the procedure with the letters *ai,* and place them about an inch to the right of the letter *p.* Repeat the procedure again with the letter *n.* Touch *p,* and say its sound. Touch *ai,* and say their sound. Touch *n,* and say its sound.

Move the letters closer together, and say their sounds, blending them slightly. Move the letters next to each other and blend the sounds to say *pain.* (You may choose to do this in several steps, moving the letters closer together to demonstrate how to blend.)

Then cover the word and spell it orally. Uncover the word and have students compare your spelling with the Touch-units. Cover the word again and write it on the whiteboard. Uncover the word and have students compare the written word with the Touch-units.

Repeat this procedure with the word *sway.*

Build Words Distribute Touch-units for the word *day.* Say *day.* Have students build it on their whiteboard using the Touch-units. Give help as necessary. After making the word, have students touch and sound each Touch-unit, then blend the sounds as they run their finger underneath the Touch-units. Have students cover the word and spell it orally, then compare their spelling to the Touch-units. Next have them cover the word again and write it on their whiteboard and then on the Build Words page of their Workbook (p. 125). Have students compare their writing to the Touch-units. Then use this procedure to have students build the following words:

	yellow	red	blue
may	m	ay	
ray	r		
rain	n	ai	
chain	ch		
stain			st
stay		ay	

Use one of the activities on page xvi to further practice sequencing and discriminating the words that students find challenging.

Read Words in Isolation Have students pair up and read all of the words they have written on Workbook page 125 aloud to their partner.

Independent Practice (Workbook page 124) For the first set of items, ask students to circle the letters that stand for the vowel sound they hear in each picture name. For the second set, ask them to circle the word that names the picture at the beginning of each row. When students complete the page, have them check their work with you or a partner.

Dictation Dictate the following sentence, and have students write it on their whiteboard or at the bottom of Workbook page 124: *You may not play in the rain.*

Reading Words in Context

Tell students that they will use what they know about words with *ai* and *ay* to read a story.

Build Words from the Story Use the Touch-units to build the following words on the whiteboard. Tell students that the words you will make together will help them read the story.

Start with the word *main.*

Substitute Touch-units to build the following words: *grain, chain, plain, vain, rain, strain, train, trail, wail, quail, hail, fail, frail, pail, snail, tail, day, lay, hay, say, gray, stay, way, sway, play.*

As a prereading activity, you may want to have students find the words in the text and read them aloud.

Read the Story Give students a copy of *A Baby Quail's Day*. Have them read it independently or with a partner. If necessary, you can support students as they read the story by identifying sight words or helping them to blend sounds to read words.

Respond to the Story After students read *A Baby Quail's Day*, have them complete Workbook page 126. Have students share their work with the rest of the group.

Lesson 43: Vowel Combinations: *au, aw*

Remind students that they have learned many of the different sounds that vowels make.

Tell students that today they will learn the sounds that *au* and *aw* make.

Phonemic Awareness Say the word *raw.* Emphasize the sound that *aw* makes.

Then say the following words, and have students listen for the vowel sound in each one: *slaw, caw, pause, launch.*

Link Sound to Letters Distribute the *aw* Touch-unit. Have students trace its shape with their finger as they make the *aw* sound together.

Form the following word on a whiteboard: *paw.* Say the word, emphasizing the *aw* sound. Then underline the *aw* in the word.

Tell students that the *aw* makes the vowel sound they hear at the end of *paw.* Isolate the sound for students, and then have them repeat it after you.

Now distribute the *au* Touch-unit. Repeat the procedure above to form the word *Paul.* Point out that *aw* and *au* make the same sound.

Form these words on the whiteboard: *flaw, slaw, cause, fault.* Say each word for students, and have them take turns underlining the *aw* or *au,* saying the sound, and then saying the word.

Build Words (Model) Tell students that they can use what they know about the *aw* and *au* sounds to build words.

Say *dawn.* Tell students you are going to build *dawn.* Use Touch-units or Magtiles to model.

Pick up the letter *d,* and say its sound as you place it on the whiteboard. Repeat the procedure with the letters *aw,* and place them about an inch to the right of the letter *d.* Repeat the procedure again with the letter *n.* Touch *d,* and say its sound. Touch *aw,* and say their sound. Touch *n,* and say its sound.

Move the letters closer together, and say their sounds, blending them slightly. Move the letters next to each other and blend the sounds to say *dawn.* (You may choose to do this in several steps, moving the letters closer together to demonstrate how to blend.)

Then cover the word and spell it orally. Uncover the word and have students compare your spelling with the Touch-units. Cover the word again and write it on the whiteboard. Uncover the word and have students compare the written word with the Touch-units.

Repeat this procedure with the word *pause.*

Build Words Distribute Touch-units for the word *straw.* Say *straw.* Have students build it on their whiteboard using the Touch-units. Give help as necessary. After making the word, have students touch and sound each Touch-unit, then blend the sounds as they run their finger underneath the Touch-units. Have students cover the word and spell it orally, then compare their spelling to the Touch-units. Next have them cover the word again and write it on their whiteboard and then on the Build Words page of their Workbook (p. 128). Have students compare their writing to the Touch-units. Then use this procedure to have students build the following words:

	yellow	red	blue
law	l	aw	
claw			cl
paw	p		
Paul	l	au	
Saul	s		
saw		aw	
yawn	y, n		

Use one of the activities on page xvi to further practice sequencing and discriminating the words that students find challenging.

Independent Practice Have students pair up and read all of the words they have written on Workbook page 128 aloud to their partner.

Independent Practice (Workbook page 127) Ask students to write the word that completes each sentence. When students complete the page, have them check their work with you or a partner.

Dictation Dictate the following sentence, and have students write it on their whiteboard or at the bottom of Workbook page 127: *Paul saw a hawk at dawn.*

Reading Words in Context

Tell students that they will use what they know about words with *au* and *aw* to read a story.

Build Words from the Story Use the Touch-units to build the following words on the whiteboard. Tell students that the words you will make together will help them read the story.

Start with the word *jaw.*

Substitute Touch-units to build the following words: *flaw, law, raw, slaw, saw, caw, straw, claw, bawl, brawl, brawn, dawn, hawk, Paul, pause, Claude, caught, taught, flaunt, fault.*

As a prereading activity, you may want to have students find the words in the text and read them aloud.

Read the Story Give students a copy of *Claude and Paul.* Have them read it independently or with a partner. If necessary, you can support students as they read the story by identifying sight words or helping them to blend sounds to read words.

Respond to the Story After students read *Claude and Paul,* have them complete Workbook page 129. Have students share their work with the rest of the group.

Lesson 44: Vowel Combinations: *oi, oy*

Remind students that they have learned many of the different sounds that vowels make.

Tell students that today they will learn the sounds that *oi* and *oy* make.

Phonemic Awareness Say the word *join.* Emphasize the sound that *oi* makes.

Then say the following words, and have students listen for the vowel sound in each one: *joy, coy, voice.*

Link Sound to Letters Distribute the *oi* Touch-unit. Have students trace its shape with their finger as they make the *oi* sound together.

Form the following word on a whiteboard: *boil.* Say the word, emphasizing the *oi* sound. Then underline the *oi* in the word.

Tell students that the *oi* makes the vowel sound they hear in the middle of *boil.* Isolate the sound for students, and then have them repeat it after you.

Now distribute the *oy* Touch-unit. Repeat the procedure above to form the word *coy.* Point out that *oy* and *oi* make the same sound.

Form these words on the whiteboard: *coin, boy, spoil, soy.* Say each word for students, and have them take turns underlining the *oi* or *oy*, saying the sound, and then saying the word.

Build Words (Model) Tell students that they can use what they know about the *oi* and *oy* sound to build words.

Say *coil.* Tell students you are going to build *coil.* Use Touch-units or Magtiles to model.

Pick up the letter *c*, and say its sound as you place it on the whiteboard. Repeat the procedure with the letters *oi*, and place them about an inch to the right of the letter *c.* Repeat the procedure again with the letter *l.* Touch *c*, and say its sound. Touch *oi*, and say their sound. Touch *l*, and say its sound.

Move the letters closer together, and say their sounds, blending them slightly. Move the letters next to each other and blend the sounds to say *coil.* (You may choose to do this in several steps, moving the letters closer together to demonstrate how to blend.)

Then cover the word and spell it orally. Uncover the word and have students compare your spelling with the Touch-units. Cover the word again and write it on the whiteboard. Uncover the word and have students compare the written word with the Touch-units.

Repeat this procedure with the word *Roy.*

Build Words Distribute Touch-units for the word *void.* Say *void.* Have students build it on their whiteboard using the Touch-units. Give help as necessary. After making the word, have students touch and sound each Touch-unit, then blend the sounds as they run their finger underneath the Touch-units. Have students cover the word and spell it orally, then compare their spelling to the Touch-units. Next have them cover the word again and write it on their whiteboard and then on the Build Words page of their Workbook (p. 131). Have students compare their writing to the Touch-units. Then use this procedure to have students build the following words:

	yellow	red	blue
toy	t	oy	
boy	b		
boil		oi	
broil			br
spoil			sp
coin	c, n		
join	j		
joy		oy	

Use one of the activities on page xvi to further practice sequencing and discriminating the words that students find challenging.

Read Words in Isolation Have students pair up and read all of the words they have written on Workbook page 131 aloud to their partner.

Independent Practice (Workbook page 130) For the first set of items, ask students to circle the letters that stand for the vowel sound they hear in each picture name. For the second set, ask them to write the word that completes each sentence. When students complete the page, have them check their work with you or a partner.

Dictation Dictate the following sentence, and have students write it on their whiteboard or at the bottom of Workbook page 130: *The boy used coins to get a toy.*

Reading Words in Context

Tell students that they will use what they know about words with *oi* and *oy* to read a story.

Build Words from the Story Use the Touch-units to build the following words on the whiteboard. Tell students that the words you will make together will help them read the story.

Start with the word *boy.*

Substitute Touch-units to build the following words: *Roy, joy, coin, join, loin, Lloyd, boil, soil, toil, coil, broil, spoil, joint, point, void, moist.*

As a prereading activity, you may want to have students find the words in the text and read them aloud.

Read the Story Give students a copy of *Mr. Lloyd's Royal Meat Shop.* Have them read it independently or with a partner. If necessary, you can support students as they read the story by identifying sight words or helping them to blend sounds to read words.

Respond to the Story After students read *Mr. Lloyd's Royal Meat Shop*, have them complete Workbook page 132. Have students share their work with the rest of the group.

Lesson 45: Vowel Combinations: *ow*

Remind students that they have learned some of the sounds that two letters make when they are next to each other in a word. Tell them that sometimes the same combination of letters can make different sounds.

Tell students that today they will learn the different sounds that *ow* makes.

Phonemic Awareness Say the word *cow*, Emphasize the sound that *ow* makes. Then say the following words, and have students listen for the *ow* sound in each one: *brown, how, howl, bow.*

Now say the word *mow.* Emphasize the sound that *ow* makes. Then say the following words, and have students listen for the other sound that *ow* makes: *grow, row, bowl, blow.*

Link Sound to Letters Distribute the *ow* Touch-unit. Have students trace its shape with their finger as they make the sound for *ow* as in *now* together.

Form the following word on a whiteboard: *now.* Say the word, emphasizing the *ow* sound. Then underline the *ow* in the word.

Tell students that the *ow* makes the sound they hear at the end of *now.* Isolate the sound for students, and then have them repeat it after you.

Repeat the procedure above to form the word *low.* Tell students that the *ow* in *low* makes a different sound than it does in *now.*

Form these words on the whiteboard: *gown, flow, how, blow.* Say each word for students, and have them take turns underlining the *ow*, saying the appropriate sound for *ow*, and then saying the word.

Build Words (Model) Tell students that they can use what they know about the *ow* sounds to build words.

Say *gown.* Tell students you are going to build *gown.* Use Touch-units or Magtiles to model.

Pick up the letter *g*, and say its sound as you place it on the whiteboard. Repeat the procedure with the letters *ow*, and place them about an inch to the right of the letter *g*. Repeat the procedure again with the letter *n*. Touch *g*, and say its sound. Touch *ow*, and say their sound. Touch *n*, and say its sound.

Move the letters closer together, and say their sounds, blending them slightly. Move the letters next to each other and blend the sounds to say *gown.* (You may choose to do this in several steps, moving the letters closer together to demonstrate how to blend.)

Then cover the word and spell it orally. Uncover the word and have students compare your spelling with the Touch-units. Cover the word again and write it on the whiteboard. Uncover the word and have students compare the written word with the Touch-units.

Repeat this procedure with the word *crow.*

Build Words Distribute Touch-units for the word *low.* Say *low.* Have students build it on their whiteboard using the Touch-units. Give help as necessary. After making the word, have students touch and sound each Touch-unit, then blend the sounds as they run their finger underneath the Touch-units. Have students cover the word and spell it orally, then compare their spelling to the Touch-units. Next have them cover the word again and write it on their whiteboard and then on the Build Words page of their Workbook (p. 134). Have students compare their writing to the Touch-units. Then use this procedure to have students build the following words:

	yellow	red	blue
row	r	ow	
tow	t		
town	n		
down	d		
brown			br
grow			gr
grown	n		

Use one of the activities on page xvi to further practice sequencing and discriminating the words that students find challenging.

Read Words in Isolation Have students pair up and read all of the words they have written on Workbook page 134 aloud to their partner.

Independent Practice (Workbook page 133) Ask students to write the word that completes each sentence. When students complete the page, have them check their work with you or a partner.

Dictation Dictate the following sentence, and have students write it on their whiteboard or at the bottom of Workbook page 133: *The brown cow lay down in the low grass.*

Reading Words in Context

Tell students that they will use what they know about words with *ow* to read a story.

Build Words from the Story Use the Touch-units to build the following words on the whiteboard. Tell students that the words you will make together will help them read the story.

Start with the word *cow.*

Substitute Touch-units to build the following words: *sow, now, how, wow, bow, chow, plow, down, town, brown, frown, crowd, howl, mow, row, sow, low, blow, grow, flow, know, known, grown, bowl.*

As a prereading activity, you may want to have students find the words in the text and read them aloud.

Read the Story Give students a copy of *The Cow and the Sow.* Have them read it independently or with a partner. If necessary, you can support students as they read the story by identifying sight words or helping them to blend sounds to read words.

Respond to the Story After students read *The Cow and the Sow,* have them complete Workbook page 135. Have students share their work with the rest of the group.

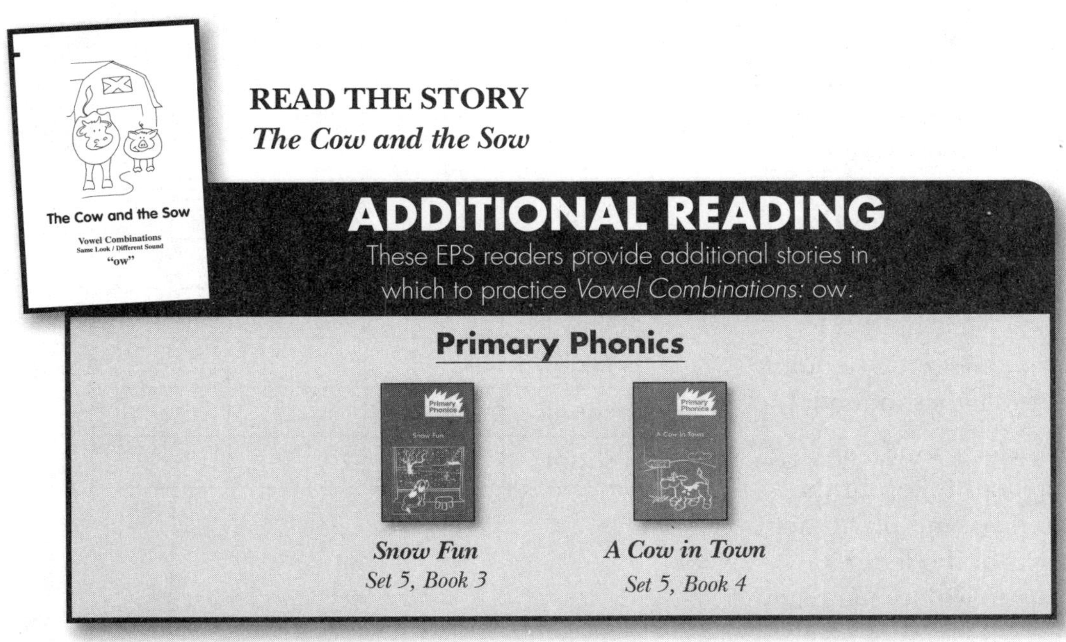

Lesson 46: Vowel Combinations: oo

Remind students that they have learned that the same combination of letters can sometimes make different sounds.

Tell students that today they will learn the different sounds that *oo* makes.

Phonemic Awareness Say the word *moon.* Emphasize the sound that *oo* makes. Then say the following words, and have students listen for the *oo* sound in each one: *noon, cool, broom.*

Now say the word *look.* Emphasize the sound that *oo* makes. Then say the following words, and have students listen for the other sound that *oo* makes: *shook, stood, wool.*

Link Sound to Letters Distribute the *oo* Touch-unit. Have students trace its shape with their finger as they make the sound for *oo* as in *pool* together.

Form the following word on a whiteboard: *pool.* Say the word, emphasizing the *oo* sound. Then underline the *oo* in the word.

Tell students that the *oo* makes the sound they hear in the middle of *pool.* Isolate the sound for students, and then have them repeat it after you.

Repeat the procedure above to form the word *cook.* Point out that the *oo* in *cook* makes a different sound than it does in *pool.*

Form these words on the whiteboard: *room, too, wood, hook.* Say each word for students, and have them take turns underlining the *oo*, saying the appropriate sound, and then saying the word.

Build Words (Model) Tell students that they can use what they know about the *oo* sounds to build words.

Say *soon.* Tell students you are going to build *soon.* Use Touch-units or Magtiles to model.

Pick up the letter *s*, and say its sound as you place it on the whiteboard. Repeat the procedure with the letters *oo*, and place them about an inch to the right of the letter *s*. Repeat the procedure again with the letter *n*. Touch *s*, and say its sound. Touch *oo*, and say their sound. Touch *n*, and say its sound.

Move the letters closer together, and say their sounds, blending them slightly. Move the letters next to each other and blend the sounds to say *soon.* (You may choose to do this in several steps, moving the letters closer together to demonstrate how to blend.)

Then cover the word and spell it orally. Uncover the word and have students compare your spelling with the Touch-units. Cover the word again and write it on the whiteboard. Uncover the word and have students compare the written word with the Touch-units.

Repear this procedure with the word *foot.*

Build Words Distribute Touch-units for the word *wool.* Say *wool.* Have students build it on their whiteboard using the Touch-units. Give help as necessary. After making the word, have students touch and sound each Touch-unit, then blend the sounds as they run their finger underneath the Touch-units. Have students cover the word and spell it orally, then compare their spelling to the Touch-units. Next have them cover the word again and write it on their whiteboard and then on the Build Words page of their Workbook (p. 137). Have students compare their writing to the Touch-units. Then use this procedure to have students build the following words:

	yellow	red	blue
took	t, k	oo	
book	b		
boom	m		
broom			br
brook	k		
shook			sh
shoot	t		

Use one of the activities on page xvi to further practice sequencing and discriminating the words that students find challenging.

Read Words in Isolation Have students pair up and read all of the words they have written on Workbook page 137 aloud to their partner.

Independent Practice (Workbook page 136) For the first set of items, ask students to circle the letters that stands for the vowel sound they hear in each picture. For the second set, ask them to write the word that completes each sentence. When students complete the page, have them check their work with you or a partner.

Dictation Dictate the following sentence, and have students write it on their whiteboard or at the bottom of Workbook page 136: *I took the broom to the cool room.*

Reading Words in Context

Tell students that they will use what they know about words with *oo* to read a story.

Build Words from the Story Use the Touch-units to build the following words on the whiteboard. Tell students that the words you will make together will help them read the story.

Start with the word *too.*

Substitute Touch-units to build the following words: *moon, soon, noon, cool, pool, boom, room, broom, groom, hoop, snoop, scoop, root, loot, food, look, book, took, hook, cook, brook, shook, good, wood, stood, foot, wool.*

As a prereading activity, you may want to have students find the words in the text and read them aloud.

Read the Story Give students a copy of *Camping at the Brook.* Have them read it independently or with a partner. If necessary, you can support students as they read the story by identifying sight words or helping them to blend sounds to read words.

Respond to the Story After students read *Camping at the Brook,* have them complete Workbook page 138. Have students share their work with the rest of the group.

Lesson 47: Vowel Combinations: ew

Remind students that they have learned that the same combination of letters can sometimes make different sounds.

Tell students that today they will learn the different sounds that *ew* makes.

Phonemic Awareness Say the word *dew.* Emphasize the sound that *ew* makes. Then say the following words, and have students listen for the *ew* sound in each one: *blew, grew, new.*

Now say the word *few.* Emphasize the sound that *ew* makes. Then say the following words, and have students listen for the other sound that *ew* makes: *grew, pew, stew, shrewd.*

Link Sound to Letters Distribute the *ew* Touch-unit. Have students trace its shape with their finger as they make the sound for *ew* as in *grew* together.

Form the following word on a whiteboard: *grew.* Say the word, emphasizing the *ew* sound. Then underline the *ew* in the word.

Tell students that the *ew* makes the sound they hear at the end of *grew.* Isolate the sound for students. Then have them repeat it after you.

Repeat the procedure above to form the word *few.* Point out that the *ew* in *few* makes a slightly different sound than it does in *grew.*

Form these words on the whiteboard: *chew, threw, knew.* Say each word for students, and have them take turns underlining the *ew,* saying the appropriate sound for *ew,* and then saying the word.

Build Words (Model) Tell students that they can use what they know about the *ew* sounds to build words.

Say *dew.* Tell students you are going to build *dew.* Use Touch-units or Magtiles to model.

Pick up the letter *d,* and say its sound as you place it on the whiteboard. Repeat the procedure with the letters *ew,* and place them about an inch to the right of the letter *d.* Touch *d,* and say its sound. Touch *ew,* and say their sound.

Move the letters closer together, and say their sounds, blending them slightly. Move the letters next to each other and blend the sounds to say *dew.* (You may choose to do this in several steps, moving the letters closer together to demonstrate how to blend.)

Then cover the word and spell it orally. Uncover the word and have students compare your spelling with the Touch-units. Cover the word again and write it on the whiteboard. Uncover the word and have students compare the written word with the Touch-units.

Repeat this procedure with the word *skew.*

Build Words Distribute Touch-units for the word *pew.* Say *pew.* Have students build it on their whiteboard using the Touch-units. Give help as necessary. After making the word, have students touch and sound each Touch-unit, then blend the sounds as they run their finger underneath the Touch-units. Have students cover the word and spell it orally, then compare their spelling to the Touch-units. Next have them cover the word again and write it on their whiteboard and then on the Build Words page of their Workbook (p. 140). Have students compare their writing to the Touch-units. Then use this procedure to have students build the following words:

	yellow	red	blue
new	n	ew	
blew			bl
crew			cr
slew			sl
stew			st
few	f		

Use one of the activities on page xvi to further practice sequencing and discriminating the words that students find challenging.

Read Words in Isolation Have students pair up and read all of the words they have written on Workbook page 140 aloud to their partner.

Independent Practice (Workbook page 139) Ask students to write the word that completes each sentence. When students complete the page, have them check their work with you or a partner.

Dictation Dictate the following sentence, and have students write it on their whiteboard or at the bottom of Workbook page 139: *The crew chews stew.*

Reading Words in Context

Tell students that they will use what they know about words with *ew* to read a story.

Build Words from the Story Use the Touch-units to build the following words on the whiteboard. Tell students that the words you will make together will help them read the story.

Start with the word *new.*

Substitute Touch-units to build the following words: *knew, dew, drew, brew, blew, chew, crew, grew, stew, slew, screw, threw, shrewd.*

As a prereading activity, you may want to have students find the words in the text and read them aloud.

Read the Story Give students a copy of *Buckaroo Stew.* Have them read it independently or with a partner. If necessary, you can support students as they read the story by identifying sight words or helping them to blend sounds to read words.

Respond to the Story After students read *Buckaroo Stew,* have them complete Workbook page 141. Have students share their work with the rest of the group.

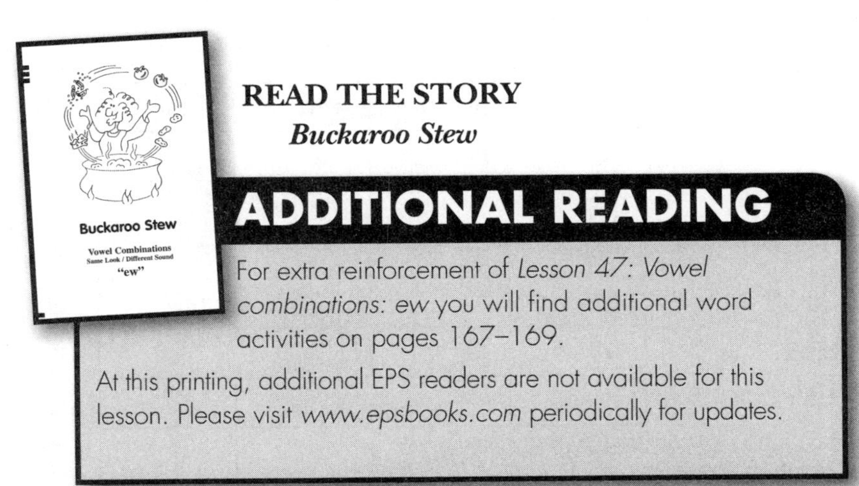

READ THE STORY
Buckaroo Stew

ADDITIONAL READING

For extra reinforcement of *Lesson 47: Vowel combinations: ew* you will find additional word activities on pages 167–169.

At this printing, additional EPS readers are not available for this lesson. Please visit *www.epsbooks.com* periodically for updates.

Lesson 48: Vowel Combinations: *ea*

Remind students that they have learned that the same combination of letters can sometimes make different sounds.

Tell students that today they will learn the different sounds that *ea* makes.

Phonemic Awareness Say the word *beat.* Emphasize the sound that *ea* makes. Then say the following words, and have students listen for the long *e* sound in each one: *peak, team.*

Now say the word *spread.* Emphasize the short *e* sound that *ea* sometimes makes. Then say the following words, and have students listen for the short *e* sound in each one: *bread, tread.*

Finally, say the word *great.* Emphasize the long *a* sound that *ea* sometimes makes. Then say the following words, and have students listen for the long *a* sound in each one: *great, steak.*

Link Sound to Letters Distribute the *ea* Touch-unit. Have students trace its shape with their finger as they make the sound for *ea* as in *neat* together.

Form the following word on a whiteboard: *neat.* Say the word, emphasizing the *ea* sound. Then underline the *ea* in the word.

Tell students that the *ea* often makes the long *e* sound they hear in the middle of *neat.* Isolate the sound for students, and then have them repeat it after you.

Repeat the procedure above to form the word *head.* Point out that the *ea* sometimes makes the short *e* sound they hear in the middle of *head.*

Repeat the procedure again to form the word *steak.* Point out that the *ea* sometimes makes the long *a* sound they hear in the middle of *steak.*

Build Words (Model) Tell students that they can use what they know about the different sounds for *ea* to build words.

Say *deal.* Tell students you are going to build *deal.* Use Touch-units or Magtiles to model.

Pick up the letter *d,* and say its sound as you place it on the whiteboard. Repeat the procedure with the letters *ea,* and place them about an inch to the right of the letter *d.* Repeat the procedure again with the letter *l.* Touch *d,* and say its sound. Touch *ea,* and say their sound. Touch *l,* and say its sound.

Move the letters closer together, and say their sounds, blending them slightly. Move the letters next to each other and blend the sounds to say *deal.* (You may choose to do this in several steps, moving the letters closer together to demonstrate how to blend.)

Then cover the word and spell it orally. Uncover the word and have students compare your spelling with the Touch-units. Cover the word again and write it on the whiteboard. Uncover the word and have students compare the written word with the Touch-units.

Repeat this procedure with *sweat* and *break.*

Build Words Distribute Touch-units for the word *pea.* Say *pea.* Have students build it on their whiteboard using the Touch-units. Give help as necessary. After making the word, have students touch and sound each Touch-unit, then blend the sounds as they run their finger underneath the Touch-units. Have students cover the word and spell it orally, then compare their spelling to the Touch-units. Next have them cover the word again and write it on their whiteboard and then on the Build Words page of their Workbook (p. 143). Have students compare their writing to the Touch-units. Then use this procedure to have students build the following words:

	yellow	red	blue
sea	s	ea	
tea	t		
team	m		
treat			tr
tread	d		
bread			br
break	k		

Use one of the activities on page xvi to further practice sequencing and discriminating the words that students find challenging.

Read Words in Isolation Have students pair up and read all of the words they have written on Workbook page 143 aloud to their partner.

Independent Practice (Workbook page 142) For the first set of items, ask students to write the letters that complete each picture name. For the second set, ask them to write the word that completes each sentence. When students complete the page, have them check their work with you or a partner.

Dictation Dictate the following sentence, and have students write it on their whiteboard or at the bottom of Workbook page 142: *It was great to eat the bread.*

Reading Words in Context

Tell students that they will use what they know about words with *ea* to read a story.

Build Words from the Story Use the Touch-units to build the following words on the whiteboard. Tell students that the words you will make together will help them read the story.

Start with the word *neat.*

Substitute Touch-units to build the following words: *beat, peat, east, beam, dream, stream, team, peak, speak, creak, heap, plead, zeal, head, tread, dread, spread, break, great, steak.*

As a prereading activity, you may want to have students find the words in the text and read them aloud.

Read the Story Give students a copy of *The Eager Beavers.* Have them read it independently or with a partner. If necessary, you can support students as they read the story by identifying sight words or helping them to blend sounds to read words.

Respond to the Story After students read *The Eager Beavers*, have them complete Workbook page 144. Have students share their work with the rest of the group.

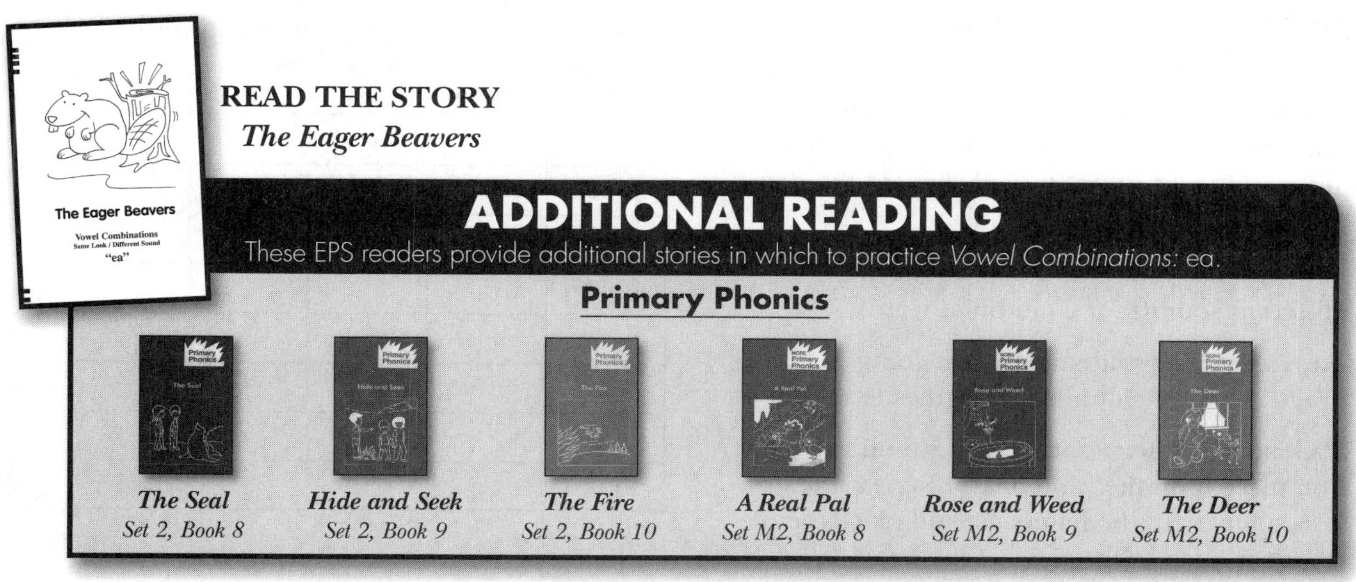

Lesson 49: Vowel Combinations: *ou*

Remind students that they have learned that the same combination of letters can sometimes make different sounds.

Tell students that today they will learn the different sounds that *ou* makes.

Phonemic Awareness Say the word *loud.* Emphasize the sound that *ou* makes. Then say the following words, and have students listen for the vowel sound in each one: *count, doubt.*

Now say the word *four,* emphasizing another vowel sound that *ou* sometimes makes. Then say the following words, and have students listen for the vowel sound: *tour, course, pour.*

Finally, say the following words and have students listen for other sounds *ou* sometimes makes: *cough, young, you, could.*

Link Sound to Letters Distribute the *ou* Touch-unit. Have students trace its shape with their finger as they make the sound for *ou* as in *stout* together.

Form the following word on a whiteboard: *stout.* Say the word, emphasizing the *ou* sound. Then underline the *ou* in the word.

Tell students that the *ou* often makes the sound they hear in the middle of *stout.* Isolate the sound for students, and then have them repeat it after you.

Repeat the procedure above to form the word *pour.* Point out that the *ou* sometimes makes the vowel sound they hear in *pour.*

Finally, say the following words and have students listen for other sounds *ou* sometimes makes: *thought, rough, through, would.*

Build Words (Model) Tell students that they can use what they know about the different sounds for *ou* to build words.

Say *mouth.* Tell students you are going to build *mouth.* Use Touch-units or Magtiles to model.

Pick up the letter *m,* and say its sound as you place it on the whiteboard. Repeat the procedure with the letters *ou,* and place them about an inch to the right of the letter *m.*

Repeat the procedure again with the letters *th.* Touch *m,* and say its sound. Touch *ou,* and say their sound. Touch *th,* and say their sound.

Move the letters closer together, and say their sounds, blending them slightly. Move the letters next to each other and blend the sounds to say *mouth.* (You may choose to do this in several steps, moving the letters closer together to demonstrate how to blend.)

Then cover the word and spell it orally. Uncover the word and have students compare your spelling with the Touch-units. Cover the word again and write it on the whiteboard. Uncover the word and have students compare the written word with the Touch-units.

Repeat this procedure with the word *tour.*

Build Words Distribute Touch-units for the word *tout.* Say *tout.* Have students build it on their whiteboard using the Touch-units. Give help as necessary. After making the word, have students touch and sound each Touch-unit, then blend the sounds as they run their finger underneath the Touch-units. Have students cover the word and spell it orally, then compare their spelling to the Touch-units. Next have them cover the word again and write it on their whiteboard and then on the Build Words page of their Workbook (p. 146). Have students compare their writing to the Touch-units. Then use this procedure to have students build the following words:

	yellow	red	blue	green
bout	b, t	ou		
pout	p			
grout			gr	
group	p			
young	y			ng
your	r			
four	f			
found				nd

Use one of the activities on page xvi to further practice sequencing and discriminating the words that students find challenging.

Read Words in Isolation Have students pair up and read all of the words they have written on Workbook page 146 aloud to their partner.

Independent Practice (Workbook page 145) Ask students to write the word that completes each sentence. When students complete the page, have them check their work with you or a partner.

Dictation Dictate the following sentence, and have students write it on their whiteboard or at the bottom of Workbook page 145: *The group thought we would go to your house.*

Reading Words in Context

Tell students that they will use what they know about words with *ou* to read a story.

Build Words from the Story Use the Touch-units to build the following words. Tell students that the words you will make together will help them read the story.

Start with the word *course.*

Substitute Touch-units to build the following words: *four, pour, tour, your, found, mound, pound, sound, bound, count, house, mouse, out, snout, spout, stout, trout, shout, scout, crouch, pouch, slouch, mouth, south, proud, loud, sought, trough, thought, rough, tough, young, touch, group, through, could, would.*

As a prereading activity, you may want to have students find the words in the text and read them aloud.

Read the Story Give students a copy of *Scout the Hound Dog.* Have them read it independently or with a partner. If necessary, you can support students as they read the story by identifying sight words or helping them to blend sounds to read words.

Respond to the Story After students read *Scout the Hound Dog,* have them complete Workbook page 147. Have students share their work with the rest of the group.

Lesson 50: Vowel Combinations: ey

Remind students that they have learned that the same combination of letters can sometimes make different sounds.

Tell students that today they will learn the different sounds that *ey* makes.

Phonemic Awareness Say the word *hey*. Emphasize the long *a* sound that *ey* makes. Then say the following words, and have students listen for the long *e* sound in each one: *grey, prey, obey*.

Now say the word *key*. Emphasize the long *e* sound that *ey* sometimes makes. Then say the following words, and have students listen for the long *e* sound in each one: *turkey, money, valley*.

Link Sound to Letters Distribute the *ey* Touch-unit. Have students trace its shape with their finger as they make the sound for *ey* as in *hey* together.

Form the following word on a whiteboard: *hey*. Say the word, emphasizing the *ey* sound. Then underline the *ey* in the word.

Tell students that the *ey* often makes the long *a* sound they hear at the end of *hey*. Isolate the sound for students, and then have them repeat it after you.

Repeat the procedure to form the word *key*. Point out that the *ey* sometimes makes the long *e* sound they hear in *key*.

Form these words on the whiteboard: *survey, alley, turkey*. Say each word for students, and have them take turns underlining the *ey*, saying the appropriate sound for *ey*, and then saying the word.

Build Words (Model) Tell students that they can use what they know about the *ey* sound to build words.

Say *obey*. Tell students you are going to build *obey*. Use Touch-units or Magtiles to model.

Pick up the letter *o*, and say its sound as you place it on the whiteboard. Repeat the procedure with the letter *b*, and place it about an inch to the right of the letter *o*. Repeat the procedure again with the letters *ey*. Touch *o*, and say its sound. Touch *b*, and say its sound. Touch *ey*, and say their sound.

Move the letters closer together, and say their sounds, blending them slightly. Move the letters next to each other and blend the sounds to say *obey*. (You may choose to do this in several steps, moving the letters closer together to demonstrate how to blend.)

Then cover the word and spell it orally. Uncover the word and have students compare your spelling with the Touch-units. Cover the word again and write it on the whiteboard. Uncover the word and have students compare the written word with the Touch-units.

Repeat this procedure with the word *key*.

Build Words Distribute Touch-units for the word *they*. Say *they*. Have students build it on their whiteboard using the Touch-units. Give help as necessary. After making the word, have students touch and sound each Touch-unit, then blend the sounds as they run their finger underneath the Touch-units. Have students cover the word and spell it orally, then compare their spelling to the Touch-units. Next have them cover the word again and write it on their whiteboard and then on the Build Words page of their Workbook (p. 149). Have students compare their writing to the Touch-units. Then use this procedure to have students build the following words:

	yellow	red	blue
grey		ey	gr
prey			pr
whey	wh		
key	k		

Use one of the activities on page xvi to further practice sequencing and discriminating the words that students find challenging.

Read Words in Isolation Have students pair up and read all of the words they have written on Workbook page 149 aloud to their partner.

Independent Practice (Workbook page 148) Ask students to write the word that completes each sentence. When students complete the page, have them check their work with you or a partner.

Dictation Dictate the following sentence, and have students write it on their whiteboard or at the bottom of Workbook page 148: *They need the key to get in the room.*

Reading Words in Context

Tell students that they will use what they know about words with *ey* to read a story.

Build Words from the Story Use the Touch-units to build the following words on the whiteboard. Tell students that the words you will make together will help them read the story.

Start with the word *they.*

Substitute Touch-units to build the following words: *grey, prey, whey, obey, osprey, survey, key, turkey, monkey, money, journey, alley, valley, galley, barley, jersey, dopey, mopey.*

As a prereading activity, you may want to have students find the words in the text and read them aloud.

Read the Story Give students a copy of *The Happy Valley Zoo.* Have them read it independently or with a partner. If necessary, you can support students as they read the story by identifying sight words or helping them to blend sounds to read words.

Respond to the Story After students read *The Happy Valley Zoo,* have them complete Workbook page 150. Have students share their work with the rest of the group.

Lesson 51: Vowel Combinations: *ei*

Remind students that they have learned that the same combination of letters can sometimes make different sounds.

Tell students that today they will learn the different sounds that *ei* makes.

Phonemic Awareness Say the word *weigh.* Emphasize the long *a* sound that *ei* makes. Then say the following words, and have students listen for long *a* sound in each one: *weight, sleigh, veil.*

Now say the word *ceiling.* Emphasize the long *e* sound that *ei* sometimes makes. Then say the following words, and have students listen for the long *e* sound: *seize, either, receive.*

Finally, say the following words and have students listen for other sounds that *ei* sometimes makes: *height, heifer, foreign.*

Link Sound to Letters Distribute the *ei* Touch-unit. Have students trace its shape with their finger as they make the sound for *ei* as in *vein* together.

Form the following word on a whiteboard: *vein.* Say the word, emphasizing the *ei* sound. Then underline the *ei* in the word.

Tell students that the *ei* often makes the long *a* sound they hear in the middle of *vein.* Isolate the sound for students, and then have them repeat it after you.

Repeat the procedure above to form the word *seize.* Point out that the *ei* sometimes makes the long *e* sound they hear in *seize.*

Finally, say the following words and have students listen for other sounds *ei* sometimes makes: *height, heifer, foreign.*

Build Words (Model) Tell students that they can use what they know about the different sounds for *ei* to build words.

Say *weigh.* Tell students you are going to build *weigh.* Use Touch-units or Magtiles to model.

Pick up the letter *w,* and say its sound as you place it on the whiteboard. Repeat the procedure with the letters *ei,* and place them about an inch to the right of the letter *w.* Repeat the procedure again with the letters *gh.* Touch *w,* and say its sound. Touch *ei,* and say their sound. Touch *gh,* and remind students that they are silent.

Move the letters closer together, and say their sounds, blending them slightly. Move the letters next to each other and blend the sounds to say *weigh.* (You may choose to do this in several steps, moving the letters closer together to demonstrate how to blend.)

Then cover the word and spell it orally. Uncover the word and have students compare your spelling with the Touch-units. Cover the word again and write it on the whiteboard. Uncover the word and have students compare the written word with the Touch-units.

Repeat this procedure with the word *seize.*

Build Words Distribute Touch-units for the word *eight.* Say *eight.* Have students build it on their whiteboard using the Touch-units. Give help as necessary. After making the word, have students touch and sound each Touch-unit, then blend the sounds as they run their finger underneath the Touch-units. Have students cover the word and spell it orally, then compare their spelling to the Touch-units. Next have them cover the word again and write it on their whiteboard and then on the Build Words page of their Workbook (p. 152). Have students compare their writing to the Touch-units. Then use this procedure to have students build the following words:

	yellow	red	blue	white
weight	w, t	ei		gh
freight			fr	
reign	r, n			
sheik	sh, k			
skein	n		sk	

Use one of the activities on page xvi to further practice sequencing and discriminating the words that students find challenging.

Read Words in Isolation Have students pair up and read all of the words they have written on Workbook page 152 aloud to their partner.

Independent Practice (Workbook page 151) Ask students to write the word that completes each sentence. When students complete the page, have them check their work with you or a partner.

Dictation Dictate the following sentence, and have students write it on their whiteboard or at the bottom of Workbook page 151: *They will seize eight freight trains.*

Reading Words in Context

Tell students that they will use what they know about words with *ei* to read a story.

Build Words from the Story Use the Touch-units to build the following words on the whiteboard. Tell students that the words you will make together will help them read the story.

Start with the word *eight.*

Substitute Touch-units to build the following words: *eighth, freight, weight, weigh, sleigh, vein, reign, lei, veil, seize, sheik, skein.*

As a prereading activity, you may want to have students find the words in the text and read them aloud.

Read the Story Give students a copy of *Larry the Library Spider.* Have them read it independently or with a partner. If necessary, you can support students as they read the story by identifying sight words or helping them to blend sounds to read words.

Respond to the Story After students read *Larry the Library Spider,* have them complete Workbook page 153. Have students share their work with the rest of the group.

Word Lists

Vowel Combinations: CVVC							
Consistent Sounds							
ee				**oa**		**ie**	**ui**
wee	deem	thee	wheel	goad	coach	field	fruit
bee	teem	flee	kneel	load	poach	wield	guise
fee	seem	glee	creel	road	roach	yield	juice
lee		knee	steel	toad			quiet
tee	seen	free			boast	niece	sluice
see	teen	tree	sheen	loaf	coast	piece	suit
	keen		green		roast		
seed		beech	preen	soak	toast	siege	
feed	keep	leech	queen				
heed	peep			coal	broach	tier	
need	seep	geese	sheep	foal			
eed	weep		sleep	goal	cloak	shield	
deed	deep	teeth	creep		croak		
reed	jeep		steep	foam		grieve	
	beep	bleed	sweep	loam	shoal		
reef		kneed	cheep	roam	groan	chief	
beef	beet	speed				thief	
	feet	breed	cheer	Joan	bloat	brief	
leek	meet	creed	sneer	loan	float	grief	
meek		freed	steer	moan	gloat		
reek		greed				quiet	
seek		steed	jeer	soap	coarse		
week		tweed	seer			priest	
peek			deer	soar	oar		
		sleeve		roar	board		
peel			sheet	boar	hoard		
heel		sneeze	skeet				
keel		breeze	fleet	boat			
reel		freeze	sleet	coat			
feel			greet	goat			
		speech	sweet	moat			
		breech	tweet				
				coax			
		cheek		hoax			
		sleek					
		creek					
		Greek					

Vowel Combinations: CVVC						
Same Sound/Different Look						
ai		**ay**	**au**	**aw**	**oi**	**oy**
laid	braid	bay	sauce	caw	void	boy
maid	staid	day	pause	jaw		joy
paid		gay		law	boil	toy
raid	flail	hay	gauze	paw	coil	Roy
faith	snail	jay		raw	soil	ploy
	frail	lay	haunch	saw	toil	Troy
bail	trail	may	launch			soy
fail	quail	nay	paunch	dawn	coin	
Gail		pay		fawn	join	
hail	claim	Ray	caulk	lawn	loin	
jail		say		pawn		
mail	chain	way	haul	sawn	joint	
nail	plain		maul	yawn	point	
pail	slain	clay	Paul			
rail	Spain	play		hawk	joist	
sail	brain	slay	caught		moist	
rail	drain		taught	bawl		
wail	grain	bray			broil	
	train	fray	fault	thaw	spoil	
gain	stain	gray	vault	claw		
lain		pray		flaw	choice	
main	chair	tray	daunt	slaw	voice	
pain	stair	stay	gaunt	gnaw		
rain		quay	haunt	draw	poise	
vain	trait	sway	jaunt			
				shawl		
bait			taut	brawl		
gait				crawl		
wait			clause	drawl		
			flaunt	trawl		
faint			fraud			
paint			staunch	spawn		
saint				brawn		
taint				drawn		
waist				prawn		

Vowel Combinations: CVVC						
Same Look/Different Sounds						
oo			**ow**		**ew**	
oo as in *book*	**oo as in *moon***		**ow as in *snow***	**ow as in *cow***	**ew as in *few***	**ew as in *new***
good	food	booth	bow	cow	few	new
hood	mood	tooth	low	vow	hew	dew
wood			mow	pow	mew	blew
	goof	brood	row	now	pew	brew
hoof	roof		sow	bow	skew	chew
		proof	tow	how	spew	crew
book	cool	spoof				drew
cook	fool		bowl	town		flew
hook	pool	spook		gown		grew
look	tool		mown	down		knew
nook		spool	sown			slew
rook	boom	drool		yowl		stew
took	doom	stool	slow	jowl		
	loom		snow	howl		
wool	room	stoop	stow			
	zoom	scoop	glow	scow		
foot		whoop	crow	chow		
soot	boon	sloop		plow		
	moon	snoop	blow	brow		
stood	noon	droop	blown	prow		
shook	soon	troop				
brook		swoop	clow	clown		
crook	boo		flown	brown		
	coo	swoon		crown		
	moo	spoon	grow	drown		
	too	croon	grown	frown		
	zoo		growth			
		shoo		crowd		
	coop		know			
	hoop	scoot	known	growl		
	loop	shoot		prowl		
	boot		show	scowl		
	hoot	smooth	shown			
	loot					
	moot	bloom				
	root	gloom				
	toot	broom				
		groom				

Vowel Combinations: CVVC			
Same Look/Different Sounds (continued)			
ey		**ei**	
ey as in *they*	**ey as in *key***	**ei as in *eight***	**ei as in *seize***
grey	key	sleigh	seize
hey		neigh	sheik
prey		weigh	
they		eighth	
whey		veil	
fey		feign	
prey		reign	
		skein	
		rein	
		vein	
		eight	
		freight	
		weight	

Vowel Combinations				
Multiple Sounds				
ea				
ea as in *eat*			**ea as in *bread***	**ea as in *steak***
pea			dead	steak
sea	beam	flea	head	break
tea	ram	plea	bread	
	seam	plead	dread	great
bead	team	knead	tread	
lead			deaf	
read	bean	breathe	death	
	dean		health	
leaf	Jean	please	sweat	
	lean		dealth	
beach	mean	grease	meant	
leach	wean		breast	
peach		bleach		
reach	heap	breach	breath	
teach	leap	preach		
	reap		wealth	
leash		sheath		
	beat	wreath		
beak	feat			
leak	heat	bleak		
peak	meat	sneak		
teak	nat	speak		
weak	peat	creak		
	seat	freak		
deal		tweak		
heal	beast	steal		
meal	feast	gleam		
peal	least	cream		
real	yeast	dream		
seal		steam		
teal		clean		
veal		glean		
zeal		cheap		
		cheat		
		sheat		
		bleat		
		cleat		
		pleat		
		treat		

Vowel Combinations:					
CVVC, Multiple Sounds (continued)					
ou					
ou as in *four*	**ou as in *loud***		**ou as in *cough***	**ou as in *trouble***	**ou as in *you***
four	loud	joust	cough	touch	you
your		bout	trough	rough	soup
pour	bound	gout	bought	tough	youth
court	found	pout	fought		troupe
mourn	hound	tout	sought		group
soul	mound	rout			route
though	pound		brought		
course	round	ground			
gourd	sound				
		cloud			
	bounce	proud			
	pounce	blouse			
	house	slouch			
	mouse	crouch			
		grouch			
	route				
		flour			
	couch	drought			
	pouch				
	vouch	scout			
		shout			
	mouth	clout			
	south	flout			
	foul	snout			
	noun	spout			
	sour	grout			
	doubt	trout			
	count	stout			
	mount				

Lesson 52: Compound Words

Tell students that today they will learn about special kinds of words called compound words.

Explain that compound words are words that are made up of two words. Breaking the word into parts can help them read, write, and understand the words.

Phonemic Awareness Say the word *ballpark*. Emphasize the pause between *ball* and *park*. Have students repeat the compound word, emphasizing the pause between its two words.

Follow the same procedure with these words: *birthday, daytime, bulldog.*

Link Sounds to Letters Distribute the Touch-units for the word *haircut* (*h, air, c, u, t*). Have students trace each Touch-unit with their finger as they make the sounds together.

Form the word *haircut* on a whiteboard. Underline *hair*, say it, and then have students repeat it. Follow the same procedure with *cut.* Follow the procedure again with *haircut.* Tell students that *haircut* is a compound word made up of the words *hair* and *cut.*

Then form these compound words on a whiteboard: *cannot, football, playground.* Say each word for students. Have them take turns underlining the two words in each compound, saying each word, and then saying the whole word.

Build Words (Model) Tell students that they can use what they know about compound words to build words.

Say *railroad.* Tell students you are going to build *railroad.* Use Touch-units or Magtiles to model.

Pick up the letter *r*, and say its sound as you place it on the whiteboard. Repeat the procedure with the letters *ai*, and place them about an inch to the right of the letter *r*. Repeat the procedure again with the letter *l*. Touch *r*, and say its sound. Touch *ai*, and say their sound. Touch *l*, and say its sound.

Move the letters closer together, and say their sounds, blending them slightly. Move the letters next to each other and blend the sounds to say *rail.* (You may choose to do this in several steps, moving the letters closer together to demonstrate how to blend.)

Follow the same procedure to build *road.* Then move *rail* and *road* closer together, and read them as one word.

Now cover *railroad* and spell it orally. Uncover the word and have students compare your spelling with the Touch-units. Cover the word again and write it on the whiteboard. Uncover the word and have students compare the written word with the Touch-units.

Build Words Distribute the Touch-units for the word *homesick.* Say *homesick.* Have students build it on their whiteboard using the Touch-units. Give help as necessary. After making the word, have students touch and sound each Touch-unit, then blend the sounds as they run their finger underneath the Touch-units. Repeat this procedure with *sick.* Then have students move *home* and *sick* closer together, and then read it as one word.

Now have students cover *homesick* and spell it orally, then compare their spelling to the Touch-units. Next have them cover the word again and write it on their whiteboard and then on the Build Words page of their Workbook (p. 155). Have students compare their writing to the Touch-units. Then use this procedure to have students build the following words: *without, breakfast, afternoon, outside, earthquake.*

Use one of the activities on page xvi to further practice sequencing and discriminating the words that students find challenging.

Read Words in Isolation Have students pair up and read all of the words they have written on Workbook page 155 aloud to their partner.

Independent Practice (Workbook page 154) For the first set of items, ask students to write the word that names each picture. For the second set, ask them to write the word that completes each sentence. When students complete the page, have them check their work with you or a partner.

Dictation Dictate the following sentence, and have students write on their whiteboard or at the bottom of Workbook page 154: *We play baseball in the hot sunshine.*

Reading Words in Context

Tell students that they will use what they know about compound words to read a story.

Build Words from the Story Use the Touch-units to build the following words on the whiteboard. Tell students that the words you will make together will help them read the story.

Start with the word *afternoon.*

Then build the following words: *afternoon, airplane, ballpark, ballplayer, baseball, basketball, blackburn, blueberry, breakfast, bulldog, daytime, downstairs.*

As a prereading activity, you may want to have students find the words in the text and read them aloud.

Read the Story Give students a copy of *Greg's Birthday at the Ballpark.* Have them read it independently or with a partner. If necessary, you can support students as they read the story by identifying sight words or helping them to blend sounds to read words.

Respond to the Story After students read *Greg's Birthday at the Ballpark,* have them complete Workbook page 156. Have students share their work with the rest of the group.

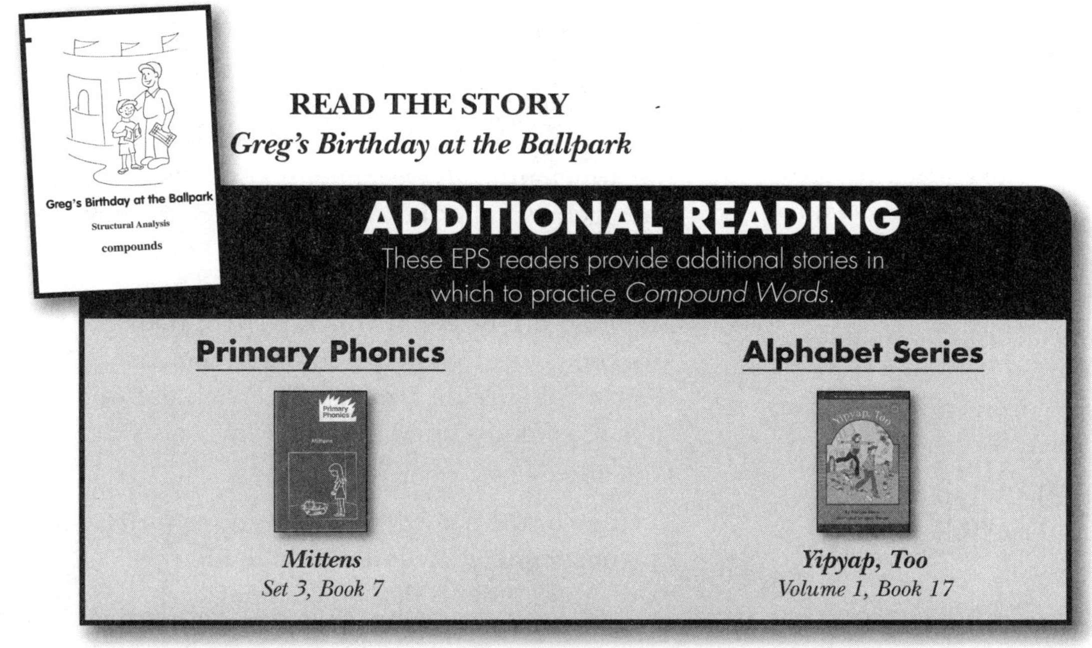

Lesson 53: Contractions

Remind students that learning about compound words helped them to read and write words.

Tell students that today they will learn about another special kind of word called a contraction.

Explain that a contraction is one word that takes the place of two words. The two words are joined together and made shorter by leaving out some letters. A punctuation mark called an apostrophe shows where the letters are left out.

Phonemic Awareness Say the words *can* and *not,* and have students repeat them. Then say the word *can't,* and have students repeat it. Tell them that *can't* means the same thing as *can not.*

Follow the same procedure with these sets of words: *was, not, wasn't; she, will, she'll; he, is, he's; we, are, we're.*

Link Sounds to Letters Distribute the Touch-units for the words *did* and *not* (*d, i, d, n, o, t*). Have students trace each Touch-unit with their finger as they make the sounds together.

Form the words *did* and *not* side by side on a whiteboard. Say each word and have students repeat them.

Remove the *n* and *o* Touch-units from *not* and put an apostrophe Touch-unit in their place. Read the new word aloud. Then use it in a sentence. Repeat the sentence using the two words that the contraction stands for: *did, not.*

Then form these contractions on a whiteboard: *I'll, it's when's, we're.* Say each contraction for students. Have them take turns saying the words that make up each contraction, saying the contraction, and then using the contraction in a sentence.

Build Words (Model) Tell students that they can use what they know about contractions to build words.

Say *isn't.* Tell students you are going to build *isn't.* Use Touch-units or Magtiles to model.

Pick up the letter *i,* and say its sound as you place it on the whiteboard. Repeat the procedure with the letter *s,* and place it about an inch to the right of the letter *i.* Touch *i,* and say its sound. Touch *s,* and say its sound.

Move the letters closer together, and say their sounds, blending them slightly. Move the letters next to each other and blend the sounds to say *is.* (You may choose to do this in several steps, moving the letters closer together to demonstrate how to blend.)

Follow the same procedure to build *not* to the right of *is.* Use the apostrophe Touch-unit to push the *o* out of *not.* Then place the apostrophe between *n* and *t.* Explain that the apostrophe takes the place of the letters you took away. Say the contraction for students.

Then cover the word and spell it orally. Uncover the word and have students compare your spelling with the Touch-units. Cover the word again and write it on the whiteboard. Uncover the word and have students compare the written word with the Touch-units.

Build Words Distribute the Touch-units for the word *wasn't.* Say *wasn't.* Have students build it on their whiteboard using the Touch-units. Give help as necessary. After making the word, have students touch and sound each Touch-unit, then blend the sounds as they run their finger underneath the Touch-units. Have students cover the word and spell it orally, then compare their spelling to the Touch-units. Next have them cover the word again and write it on their whiteboard and then on the Build Words page of their Workbook (p. 158). Have students compare their writing to the Touch-units. Then use this to have students build the following words: *didn't, couldn't, I'll, she'll, he's, how's, you're.*

Use one of the activities on page xvi to further practice sequencing and discriminating the words that students find challenging.

Read Words in Isolation Have students pair up and read all of the words they have written on Workbook page 158 aloud to their partner.

Independent Practice (Workbook page 157) Ask students to write the word that completes each sentence. When students complete the page, have them check their work with you or a partner.

Dictation Dictate the following sentence, and have students write it on their whiteboard or at the bottom of Workbook page 157: *It's something we couldn't do.*

Reading Words in Context

Tell students that they will use what they know about contractions to read a story.

Build Words from the Story Use the Touch-units to build the following words. Tell students that the words you will make together will help them read the story. Start with the word *aren't.*

Then build the following words: *can't, couldn't, didn't, doesn't, don't, haven't, isn't, wasn't, wouldn't, here's, it's, she's, there's, they're, we're, you're, I've, we've, they've, let's, he'll, I'll, she'll, we'll.*

As a prereading activity, you may want to have students find the words in the text and read them aloud.

Read the Story Give students a copy of *Julie's Gymnastics Class.* Have them read it independently or with a partner. If necessary, you can support students as they read the story by identifying sight words or helping them to blend sounds to read words.

Respond to the Story After students read *Julie's Gymnastics Class,* have them complete Workbook page 159. Have students share their work with the rest of the group.

Lesson 54: Open and Closed Syllables

Remind students that they have learned about different kinds of special words.

Tell students that today they will learn about word parts called syllables.

Explain that a syllable is a word part that has only one vowel sound. It can have more than one vowel, but only one vowel sound.

Phonemic Awareness Say the word *boat*. Emphasize the vowel sound. Say it again as you clap once for the syllable.

Then say the word *pepper*. Emphasize the vowel sounds in each syllable: *pepper*. Say it again as you clap once for each syllable.

Then say the following words as you clap out the syllables for each one: *window, letter, desk, shelf, crayon, pen*. Repeat the words and have students clap out the syllables with you.

Link Sounds to Letters Distribute the Touch-units for the word *begin* (*b, e, g, i, n*). Have students trace each Touch-unit with their finger as they make the sounds together.

Form the word *begin* on a whiteboard. Underline the first syllable *be* and say it, emphasizing the vowel sound. Point out that the first syllable ends with a long vowel sound. Have students repeat it back to you.

Now underline the second syllable *gin* and say it, emphasizing the vowel sound. Point out that the vowel sound is in the middle of the second syllable. Have students repeat it back to you.

Finally, say the syllables together as a word: *begin*. Have students repeat it back to you.

Build Words (Model) Tell students that they can use what they know about syllables to build words.

Say *forget*. Tell students you are going to build *forget*. Use Touch-units or Magtiles to model.

Pick up the letter *f*, and say its sound as you place it on the whiteboard. Repeat the procedure with the letters *or*, and place it about an inch to the right of the letter *f*.

Touch *f*, and say its sound. Touch *or*, and say their sound.

Move the letters closer together, and say their sounds, blending them slightly. Move the letters next to each other and blend the sounds to say *for*. (You may choose to do this in several steps, moving the letters closer together to demonstrate how to blend.)

Repeat this procedure to build *get*. Then move *for* and *get* closer together, and read them as one word.

Then cover the word and spell it orally. Uncover the word and have students compare your spelling with the Touch-units. Cover the word again and write it on the whiteboard. Uncover the word and have students compare the written word with the Touch-units.

Build Words Distribute the Touch-units for the word *zebra*. Say *zebra*. Have students build it on their whiteboard using the Touch-units. Give help as necessary. After making the word, have students touch and sound each Touch-unit, then blend the sounds as they run their finger underneath the Touch-units. Have students cover the word and spell it orally, then compare their spelling to the Touch-units. Next have them cover the word again and write it on their whiteboard and then on the Build Words page of their Workbook (p. 161). Have students compare their writing to the Touch-units. Then use this procedure to build the following words: *finish, puppy, counter, tunnel, hamster*.

Use one of the activities on page xvi to further practice sequencing and discriminating the words that students find challenging.

Read Words in Isolation Have students pair up and read all of the words they have written on Workbook page 161 aloud to their partner.

Independent Practice (Workbook page 160) For the first set of items, ask students to circle the word that names the picture at the beginning of each row. For the second set of items, ask them to write the word that completes each sentence. When students complete the page, have them check their work with you or a partner.

Dictation Dictate the following sentence, and have students write it on their whiteboard or at the bottom of Workbook page 160: *I forgot my paper on the kitchen counter.*

Reading Words in Context

Tell students that they will use what they know about syllables to read a selection.

Build Words from the Selection Use the Touch-units to build the following words on the whiteboard. Tell students that the words you will make together will help them read the selection.

Start with the word *pilot.*

Then build the following words: *final, tiger, lion, hammer, arrow, velvet, circus, camel, wagon, artist, floppy, city.*

As a prereading activity, you may want to have students find the words in the text and read them aloud.

Read the Selection Give students a copy of *The Circus*. Have them read it independently or with a partner. If necessary, you can support students as they read the selection by identifying sight words or helping them to blend sounds to read words.

Respond to the Selection After students read *The Circus,* have them complete Workbook page 162. Have students share their work with the rest of the group.

Lesson 55: Syllables with *le*

Remind students that they have learned to read words with different syllables.

Tell students that today they will learn about syllables with the sound for *le*.

Phonemic Awareness Say the following word, emphasizing the sound that *le* makes in the second syllable: *apple*. Ask students to tell you what vowel sound they hear in the second syllable. If they said that it was a short *u* sound, tell them that they made a good guess. Tell them that the vowel sound is a ə sound, which is similar to a short *u* sound, but can be spelled with any vowel letter.

Then say the following words, and have students listen for the *le* sound at the end of each one: *circle, pickle, kettle, able, handle.*

Link Sounds to Letters Distribute the *l* and *e* Touch-units. Have students trace the shapes with their finger as they make the sounds for *le* together.

Form the following word on a whiteboard: *nibble*. Say the word, emphasizing the *le* sounds. Then underline the *le* in the word.

Tell students that the *le* has the ə sound and the *l* sound they hear at the end of *nibble*. Isolate the sounds for students, and have them repeat the sounds after you.

Form these words on the whiteboard: *uncle, middle, tumble, purple, little.* Say each word for students, and have them take turns underlining the *le*, saying the sounds that *le* makes, and then saying the word.

Build Words (Model) Tell students that they can use what they know about the *le* sounds to build words.

Say *bridle*. Tell students you are going to build *bridle*. Use Touch-units or Magtiles to model.

Break the word into two syllables for students: *bri, dle.*

Pick up the letters *br*, and say their sounds as you place them on the whiteboard. Repeat the procedure with the letter *i*, and place it about an inch to the right of the letters *br*. Touch *br*, and say their sounds. Touch *i*, and say its sound.

Move the letters closer together, and say their sounds, blending them slightly. Move the letters next to each other and blend the sounds to say *bri*. (You may choose to do this in several steps, moving the letters closer together to demonstrate how to blend.)

Repeat this procedure to build the second syllable, *dle*. Place the brown ə Touch-unit on top of the *le* Touch-unit to show the pronunciation of the vowel. Then move the syllables closer together, and read them as one word.

Then cover the word and spell it orally. Uncover the word and have students compare your spelling with the Touch-units. Cover the word again and write it on the whiteboard. Uncover the word and have students compare the written word with the Touch-units.

Build Words Distribute the Touch-units for the word *bundle*. Say *bundle*. Have students build it on their whiteboard using the Touch-units. Give help as necessary. Remind students to place the brown ə Touch-unit on top of the *le* to show the pronunciation of the vowel.

After making the word, have students touch and sound each Touch-unit, then blend the sounds as they run their finger underneath the Touch-units. Have students cover the word and spell it orally, then compare their spelling to the Touch-units. Next have them cover the word again and write it on their whiteboard and then on the Build Words page of their Workbook (p. 164). Have students compare their writing to the Touch-units.

Then use the same procedure to have students build the following words: *single, bottle, kettle, settle, cuddle, brittle.*

Use one of the activities on page xvi to further practice sequencing and discriminating the words that students find challenging.

Read Words in Isolation Have students pair up and read all of the words they have written on Workbook page 164 aloud to their partner.

Independent Practice (Workbook page 163) For the first set of items, ask students to connect all the picture names that have the *le* sound to find their way through the maze. For the second set, ask them to write the word that completes each sentence. When students complete the page, have them check their work with you or a partner.

Dictation Dictate the following sentence, and have students write it on their whiteboard or at the bottom of Workbook page 163: *My uncle was able to saddle the horse.*

Reading Words in Context

Tell students that they will use what they know about the sounds for *le* to read a story.

Build Words from the Story Use the Touch-units to build the following words on the whiteboard. Tell students that the words you will make together will help them read the story.

Start with the word *amble.*

Then build the following words: *crumble, stable, stumble, bridle, bundle, cuddle, apple, maple, sample, circle, uncle, bottle, brittle, snuggle, single.*

As a prereading activity, you may want to have students find the words in the text and read them aloud.

Read the Story Give students a copy of *Apple Time with Annie.* Have them read it independently or with a partner. If necessary, you can support students as they read the story by identifying sight words or helping them to blend sounds to read words.

Respond to the Story After students read *Apple Time with Annie,* have them complete Workbook page 165. Have students share their work with the rest of the group.

Lesson 56: Suffixes

Remind students that they have learned about word parts called syllables.

Tell students that today they will learn about word parts that come at the end of words. These are called suffixes.

Phonemic Awareness Say the word *powerful.* Emphasize the pause between *power* and *ful.* Have students repeat the word, emphasizing the pause between the root word and the suffix.

Follow the same procedure with these words: *golden, joyous, foolish.*

Link Sounds to Letters Distribute the Touch-units for the word *thankful* (*th, a, nk, ful*). Have students trace each Touch-unit with their finger as they make the sounds together.

Form the word *thankful* on a whiteboard. Underline *thank,* say it, and then have students repeat it. Follow the same procedure with *ful.* Tell students that this suffix means "full of."

Now underline the whole word, *thankful,* say it, and then have students repeat it. Explain to students that the suffix changes the meaning of the root word *thank* to "full of thanks."

Form these words on a whiteboard: *joyous, kindness, likeable.* Place the brown ə Touch-unit on top of a vowel if the vowel has a ə sound. Say each word for students. Have them take turns underlining the root word and suffix in each one, saying each word part, and then saying the whole word. You may also want to review how each suffix changes the meaning of the root word.

Model Tell students that they can use what they know about suffixes to build words.

Say *sadly.* Tell students you are going to build *sadly.* Use Touch-units or Magtiles to model.

Pick up the letter *s,* and say its sound as you place it on the whiteboard. Repeat the procedure with the letter *a,* and place it about an inch to the right of the letter *s.* Repeat the procedure again with the letter *d.* Touch *s,* and say its sound. Touch *a,* and say its sound. Touch *d,* and say its sound.

Move the letters closer together, and say their sounds, blending them slightly. Move the letters next to each other and blend the sounds to say *sad.* (You may choose to do this in several steps, moving the letters closer together to demonstrate how to blend.)

Now pick up the letters *ly,* and say their sounds as you place them about an inch to the right of the root word. Touch *ly,* and say their sounds. Tell students that this suffix means "in a certain way."

Move the root word and the suffix together, blending them slightly. Move them next to each other and blend the sounds to say *sadly.* Explain that the suffix changes the meaning of the root word *sad* to "in a sad way."

Then cover the word and spell it orally. Uncover the word and have students compare your spelling with the Touch-units. Cover the word again and write it on the whiteboard. Uncover the word and have students compare the written word with the Touch-units.

Build Words Distribute the Touch-units for the word *useful.* Say *useful.* Have students build it on their whiteboard using the Touch-units. Give help as necessary. Remind students to place the brown ə Touch-unit on top of the second *u* to show the pronunciation of the vowel. After making the word, have students touch and sound each Touch-unit, then blend the sounds as they run their finger underneath the Touch-units. Have students cover the word and spell it orally, then compare their spelling to the Touch-units. Next have them cover the word again and write it on their whiteboard and then on the Build Words page of their Workbook (p. 167). Have students compare their writing to the Touch-units. Then use the same procedure to have students build the following words: *kindness, bendable, action, picture, hardly.*

Use one of the activities on page xvi to further practice sequencing and discriminating the words that students find challenging.

Read Words in Isolation Have students pair up and read all of the words they have written on Workbook page 167 aloud to their partner.

Independent Practice (Workbook page 166) Ask students to write the word that completes each sentence. When students complete the page, have them check their work with you or a partner.

Dictation Dictate the following sentence, and have students write it on their whiteboard or at the bottom of Workbook page 166: *I got a lovely invitation to a wonderful celebration.*

Reading Words in Context

Tell students that they will use what they know about suffixes to read a story.

Build Words from the Story Use the Touch-units to build the following words on the whiteboard. Tell students that the words you will make together will help them read the story.

Start with the word *respectfully.*

Then build the following words: *powerful, golden, dimly, gladly, squeamish, joyous, unforgettable, classical.*

As a prereading activity, you may want to have students find the words in the text and read them aloud.

Read the Story Give students a copy of *Wilhelmina Walrus.* Have them read it independently or with a partner. If necessary, you can support students as they read the story by identifying sight words or helping them to blend sounds to read words.

Respond to the Story After students read *Wilhelmina Walrus,* have them complete Workbook page 168. Have students share their work with the rest of the group.

Lesson 57: Inflectional and Comparison Suffixes

Remind students that they have learned about suffixes that change the meaning of words.

Tell students that today they will learn about more suffixes.

Phonemic Awareness Say the word *dogs.* Emphasize the suffix *s.*

Then say the following words, and have students listen for the suffix in each one: *brushes, paying, asked.*

Link Sounds to Letters Distribute the Touch-units for the word *teacher* (*t, ea, ch, er*). Have students trace each Touch-unit with their finger as they make the sounds together.

Form the word *teacher* on a whiteboard. Underline *teach,* say it, and then have students repeat it. Follow the same procedure with *er.* Tell students that this suffix means "a person who."

Now underline the whole word, *teacher,* say it, and have students repeat it. Explain to them that the suffix changes the meaning of the root word *teach* to "a person who teaches."

Form these words on a whiteboard: *pets, older, fastest.* Say each word for students. Have them take turns underlining the root word and suffix in each one, saying each word part, and then saying the whole word. You may also want to review how each suffix changes the meaning of the root word.

Build Words (Model) Tell students that they can use what they know about suffixes to build words.

Say *longer.* Tell students you are going to build *longer.* Use Touch-units or Magtiles to model.

Pick up the letter *l,* and say its sound as you place it on the whiteboard. Repeat the procedure with the letter *o,* and place it about an inch to the right of the letter *l.* Repeat the procedure again with the letters *ng.* Touch *l,* and say its sound. Touch *o,* and say its sound. Touch *ng,* and say their sounds.

Move the letters closer together, and say their sounds, blending them slightly. Move the letters next to each other and blend the sounds to say *long.* (You may choose to do this in several steps, moving the letters closer together to demonstrate how to blend.)

Now pick up the letters *er,* and say their sound as you place them about an inch to the right of the root word. Touch *er,* and say their sound.

Move the root word and the suffix together, blending them slightly. Move them next to each other and blend the sounds to say *longer.*

Then cover the word and spell it orally. Uncover the word and have students compare your spelling with the Touch-units. Cover the word again and write it on the whiteboard. Uncover the word and have students compare the written word with the Touch-units.

Build Words Distribute the Touch-units for the word *standing.* Say *standing.* Have students build it on their whiteboard using the Touch-units. Give help as necessary. After making the word, have students touch and sound each Touch-unit, then blend the sounds as they run their finger underneath the Touch-units. Have students cover the word and spell it orally, then compare their spelling to the Touch-units. Next have them cover the word again and write it on their whiteboard and then on the Build Words page of their Workbook (p. 170). Have students compare their writing to the Touch-units. Then use the same procedure to have students build the following words: *takes, dresses, desks, asked, helping, taller, younger.*

Use one of the activities on page xvi to further practice sequencing and discriminating the words that students find challenging.

Read Words in Isolation Have students pair up and read all of the words they have written on Workbook page 170 aloud to their partner.

Independent Practice (Workbook page 169) Ask students to write the word that completes each sentence. When students complete the page, have them check their work with you or a partner.

Dictation Dictate the following sentence, and have students write it on their whiteboard or at the bottom of Workbook page 169: *The birds landed in the highest branches of the tree.*

Reading Words in Context

Tell students that they will use what they know about suffixes to read a selection.

Build Words from the Selection Use the Touch-units to build the following words on the whiteboard. Tell students that the words you will make together will help them read the selection.

Start with the word *lower.*

Then build the following words: *means, shines, becomes, beaches, branches, bunches, beaks, bubbles, crabs, calming, crashing, bolder, closer, thinkers, cluster, dearest.*

As a prereading activity, you may want to have students find the words in the text and read them aloud.

Read the Selection Give students a copy of *The Pacific Coast.* Have them read it independently or with a partner. If necessary, you can support students as they read the selection by identifying sight words or helping them to blend sounds to read words.

Respond to the Selection After students read *The Pacific Coast,* have them complete Workbook page 171. Have students share their work with the rest of the group.

Lesson 58: Prefixes with Meanings

Remind students that they have learned about word parts called suffixes that come at the end of words.

Tell them that today they are going to learn about word parts that come at the beginning of words. These are called prefixes.

Phonemic Awareness Say the word *unkind.* Emphasize the prefix *un.*

Then say the following words, and have students listen for the prefix in each one: *recap, inform, uncommon.*

Link Sounds to Letters Distribute the Touch-units for the word *rewrite* (*re, wr, i, t,* silent *e*). Have students trace each Touch-unit with their finger as they make the sounds together.

Form the word *rewrite* on a whiteboard. Underline the prefix *re,* say it, and then have students repeat it. Tell students that this prefix means "again" or "back." Follow the same procedure with *write.*

Now underline the whole word, *rewrite,* say it, and then have students repeat it. Explain to students that the suffix changes the meaning of the root word *write* to "write again."

Form these words on a whiteboard: *defrost, explode, across, impossible, perform, progress, preview, confuse, endanger, disappear.* Say each word for students, and have them take turns underlining the prefix and root word, saying each word part, and then saying the whole word. You may also want to review how each prefix changes the meaning of the root word.

Build Words (Model) Tell students that they can use what they know about prefixes to build words.

Say *resend.* Tell students you are going to build *resend.* Use Touch-units or Magtiles to model.

Pick up the letters *re,* and say their sound as you place them on the whiteboard.

Then pick up the letter *s,* and say its sound as you place it on the whiteboard. Repeat the procedure with the letter *e,* and place it about an inch to the right of the letter *s.* Repeat the procedure again with the letters *nd.* Touch *s,* and say its sound. Touch *e,* and say its sound. Touch *nd,* and say their sounds

Move the letters in the root word closer together, and say their sounds, blending them slightly. Move the letters next to each other and blend the sounds to say *send.*

Now move the prefix and root word together, blending them slightly. Move them next to each other and blend the sounds to say *resend.*

Then cover the word and spell it orally. Uncover the word and have students compare your spelling with the Touch-units. Cover the word again and write it on the whiteboard. Uncover the word and have students compare the written word with the Touch-units.

Build Words Distribute the Touch-units for the word *depart.* Say *depart.* Have students build it on their whiteboard using the Touch-units. Give help as necessary. After making the word, have students touch and sound each Touch-unit, then blend the sounds as they run their finger underneath the Touch-units. Have students cover the word and spell it orally, then compare their spelling to the Touch-units. Next have them cover the word again and write it on their whiteboard and then on the Build Words page of their Workbook (p. 173). Have students compare their writing to the Touch-units. Then use this procedure to have students build the following words: *extend, around, unable, permit, predict, contest.*

Use one of the activities on page xvi to further practice sequencing and discriminating the words that students find challenging.

Read Words in Isolation Have students pair up and read all of the words they have written on Workbook page 173 aloud to their partner.

Independent Practice (Workbook page 172) Ask students to write the word that completes each sentence. When students complete the page, have them check their work with you or a partner.

Dictation Dictate the following sentence, and have students write it on their whiteboard or at the bottom of Workbook page 172: *I'm unable to recall the time they will depart on their trip.*

Reading Words in Context

Tell students that they will use what they know about prefixes to read a selection.

Build Words from the Selection Use the Touch-units to build the following words on the whiteboard. Tell students that the words you will make together will help them read the selection.

Start with the word *aboard.*

Then build the following words: *describe, disgusting, expect, impressed, inform, submerged, predict, persuade, recap, uncommon, composed, confused, production.*

As a prereading activity, you may want to have students find the words in the text and read them aloud.

Read the Selection Give students a copy of *The Whale Event.* Have them read it independently or with a partner. If necessary, you can support students as they read the selection by identifying sight words or helping them to blend sounds to read words.

Respond to the Selection After students read *The Whale Event,* have them complete Workbook page 174. Have students share their work with the rest of the group.

READ THE STORY
The Whale Event

ADDITIONAL READING
This EPS reader provides an additional story in which to practice *Prefixes with Meanings.*

SPIRE Decodables

The Shark
Set 6A, Book 1

Lesson 59: Borrowed Sounds

Remind students that they have learned that different letter combinations make different sounds.

Tell students that today they will learn the sounds that some combinations make. These combinations sound like other sounds that they already know. They borrow their sounds.

Phonemic Awareness Say the word *action.* Emphasize the *sh* sound that *ti* makes. Then say the following words, and have students listen for the *sh* sound in each one: *delicious, chef, surely.*

Now say the word *adventure.* Emphasize the *ch* sound that *tu* makes. Then say the following words, and have students listen for the *ch* sound in each one: *mixture, ancient.*

Finally, say the word *laugh.* Emphasize the *f* sound that *gh* makes. Then say the following words, and have students listen for the *f* sound in each one: *cough, photo.*

Link Sound to Letters Distribute the *si* Touch-unit. Have students trace its shape with their finger as they make the sound for *si* together.

Form the following word on a whiteboard: *vision.* Say the word, emphasizing the *si* sound. Then underline the *si* in the word.

Tell students that the *si* sometimes makes the sound they hear in the middle of *vision.* Isolate the sound for students, and then have them repeat it after you.

Distribute the *ti* and *ci* Touch-units and repeat the procedure above with the words *direction* and *musician.* Explain to students that *ti* and *ci* sometimes make the *sh* sound.

Now distribute the *t* and *u* Touch-units. Repeat the procedure again to form the word *mixture.* Tell students that *tu* can sometimes make the *ch* sound they hear in the middle of *mixture.*

Repeat the procedure again with the word *ancient.* Explain to students that the *ci* sometimes also makes the *ch* sound.

Then distribute the *gh* Touch-unit. Repeat the procedure again to form the word *cough.* Tell students that the *gh* sometimes makes the *f* sound they hear at the end of *cough.*

Finally, distribute the *ph* Touch-unit. Repeat the procedure again to form the word *photo.* Explain to students that the *ph* sometimes also makes the *f* sound.

Build Words (Model) Tell students that they can use what they know about borrowed sounds to build words.

Say *chef.* Tell students you are going to build *chef.* Use Touch-units or Magtiles to model.

Pick up the letters *ch,* and say their sound as you place them on the whiteboard. Repeat the procedure with the letter *e,* and place it about an inch to the right of the letters *ch.* Repeat the procedure again with the letter *f.* Touch *ch,* and say their sound. Touch *e,* and say its sound. Touch *f,* and say its sound.

Move the letters closer together, and say their sounds, blending them slightly. Move the letters next to each other and blend the sounds to say *chef.*

Then cover the word and spell it orally. Uncover the word and have students compare your spelling with the Touch-units. Cover the word again and write it on the whiteboard. Uncover the word and have students compare the written word with the Touch-units.

Repeat the procedure with the words *attention* and *phantom.*

Build Words Distribute Touch-units. Say the word *attraction.* Have students build it on their whiteboard using the Touch-units. Give help as necessary. After making the word, have students touch and sound each Touch-unit, then blend the sounds as they run their finger underneath the Touch-units. Have students cover the word and spell it orally, then compare their spelling to the Touch-units. Next have them cover the word again and write it on their whiteboard and then on the Build Words page of their Workbook

(p. 176). Have students compare their writing to the Touch-units.

Then use the same procedure to have students build the following words: *measure, fixture, phone, tough, mansion.* Help students understand that you can change words by substituting letters.

Use one of the activities on page xvi to further practice sequencing and discriminating the words that students find challenging.

Read Words in Isolation Have students pair up and read all of the words they have written on Workbook page 176 aloud to their partner.

Independent Practice (Workbook page 175) Ask students to write the word that completes each sentence. When students complete the page, have them check their work with you or a partner.

Dictation Dictate the following sentence, and have students write on their whiteboard or at the bottom of Workbook page 175: *The special photo machine went into action.*

Reading Words in Context

Tell students that they will use what they know about words with borrowed sounds to read a story.

Build Words from the Story Use the Touch-units to build the following words on the whiteboard. Tell students that the words you will make together will help them read the story.

Start with the word *action.*

Substitute Touch-units to build the following words: *attention, attraction, mansion, occasion, confusion, ambitious, cautious, delicious, gracious, machine, chef, measured, surely, mixture, ancient, laughed, photographer.*

As a prereading activity, you may want to have students find the words in the text and read them aloud.

Read the Story Give students a copy of *The Celebration.* Have them read it independently or with a partner. If necessary, you can support students as they read the story by identifying sight words or helping them to blend sounds to read words.

Respond to the Story After students read *The Celebration*, have them complete Workbook page 177. Have students share their work with the rest of the group.

Word Lists

Compound Words				
everybody	without	sunset	baseball	birthday
nobody	within	daytime	basketball	breakfast
anything	outside	daylight	airplane	backyard
whenever	inside	sunlight	bedroom	raincoat
however	cannot	sunshine	bathroom	fireplace
	upset	football	earthquake	

Contractions				
I've	they'll	isn't	it's	I'd
you've	I'll	didn't	here's	you'd
they've	we'll	don't	what's	they'd
we've	can't	won't	that's	he'd
you'll	wouldn't	hasn't	I'm	she'd
she'll	couldn't	weren't	they're	we'd
he'll	aren't	he's	we're	let's
		she's	you're	

Open and Closed Syllables and ə

Open Syllables	Closed Syllables	ə
pi-lot	cab-in	doll-ar
pu-pil	vel-vet	cot-ton
be-gin	sel-fish	mel-on
ho-tel	rab-bit	fav-or
ti-ger	gos-sip	anch-or
be-gan	com-mit	farm-er
go-pher	hap-pen	
va-ca-tion	tun-net	
po-ny		
di-ary		
he-ro		
ru-in		
di-et		
va-por		
la-bor		
pa-per		
ze-bra		
be-leive		
be-long		
hu-man		
de-ny		
stu-pid		
po-et		
fi-nal		

Syllables with *le*					
ple	**tle**	**dle**	**ble**	**cle**	**fle**
staple	title	idle	cable	circle	rifle
people		cradle	table	article	trifle
maple	little	bridle	stable	bicycle	stifle
triple	cattle	handle	fable	uncle	
	bottle	needle	able	oracle	baffle
apple	settle		trouble	particle	duffle
cripple		fiddle	tremble	miracle	raffle
		muddle		obstacle	scuffle
		huddle	babble	vehicle	shuffle
		meddle	dabble	icicle	sniffle
		middle	pebble	popsicle	muffle
		saddle	dribble		ruffle
		toddle	nibble		waffle
		puddle	gobble		
			cobble		
			wobble		
			bubble		

Suffixes and Prefixes: Suffixes
Beginning with a Consonant

y	ful	ness	tion cion sion	sure ture	ly
(1)	(1)	(1)	(1)	(1)	(1)
stormy	thankful	stubbornness	attention	measure	hardly
cloudy	cheerful	illness	mention	treasure	partly
rainy	cupful	kindness	question	leisure	gladly
bloody	handful	witness	contention	unsure	suddenly
lucky	harmful	blindness	emotion	picture	sadly
curly	forgetful	goodness		capture	dimly
sandy	wonderful	(3)	extension	adventure	(2)
sleepy	powerful	completeness	confusion	future	vocally
tricky	(3)	gentleness	television	mixture	personally
dirty	hopeful	(4)	explosion	(2)	especially
angry	useful	happiness		assure	respectfully
speedy	careful	laziness	coercion	reassure	carefully
(2)		steadiness	suspicion	pressure	hopefully
messy		loneliness	(2)	fissure	mentally
snappy		readiness	profession		(3)
floppy		loveliness	impression		likely
happy			confession		safely
funny			session		largely
sunny					surely
(3)					scarcely
easy					lonely
flaky					lovely
					ultimately
					completely
					attentively
					shapely
					safely
					timely
					(4)
					easily
					happily
					sleepily
					readily

1) Closed Syllable: Has consonant at the beginning and the end of the syllable.
2) Doubling: 1 syllable; 1 single vowel; 1 final consonant
3) final "e": Drop "e" with vowel suffix. Keep "e" with consonant suffix.
4) Spelling Change: Exchange "y" for "i" except with "ing". Exchange "f" for "v".

Suffixes and Prefixes: Suffixes

Beginning with a Vowel

al ə	il ə	ous us	ive	ary	ish	age
(1)	(1)	(1)	(1)	(1)	(1)	(1)
pedal	pupil	famous	sensitive	ordinary	foolish	courage
signal	fossil	nervous	attractive	stationary	boyish	damage
central		humorous	defensive	missionary	girlish	voyage
total		joyous	active	military	childish	bandage
mortal		perilous	elective	library	squeamish	manage
normal		thunderous	native	salary	finish	garbage
royal		mysterious	productive	contrary	(2)	package
several		dangerous	fugitive	ordinary	clannish	postage
magical		rigorous	detective	dictionary	reddish	image
animal		hazardous	(2)	(3)	mannish	footage
rural		mountainous	massive	primary		(2)
liberal		enormous	passive			cottage
oval		wondrous	(3)			baggage
verbal		(3)	relative			luggage
dental		courageous	repulsive			cabbage
renewal		ridiculous	expensive			passage
(3)		delicious	negative			village
bridal		contagious				message
fatal						(3)
brutal						acreage
reversal						mileage
natural						marriage
primal						carriage
(4)						
denial						
trial						
classical						
physical						
lyrical						

1) Closed Syllable: Has consonant at the beginning and the end of the syllable.
2) Doubling: 1 syllable; 1 single vowel; 1 final consonant
3) final "e": Drop "e" with vowel suffix. Keep "e" with consonant suffix.
4) Spelling Change: Exchange "y" for "i" except with "ing". Exchange "f" for "v".

Suffixes and Prefixes: Suffixes Beginning with a Vowel (continued)			
ic	**ible* able**	**en**	**ent ant* ance***
(1)	(1)	(1)	(1)
fantastic	tangible	eaten	excellent
magic	eligible	beaten	frequent
lyric	incredible	shorten	patient
phonic	corruptible	golden	sufficient
poetic	resistible	harden	efficient
comic	legible	sharpen	lenient
frantic	comfortable	frighten	expedient
heroic	readable	silken	consequent
critic	(2)	darken	delinquent
relic	possible	(2)	proficient
bionic	accessible	hidden	obedient
	horrible	gotten	client
	terrible	bitten	student
	regrettable	happen	opponent
	(3)	(3)	(4)
	invincible	taken	reliant
	producible	broken	defiant
	sensible		defiance
	forcible		ignorance
	legible		ignorant
	durable		
	movable		
	usable		
	reputable		
	variable		

1) Closed Syllable: Has consonant at the beginning and the end of the syllable.
2) Doubling: 1 syllable; 1 single vowel; 1 final consonant
3) final "e": Drop "e" with vowel suffix. Keep "e" with consonant suffix.
4) Spelling Change: Exchange "y" for "i" except with "ing". Exchange "f" for "v".

Suffixes and Prefixes: Inflectional and Comparison Suffixes

s	es	ed (/t/)	ed (/ed/)	ed (/d/)	er	est	ing
(1)	(1)	(1)	(1)	(1)	(1)	(1)	(1)
pets	fixes	asked	cheated	cleaned	farmer	slowest	eating
hats	boxes	fixed	shouted	chewed	worker	highest	beating
nuts		laughed	wanted	boiled	eater	nearest	working
birds	fishes		planted	climbed	beater	oldest	farming
ducks	dishes	cracked	landed	learned		darkest	jumping
worms	pushes	wished	acted	played	sharper	longest	starting
		walked	needed	crawled	harder	(2)	singing
walks	bunches	soaked	hunted	sailed	quicker	biggest	barking
runs	branches	helped	granted	cooled	richer	saddest	hunting
jumps	touches	romped	sifted	followed	(2)	maddest	laughing
flaps	(2)	dished	dented	(2)	upper	hottest	(2)
asks	buzzes	licked	painted	scrubbed	bigger	(3)	mopping
laughs	dresses	jumped	loaded	robbed	clipper	latest	hopping
(3)	glasses	(2)	(2)	grabbed	hotter	finest	winning
bites	(3)	stopped	batted	grinned	robber	(4)	planning
caves	horses	dropped	spotted	trimmed	sadder	cloudiest	(3)
(4)	chooses	skipped	padded	begged	madder	noisiest	dancing
cries	bases	slipped	plotted	hugged	dinner	finniest	taking
worries	(4)	flapped	fitted	plugged	(3)	sleepiest	hiding
carries	elves	hopped*	petted	(4)	taker	flakiest	hoping
cities	shelves	(3)		tried	broker		riding
	halves	raced		cried	later		(4)
		hoped		applied	diner		crying
		baked		carried	(4)		buying
		chased		worried	copier		trying
				relied	heavier		flying
				studied	easier		carrying
							obeying

1) Closed Syllable: Has consonant at the beginning and the end of the syllable.
2) Doubling: 1 syllable; 1 single vowel; 1 final consonant
3) final "e": Drop "e" with vowel suffix. Keep "e" with consonant suffix.
4) Spelling Change: Exchange "y" for "i" except with "ing". Exchange "f" for "v".

Suffixes and Prefixes: Prefixes with Meaning

a	in	un	de	ex	en	dis
	inactive	unable	debate	exact	enclose	disable
about	incapable	undo	decent	examine	encourage	discard
above	income	undone	decide	excellent	enforce	discount
across	incomplete	uneven	deduct	excess	engage	discourage
afraid	independent	unfair	defeat	excite	enjoy	discover
agree	indirect	unfold	defend	exhaust	enlarge	discuss
ahead	indoor	unguarded	defrost	exile	enlist	disgrace
alert	infer	unhappy	deject	exit	enrich	disgust
alike	infield	unkind	delay	expect	enroll	dislike
alive	insecure	unlike	deliver	explode	ensure	dismiss
along	inspect	unnatural	demand	express	entrust	disobey
aloud	intake	unopened	depart	extend		disorder
among	intend	unreal	depend	external	**pro**	displace
arise		unscrew	deport	extract	proceed	disrespect
around	**im**	unselfish	depress		process	disrupt
asleep	immature	unsettled	deserve	**pre**	produce	distract
await	immodest	unskilled	detail	predict	product	
awake	immortal	untied	detain	prefer	production	**per**
	immoral	untrue	detract	prejudge	program	perform
re	impasse	unwind		prepare	project	permit
react	impatient		**com**	prescription	promote	persist
redo	imply	**con**	combine	present	propose	
redone	import	conduct	comfort	pretend	protest	
reduce	impress	confer	comment	prevent		
Reference:	imprint	conform	commit			
refuse		confuse	common			
regret		connect	compete			
reject		consult	compose			
retract		content	compound			
return		contest				
		contract				
		control				
		convict				

Borrowed Sounds				
ti	**ci**	**si as /sh/**	**gh**	**ph**
patience	precious	mansion	coughing	elephant
substantial	vicious	suspension	laughing	phonograph
essential	gracious	session	rougher	alphabet
potential	facial	admission	tougher	phonics
ambitious	musician	compression		
fraction	special	depression		
partial	ancient	discussion		
credential	social	**si as /zh/**		
imagination	luscious	illusion		
attention	official	division		
	racial	revision		
		fusion		
		explosion		
		confusion		
		excursion		

Appendices

Prereading Activities

To decide which Prereading Activities to do with students, refer to their results on the *Touchphonics* Consonant Inventory (page 170). You can do the Letter Names and Consonant Sounds Prereading Activities with students who cannot name a significant number of letters or identify the sounds of many of the single consonants. If students are shaky on only some letter names and consonant sounds, these can be learned or rediscovered during the Consonant Warm-up and other lessons. If students know the names of every letter and the sounds of the single consonants, they are ready to start the *Touchphonics* lessons. For students who lack story and book concepts, we recommend the Book Conventions and Learning about Stories activities.

Letter Names and Consonant Sounds

The objective of these activities is to help students learn the names of all the letters and the sounds of the consonants. You can do these activities with just a few letters at a time, and repeat them as necessary to cover all the letters.

Single consonants that have their sound at the beginning of their name are easy to identify when using their name as a referent, and can be taught first. These single consonants are *b, d, j, k, p, t, v* and *z*.

Single consonants that have their sound at the end of their name are often more difficult for students to learn, and can be taught next. These single consonants are *f, l, m, n, s, r* and *x*. Teaching these sounds as a group and identifying the end of the letter name as the place to listen for the sound represented by the letter helps students become aware of the segmentation of sounds in a word. It introduces the concept that a sound can be heard in various places within a word. You can tell students, for example, to name the letter that makes the /f/ sound. Then ask them if they hear the sound /f/ at the end of the letter *f*.

Single consonants that have a sound that is unrelated to their name are often the most difficult for students to learn, and can be taught last. These single consonants are *c, g, h, qu, y* and *w*. Some students may need a personal or meaningful item as a referent to help them remember both the letter and the sound it represents. For example, you could tell students that the sound of *h* is like the sound of puffing as you are climbing a hill.

> **Note:** *q* has no sound by itself. It is taught as *qu*, decoded as the sound /kw/, and is included as a single Touch-unit phoneme.

> **Note:** Consonants must be pronounced without voicing a vowel sound at the end. Example: b is pronounced /b/, not /buh/. Single-consonant sounds that are more difficult to pronounce in isolation without a vowel added are often referred to as "plosives." They are: *b, d, k, j, p, t, w,* and *y*, the /k/ sound of *c* as in *cat*, the /g/ sound of *g* as in *got*, the *qu* sound, and the digraphs *ch, wh,* and the two sounds of *th.*

Environmental Letters Have students learn to say the letters in their names and in the names of other students in the class. This activity can be extended to learning to spell other highly meaningful words, such as students' favorite snacks, toys, or other familiar objects.

Making Sounds As students are learning the sounds of consonants, remind them to look at your mouth as you say a sound. Ask them what position your lips, tongue, and teeth are in. Have them imitate those positions and look in mirrors to see if they are doing it correctly as they make the correct sounds.

Picture-Sound Sort Draw or cut out pictures of animals, foods, or other items that start with the sounds of the consonants that you are teaching. Glue each picture on a plain 3x5 card. Have students name the picture. Ask them to say just the first sound of the picture. Write the corresponding letter under the picture or on the back of the card. Place one picture of each beginning sound in its own plastic bag or other container, or write the letter on the bag or box. Then have students put all of the picture cards that have the same sound into the correct bag or box. Then ask questions such as, "Which bag is for pictures whose names start with /k/?"

Touch-unit and Picture-Sound Sort Put 4 or 5 yellow single-consonant Touch-units that students need to learn on the table. Hand them several of the picture cards that were made for the Picture-Sound Sort. Tell students to pick out only the picture cards that start with the sounds of the letters on the table and put each set of picture cards in a pile under the appropriate Touch-unit. Place more Touch-units and picture cards on the table and follow the same procedure. Variation: Use small objects instead of picture cards.

Touch-unit Letter Practice

1. Lay out two or three Touch-units of single consonants.
2. Point to the first letter.
3. Ask students to tell you the letter name.
4. Ask students to tell you the letter sound.
5. Ask students to write the letter as you say its sound.
6. Ask students to tell you something that begins with that sound.
7. Ask students the name of the letter that says that sound.

Repeat the above steps with the next set of consonants. Spend more time with letters that give the students difficulty, but don't neglect to include known letters so that students can feel success and progress. Follow similar procedures for the single vowel Touch-units, but follow steps 1–3 only.

My Own Alphabet Book Make a little book for each letter with pictures that each student draws or cuts from a magazine and pastes on the page. Use one page for each letter. Use students' choices of pictures for the consonants, but suggest pictures for the vowels that start with the short vowel sounds. Check each one to be sure it is correct. Have each student be the author of his or her book and title the book "My Own Alphabet Book" by _____ (student's name). You can have students make the pages in alphabetic order, or you can have students start with the letters they know for the first pages of the book. This can be an "add onto" book as other pictures are found that start with the same letter sound and/or as students learn more letters by name and sound. Have each student write the letter in both upper and lower case on each page. You can help students label the pictures, but let them write the first letter of the label. As soon as it has a few pages, ask students to read the book to you and to others.

Book Conventions

Who Made This Book? Give students books that you have selected to share together. These can be books with a simple text such as an alphabet book, a concept book, or a picture book. Point out the names of the author and illustrator. Explain the role that each of these has had in making the book. Ask students to choose another book and tell where the names of the author and illustrator appear, and tell what each of them does to make the book.

Directions for Reading Show students a book with just one or two lines printed on each page. If you have a Big Book, it is useful for this activity. Demonstrate which way you go through the book as you turn the pages. Move your finger under words from left to right. At the end of the first line sweep back to the left to begin the next line. Point to each word as you read the line or lines on each page. After you have read through the entire story, re-read it asking questions such as, "Do I start here, or here?" (Point to the beginning of the line and the end of the line), "Which way do I go?" and "Where do I go now?" Have students show you which direction to turn the page.

Learning about Stories

Discover Story Structure A story structure includes:
Beginning—Characters and Setting
Middle—Plot, Problem, and Events
End—The Problem Resolution and Conclusion
Choose an appropriate and inviting book with the story elements listed above. As you read the story to students, talk about the characters, the setting, the main plot or problem and the ending/solution. Ask questions such as who did what, when, and how. Pause after you read the problem, and after each successive event and the solution to the problem.

Summarize Picture books can be used for plot strategies you have modeled, so that students can tell the stories themselves, recognizing the elements of the plot. After you finish a story, ask students to tell you about the characters and setting, summarize what happened, and tell how it ended. Guide students to focus on summarizing rather than relating less necessary details.

Reader Response Choose a book with a simple storyline for this activity. As you read the story to the class, talk about the characters, the setting, the main plot or problem, and the ending or the solution. Ask questions that cannot be answered by "yes" or "no." Ask for details of who did what, when, and how. Ask cause and effect questions, such as "What will happen if ...", or "What would have happened if ...?" Lead students to make statements that express a personal opinion, such as "I thought this happened because ...," "My favorite part was ...," "It didn't make sense when ...," "I liked the part when ...," or "I didn't like ... ." These types of questions help build critical thinking skills.

Phonemic Awareness Activities

Find the Rhyme One of the best ways for students to begin comparing and hearing sounds is for you to model rhyming. For example, say *wish* and *fish* and tell students that there are three separate sounds in both of these word, and then pronounce the sounds slowly for them: /w/, /i/, /sh/, and /f/, /i/, /sh/. Ask students if they can hear sounds that are the same in both words, then discuss how the second and last sounds are the same. You can also draw students' attention to rhymes in writing and to patterns in words. Call students' attention to rhyming with stories and poems that rhyme; then begin to ask: "Do these words rhyme: *fish* and *dish*? What about *hill* and *mop*?" When presenting pairs of words that students should recognize as nonrhyming, choose words that do not have the same ending sound or vowel sound. Only after students have a good grasp of rhyme should you start presenting nonrhyming word pairs that share some sounds.

Same Sound/Beginning Have students listen to two words and determine if the two words begin with the same sound. First model: "Listen to the words *team* and *test.* They both have the same beginning sound. Can you hear it? It is the sound /t/. *Team, test.* Now listen to the words *happy* and *soup.* They don't have the same starting sound. Can you tell?" Then encourage students' participation: "I am going to say two words. Tell me if they start with the same sound: *monkey, mother.* Listen again: *monkey, mother.*" When presenting word pairs that don't have the same beginning sound, start with words that are very different in sound like *sun* and *cat.* Move toward beginning sounds that are harder to distinguish, like these pairs: /b/ and /d/, /b/ and /v/, /t/ and /d/, /m/ and /n/. If students are having difficulty with these sounds, have them watch your lips as you pronounce the word pairs.

Break It Up Model this sound segmentation activity first: "I am going to say a word. Then I am going to say each sound in the word. The word is *top*. The sounds in *top* are /t/, /o/, /p/." (Be sure to articulate each sound separately. Do not stretch out the word or the sounds.) Then have students reproduce the sounds. Next model this procedure: "Listen to this word. This time, you tell me the sounds in the word. Listen carefully: *man*. Break up the word into its separate sounds. What sounds do you hear in *man*?" Students will produce the sounds /m/, /a/, /n/.

Sound Count While students are learning sound segmentation, have them hold up fingers for each sound they produce. Model this activity by counting on your fingers as you say each sound of a word, then looking at your fingers to see how many sounds were in the word. You can say, "How many sounds were in *cat*? How many fingers did I hold up?"

Quack, Quack, Quack Poetry, song, and rhythmic stories are helpful when modeling phonemic awareness and fluent reading. Print this poem on the chalkboard, and read it aloud to students. Then, read it again and have them read along with you, listening for the /kw/ and gesturing with a "thumbs up" sign whenever they hear it.

Quacking Is Easy
Quack very quietly. Quack Quack Quack
Quack like you're queasy. Quack Quack Quack
Quack me a question. Quack? Quack? Quack?
Quacking is easy! Quack Quack Quack

Quack very quickly. Quack Quack Quack
Quack like a duck queen. Quack Quack Quack!
Quack with a quiver. Quack Quack Quack
Quacking is keen! Quack Quack Quack

Look at the Sound Small mirrors are very effective in helping students discriminate between different sounds.

Teach students to discriminate between the /m/ and /n/ sounds, for example, with the following dialogue: "Look at me as I say /m/. Do you see how my lips come together? Now look at me as I say /n/. My lips aren't together. Now make the /m/ sound yourself. Can you feel and see in the mirror how your lips come together? Now make the /n/ sound and feel the tip of your tongue touch the roof of your mouth. Look in the mirror, and notice that your lips aren't together. Say /m/, then /n/, and look at your mouth in the mirror as you say each sound." Check for how students are pronouncing the sound, correct students, then repeat. Give some examples of words that have the sound in them. Then tell students to look in the mirror and say the sound several times, then say a word with the sound in it, looking for the sound in the mirror.

As students look in the mirror, ask them the following questions to lead them to focus on the physical aspects of making the sound:

1. What shape is your mouth as you say the sound?
2. Tell me about your teeth. Are they together? Apart? Can you even see them?
3. Where is your tongue? Is it pressing against any part of your mouth? Do you need your tongue to help you pronounce this sound?
4. Is any air coming out of your mouth? Put your hand close to your mouth and say the sound. Which way is the air coming out? Is it coming out downwards, upwards, or straight out?
5. How does your nose function when you make this sound?
6. Where do you make the sound? Touch your throat and neck area.

Additional Word Activities

These are fun activities for reinforcing concepts learned in the *Touchphonics* lessons. You can involve students in these activities when you need an instructional session to vary the routine.

Word Ladders Draw a ladder on a piece of paper. Choose a word and write it on the top rung of the ladder. Using Touch-units, make the word and have a student change one unit at a time and write the new word on the next rung of the latter. At every rung of the ladder, the student changes one letter and creates a new word (for example: farm to form, form to fort, etc.). There is nearly always more than one possibility to change. It's fun for students to see how many steps on the ladder can be filled in.

Example Word Ladder:

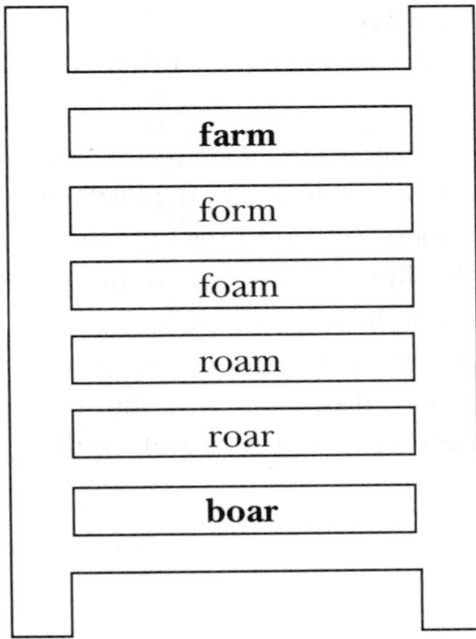

Pick a Touch-unit To prepare, choose about 15 Touch-units and place them in a box or opaque bag. Scatter 8 more Touch-units (3 consonants and one each of the 5 vowels) on the table. Situate students around a table and give each of them a sheet of lined paper and a pencil. During a turn, the student picks one Touch-unit from the box or bag, places it on the table with the scattered Touch-units, and tries to build as many words as possible from all the Touch-units on the table. You may want to set a time limit for each student's turn. At the end of the turn, the student writes the words built on the lined paper and re-scatters the Touch-units that are on the table. The game ends when there are no more Touch-units in the box. The winner is the one with the most words written down.

Tips and variations

- Acceptable words can be defined in advance; for example, you may choose to limit them to words found in the dictionary, or to not allow proper nouns or abbreviations.
- For extended play, increase the number of Touch-units in the box.
- To focus on a recently learned concept and tie the game into the current lesson, you can stipulate which Touch-units to use in words. For example, if you want to review the *th, ch,* and *sh* concepts, you can make a rule such as "Each word built must contain a *th, ch,* or *sh* Touch-unit."

Word Sorts You can make a set of index cards with words on them and ask students to sort the cards to classify the words by sound patterns or other similar attributes that you select to focus on. Sorts can include:

- phonograms
- beginning sounds
- ending sounds
- vowel sounds
- alphabetical order

Word Rings Word cards, perhaps those used in Word Sorts, are a popular way of building students' automaticity. Putting a set of cards on a ring for each student gives that student a chance to see the words repeatedly.

After working with new words, reading a story, or completing a *Touchphonics* lesson, choose words to focus on for structure and vocabulary. Give students these words on index cards to add to their Word Rings. You can take four or five minutes of class time and have students go through their Word Rings, reading each card first alone and then to a partner. This way, even though they have finished a story or lesson, students will continue to practice words and vocabulary they may not have mastered with a single exposure. If you wish, you can mark the cards with a sticker or star as students demonstrate that they have learned the word and can read it automatically.

Word Walls A Word Wall can be a useful tool for reading and writing activities. To make a Word Wall, categorize often-used words and write them on large cards, mounting them on one wall of the classroom. The words can be categorized by graphophonemic units ("s" blends, single "a" sound words, "tch" words, sight words, etc.); alphabetic order; or by theme (e.g. weather, space, animals). Students can refer to these groups of words while they are reading and writing. If you wish, you can color the target graphophonemic unit in the word to match the color of the corresponding Touch-unit.

Assessments

Assessment and evaluation should be used to guide and monitor instruction. The two *Touchphonics* inventories below can be given as diagnostics at the beginning of instruction, and as assessments after completing a part of the program or the whole program.

The *Touchphonics* Diagnostic/Assessment Tools include:

- The *Touchphonics* Consonant Inventory
- The *Touchphonics* Diagnostic Inventory
- Information about keeping Running Records for assessing reading accuracy, analyzing student errors, and establishing reading levels

Touchphonics Consonant Inventory

You can determine students' level of knowledge of the names and sounds of letters and their ability to write them by conducting a simple test. First, you will want to determine which letters a student can name, sound, and write. After completing the inventory, refer to your score sheet to take note of the letters that need special attention, and focus on them during the Prereading activities, the Consonant Warm-up, and the Reading Lessons.

The Letter Names Begin with the consonants. Place all the single consonants on the workspace in the order they appear on the Score Sheet on p.171. Point to each of the consonant letters, in order, and ask the student to say its name.

The Letter Sounds Using the same procedures as above, ask the student to say the sound of each letter as you point to it. If students respond with the letter's name, say, for example, "Yes, that's right, that letter is *m*. What sound does *m* make?" Mark the results on your score sheet.

Writing the Letters Take away the Touch-units and ask students to write each consonant as you say its name. Indicate the results on your score sheet. Then ask the student to write each letter as you say its sound. Mark the results on your score sheet.

Touchphonics Consonant Inventory Score Sheet

Name ______________________________ Date ____________

Grade ________ Age ________ Teacher ______________________

Check the boxes that students know and leave blank the ones they are not able to name, sound or write.

1. Point to each Touch-unit indicated and ask students to say its name.
2. Point to each Touch-unit indicated and ask students to say its sound.
3. Say the name of the letter and ask students to write it.
4. Say the sound of the letter and ask students to write it.

Letter	1. Say Name	2. Say Sound	3. Write Letter	4. Write Sound
b				
c				
d				
j				
k				
p				
t				
v				
z				
f				
l				
m				
n				
s				
r				
x				
g				
h				
qu				
y				
w				

Touchphonics Diagnostic Inventory

Introduction

The *Touchphonics* Diagnostic Inventory is a tool for assessing students' knowledge of phoneme and grapheme units through encoding and decoding tasks. The units that are not readily recognized and used should become the targeted units and patterns for instruction. The known units should also be practiced for positive reinforcement.

Score Sheet, Test Cards, and Instructions for Delivery

The Score Sheet and Test Cards can be reproduced. Make a copy of each and cut the Test Cards apart. Keep the cards in numerical order and separate into two packs, Decoding and Encoding.

Section 1—Decode

This section assesses to what extent the student is able to recognize word structure patterns while decoding non-words.

The test words are arranged in groups of increasing complexity. The targeted orthographic patterns being assessed are grouped on the Teacher Summary Sheet for easier analysis. For example, Decode cards 2 through 8 assess the student's recognition of the CVC pattern. The other pattern groups include VC, CVCe, C(V+r), CVVC, prefixes, and suffixes, and more.

Instructions for Delivering Section 1

Step 1: Give the student Decoding Test Card 1. It should read: **1. af**

Step 2: Say: "This is not a real word. Tell me what you think it says, and I'll write what you say."

Step 3: Repeat with the following cards. As the student responds to each card, record the exact student response in the blank on the Teacher Score Sheet, which should read: **1. af (VC) (a)** _____. Remind the student, if necessary, that these are not real words. When writing the student's responses, use phonetic spelling and/or mark the vowel sound with diacritical markings.

Note: Because the items increase in difficulty, stop testing if the student is struggling. If, after the first five items, the student has responded incorrectly, the teacher should discontinue the test and go straight to the Consonant Inventory to test the student's knowledge of the letter sounds and names.

Section 2—Encode

This section inventories the phonemes that the student can recognize and use to build a real word. This task is visually oriented and indicates spelling ability.

The test words are arranged in groups of increasing complexity. The targeted graphemes being assessed are grouped on the Teacher Summary Sheet for easier analysis. For example, encode cards 1 through 8 assess the student's recognition and use of initial consonants. The other groups are: final consonants, final vowel *y*, digraphs, single vowels, initial and final consonant blends, silent letters, r-controlled vowels, final *e*, a variety of vowel combinations, and common suffixes.

Instructions for Delivering Section 2

Step 1: Give the student Encoding Test Card 1. It should read: **_ap**

Step 2: Refer to the Score Sheet to get the cue word, *lap*. The missing letter or letters are in parentheses after the word. It looks like this on the Score Sheet: **1. _ap (l)**

Step 3: Say: "Tell me what letter needs to go in the blank to make this word say *lap*."

Step 4: Record the student's answer in the corresponding blank on the Score Sheet and give the student the next card.

Summary Sheet Instructions and Guidelines

The Summary Sheet can be reproduced, one per student, to compile and analyze the results from the Score Sheet. You can draw up this summary after the student has finished the *Touchphonics* Diagnostic Inventory.

The patterns being tested in Section One are grouped in increasing levels of complexity on the Summary Sheet. The pattern of each word being tested is in parentheses after the word. The target phonemes of the non-words are in the parenthesis next to the pattern.

The pattern code for the score sheet is as follows:

[C] may represent: a single consonant; a consonant digraph; an initial or final consonant blend.

[X] represents a silent letter.

[V] represents a single vowel.

[r] represents an r-controlled vowel.

[e] represents a silent *e*.

Section 1: Use a check mark to record the number of errors for the appropriate pattern group to indicate the number of times each pattern was missed.

Section 2: The phonemes being tested are grouped by type, and the item numbers are indicated. List the specific phonemes missed on the appropriate line.

Indicators of Strengths and Weaknesses

The skills are tested in the sequence of instruction, but students' knowledge of phonemes, patterns and principles may be spotty. A low overall score in decoding non-words coupled with a higher score in encoding real words may suggest a weakness in decoding automaticity and a reliance on memorized words, as well as possible specific phoneme/grapheme weaknesses.

When you find a pattern of errors in both encoding and decoding that shows a weakness with a certain skill, pay extra attention to this skill during instruction or focus on it during remediation.

Decoding Test Cards for Section 1

af Decoding Test Card 1	**jek** Decoding Test Card 2	**yim** Decoding Test Card 3	**quib** Decoding Test Card 4	**shoff** Decoding Test Card 5
ched Decoding Test Card 6	**whik** Decoding Test Card 7	**thop** Decoding Test Card 8	**smosk** Decoding Test Card 9	**grif** Decoding Test Card 10
glit Decoding Test Card 11	**spraf** Decoding Test Card 12	**rilp** Decoding Test Card 13	**sont** Decoding Test Card 14	**knaid** Decoding Test Card 15
wraf Decoding Test Card 16	**vo** Decoding Test Card 17	**lote** Decoding Test Card 18	**bute** Decoding Test Card 19	**hife** Decoding Test Card 20
strue Decoding Test Card 21	**vor** Decoding Test Card 22	**zar** Decoding Test Card 23	**lirt** Decoding Test Card 24	**jerg** Decoding Test Card 25

Decoding Test Cards for Section 1, continued

fean Decoding Test Card 26	**hoil** Decoding Test Card 27	**reet** Decoding Test Card 28	**hoad** Decoding Test Card 29	**wout** Decoding Test Card 30
jow Decoding Test Card 31	**taul** Decoding Test Card 32	**sook** Decoding Test Card 33	**doot** Decoding Test Card 34	**rawl** Decoding Test Card 35
poy Decoding Test Card 36	**phug** Decoding Test Card 37	**bly** Decoding Test Card 38	**digh** Decoding Test Card 39	**refib** Decoding Test Card 40
explub Decoding Test Card 41	**imlet** Decoding Test Card 42	**sidle** Decoding Test Card 43	**piction** Decoding Test Card 44	**hoffer** Decoding Test Card 45
noping Decoding Test Card 46	**jannies** Decoding Test Card 47	**poddest** Decoding Test Card 48	**ligging** Decoding Test Card 49	**zoby** Decoding Test Card 50

Encoding Test Cards for Section 2

_ap Encoding Test Card 1	**_ark** Encoding Test Card 2	**_all** Encoding Test Card 3	**_an** Encoding Test Card 4	**_et** Encoding Test Card 5
_eat Encoding Test Card 6	**_ick** Encoding Test Card 7	**_ig** Encoding Test Card 8	**fo_** Encoding Test Card 9	**hand_** Encoding Test Card 10
ben_ Encoding Test Card 11	**_ack** Encoding Test Card 12	**p_t** Encoding Test Card 13	**g_n** Encoding Test Card 14	**r_g** Encoding Test Card 15
l_t Encoding Test Card 16	**p_d** Encoding Test Card 17	**_ow** Encoding Test Card 18	**_and** Encoding Test Card 19	**_ock** Encoding Test Card 20
_ash Encoding Test Card 21	**ma_** Encoding Test Card 22	**co_** Encoding Test Card 23	**mi_** Encoding Test Card 24	**wi_** Encoding Test Card 25

Encoding Test Cards for Section 2, continued

_ife Encoding Test Card 26	**ba_** Encoding Test Card 27	**st_** Encoding Test Card 28	**st_y** Encoding Test Card 29	**gam_** Encoding Test Card 30
pil_ Encoding Test Card 31	**f_t** Encoding Test Card 32	**p_nt** Encoding Test Card 33	**g_t** Encoding Test Card 34	**p_** Encoding Test Card 35
m_n Encoding Test Card 36	**p_ch** Encoding Test Card 37	**r_** Encoding Test Card 38	**cr_** Encoding Test Card 39	**sh_k** Encoding Test Card 40
_l Encoding Test Card 41	**sh_t** Encoding Test Card 42	**n_** Encoding Test Card 43	**_l** Encoding Test Card 44	**ch_f** Encoding Test Card 45
paint_ Encoding Test Card 46	**want_** Encoding Test Card 47	**hunt_** Encoding Test Card 48	**na_** Encoding Test Card 49	**kind_** Encoding Test Card 50

Score Sheet for Section 1

Name ______________________________ Date ____________

Grade ________ Age ________ Teacher ______________________________

SECTION 1 *(Decode/Auditory): "These are not real words. Tell me what you think it says, and I'll write what you say."*

1. **af** (VC) *(a)* ____
2. **jek** (CVC) *(e)* ____
3. **yim** (CVC) *(i)* ____
4. **quib** (CVC) *(qu)* ____
5. **shoff** (CVC) *(sh)* ____
6. **ched** (CVC) *(ch)* ____
7. **whik** (CVC) *(wh)* ____
8. **thop** (CVC) *(th)* ____
9. **smosk** (CCVCC) *(sm-sk)* ____
10. **grif** (CCVC) *(gr)* ____
11. **glit** (CCVC) *(gl)* ____
12. **spraf** (CCVC) *(spr)* ____
13. **rilp** (CVCC) *(lp)* ____
14. **sont** (CVCC) *(nt)* ____
15. **knaid** (XCVVC) *(kn)(ai)* ____
16. **wraf** (XCVC) *(wr)* ____
17. **vo** (CV) *(o)* ____
18. **lote** (CVCe) *(o-e)* ____
19. **bute** (CVCe) *(u-e)* ____
20. **hife** (CVCe) *(i-e)* ____
21. **strue** (CCVe) *(u-e)* ____
22. **vor** C(V+r) *(or)* ____
23. **zar** C(V+r) *(ar)* ____
24. **lirt** C(V+r)C *(ir)* ____
25. **jerg** C(V+r)C *(er)* ____
26. **fean** (CVVC) *(ea)* ____
27. **hoil** (CVVC) *(oi)* ____
28. **reet** (CVVC) *(ee)* ____
29. **hoad** (CVVC) *(oa)* ____
30. **wout** (CVVC) *(ou)* ____
31. **jow** (CVVC) *(ow)* ____
32. **taul** (CVVC) *(au)* ____
33. **sook** (CVVC) *(oo)* ____
34. **doot** (CVVC) *(oo)* ____
35. **rawl** (CVVC) *(aw)* ____
36. **poy** *(oy)* ____
37. **phug** *(ph)* ____
38. **bly** *(y)* ____
39. **digh** *(igh)* ____

(Structural Analysis)

40. **refib** *(re)* ____
41. **explub** *(ex)* ____
42. **imlet** *(im)* ____
43. **sidle** *(le)* ____
44. **piction** *(tion)* ____
45. **hoffer** *(er)* ____
46. **noping** *(e-ing)* ____
47. **jannies** *(y-i-es)* ____
48. **poddest** (CC) *(est)* ____
49. **ligging** (CC) *(ing)* ____
50. **zoby** (CV-Cy) *(y)* ____

Score Sheet for Section 2

Name ______________________ **Date** __________

Grade ________ **Age** ________ **Teacher** ______________________

SECTION 2 *(Encode/Visual): "These are real words. Tell me what needs to go in the blank to make the word say ______."*

1. **_ap** *(l)*	26. **_ife** *(kn)*
2. **_ark** *(d)*	27. **ba_** *(ck)*
3. **_all** *(w)*	28. **st_** *(ar)*
4. **_an** *(v)*	29. **st_y** *(or)*
5. **_et** *(y)*	30. **gam_** *(e)*
6. **_eat** *(n)*	31. **pil_** *(e)*
7. **_ick** *(qu)*	32. **f_t** *(ee)*
8. **_ig** *(j)*	33. **p_nt** *(ai)*
9. **fo_** *(x)*	34. **g_t** *(oa)*
10. **hand_** *(y)*	35. **p_** *(ay)*
11. **ben_** *(ch)*	36. **m_n** *(oo)*
12. **_ack** *(wh)*	37. **p_ch** *(ea)*
13. **p_t** *(e)*	38. **r_** *(aw)*
14. **g_n** *(u)*	39. **cr_** *(ow)*
15. **r_g** *(i)*	40. **sh_k** *(oo)*
16. **l_t** *(o)*	41. **_l** *(oi)*
17. **p_d** *(a)*	42. **sh_t** *(ou)*
18. **_ow** *(gr)*	43. **n_** *(ew)*
19. **_and** *(st)*	44. **_l** *(ow)*
20. **_ock** *(bl)*	45. **ch_f** *(ie)*
21. **_ash** *(spl)*	*(Structural Analysis)*
22. **ma_** *(sk)*	46. **paint_** *(ed)*
23. **co_** *(ld)*	47. **want_** *(ing)*
24. **mi_** *(lk)*	48. **hunt_** *(er)*
25. **wi_** *(ng)*	49. **na_** *(tion)*
	50. **kind_** *(est)*

Touchphonics Diagnostic Inventory
Summary Sheet for Sections 1 and 2

Name ______________________________ Date ______________

Grade ________ Age ________ Teacher ______________________________

SECTION 1: DECODE	**SECTION 2: ENCODE**
Orthographic Patterns	*Parts and Principles*
Check the number of times a pattern was missed.	*Record the Phonemes that were missed.*
Card number:	Card number:
1 **VC Pattern** ________	1–8 **Initial Consonants** ________
2–8 **CVC Pattern** ________	9 **Final Consonants** ________
9–12 **CCVC, CCVCC Pattern** ________	10 **Ending Vowel *y*** ________
13–14 **CVCC Pattern** ________	11–12 **Initial or Final Consonants** ________
15–16 **XCVC, XCVVC Pattern** ________	13–17 **Short Vowels** ________
17 **CV Pattern** ________	18–21 **Initial Consonant Blends** ________
18–21 **CVCe, CCVCe Pattern** ________	22–25 **Final Consonant Blends** ________
22–25 **C(V+r), CV(V+r) Pattern** ________	26–27 **Silent Letter Clusters** ________
26–35 **CVVC Pattern** ________	28–29 **Vowel + *r*** ________
36–39 **Other** ________	30–31 **Final *e*** ________
40–42 **Prefixes** ________	32–45 **Vowel Combinations** ________
43–45 **Suffixes** ________	46–50 **Suffixes** ________
46–50 **Special** ________	

Running Records

To learn more about the decoding and encoding strategies a student uses, listen to the student read and record the information in a running record.

1. Select a book that you feel is close to the student's reading level.
2. Ask the student to read the selected story aloud. Listen carefully as the student reads and record any errors or miscues in a running record.
3. Tabulate and review the student's reading errors and miscues. Record the source of the errors by determining which cues the student depends on. For each error, ask yourself:
   - Did the student use visual cues from letters and words, which would result in errors such as mistaking *they* for *them*?
   - Did the student use context clues to construct meaning? Inaccurate reading that makes sense indicates that the student is using a prior knowledge base to construct meaning of the text.
   - Did the student use knowledge of the grammatical structure of language? Inaccurate reading that is grammatically similar to the student's own speech patterns indicates that the student's own oral language is influencing the response.
4. Record any additional observations of the student's reading behavior.
5. Depending on the percentage of words a student reads accurately during the assessment, instructional needs for each student will become apparent. Look for patterns that indicate what the student is paying attention to. Notice the information sources the student uses and those that may be neglected.
6. As the student reads the decodable Reader and other texts, use the results of the running record to help the student pay attention to the cues that the student may not be consistently using.